Briefcase on Family Law

Second Edition

LB Curzon
Barrister

Cavendish
Publishing
Limited

London • Sydney

Second edition first published 2001 by Cavendish Publishing Limited, The Glass House, Wharton Street, London WC1X 9PX, United Kingdom

Telephone: + 44 (0)20 7278 8000   Facsimile: + 44 (0)20 7278 8080

Email: info@cavendishpublishing.com

Website: www.cavendishpublishing.com

© Curzon, LB   2001
First edition   1997
Second edition 2001

Curzon, LB (Leslie Basil)
Briefcase on family law – 2nd ed
1 Domestic relations – England 2 Domestic relations – Wales
I Title II Family law
346.4'2'015

ISBN 1 85941 689 6

Printed and bound in Great Britain

Preface

This text, which comprises a selection of important cases in family law, is intended primarily for law students and others who are preparing for first examinations in this subject area. It is intended to provide a digest of cases which illustrate the application of principles in this field of law. The cases chosen will offer useful adjunctive material for the group of Cavendish publications concerned with family law.

For this second edition, cases which are no longer relevant have been omitted, and some 80 new cases have been added.

For students who find access to the full reports difficult, there is now a valuable set of summaries of current cases available: *Family Law* (monthly) gives full summaries of recent decisions, together with authoritative commentaries; *Current Law* (monthly) provides abstracts of the decisions of the courts in cases relating to family law; *New Law Journal* (weekly) often includes summaries of developments in the field of family law; *Student Law Review* (triannually) contains a section devoted specifically to matters of interest in family law.

LB Curzon
2001

Abbreviations

AA	Adoption Act 1976
CACA	Child Abduction and Custody Act 1985
Ch A	Children Act 1989
CLSA	Courts and Legal Services Act 1990
CSA	Child Support Act 1995
DMPA	Domestic and Matrimonial Proceedings Act 1973
DPMCA	Domestic Proceedings and Magistrates' Courts Act 1978
DVMPA	Domestic Violence and Matrimonial Proceedings Act 1976
FLA	Family Law Act 1986/1996
FLRA	Family Law Reform Act 1969
HFEA	Human Fertilisation and Embryology Act 1990
LPA	Law of Property Act 1925
LRA	Land Registration Act 1925
MA	Marriage Act 1949
MCA	Matrimonial Causes Act 1973
MFPA	Matrimonial and Family Proceedings Act 1984
MHA	Matrimonial Homes Act 1983
MWPA	Married Women's Property Act 1882
SCA	Supreme Court Act 1981

Contents

Table of Cases

Table of Statutes

1 Legal Capacity to Marry and Formalities

1.1 The basic legal principle of marriage

Note ───────────────────────────────────

A marriage can be created legally between a male and a female who possess appropriate legal capacity to marry and who comply fully with all formal requirements.

───────────────────────────────────────

Hyde v Hyde (1866)

P, the petitioner, an Englishman, took up residence in Utah, where he became a Mormon and married R, who was also a Mormon, in accordance with the marriage rites of the Mormon Church which, at that time, allowed polygamy. P later returned to England, having renounced the Mormon faith. R continued to reside in Utah and married a second husband. P sought to divorce R on the ground of her adultery.

Held: P's petition would be *refused* because English matrimonial law concerned Christian marriage only. *Per* Lord Penzance:

> I conceive that marriage, as understood in Christendom, may be defined as the voluntary union for life of one man and one woman to the exclusion of all others.

Rignell v Andrews (1991)

X had cohabited with Y for some 11 years. Y had taken X's surname. X claimed that Y was his 'common-law wife' and that he could claim the tax allowances appropriate to a husband whose wife was living with him.

Held: the term 'wife' applied only to a woman who had entered into the relationship of marriage with a man. Mere cohabitation did not give rise to marriage, and the phrase 'common-law marriage' was *inaccurate*.

1.2 The legal capacity to marry

Note
A person domiciled in England has capacity to marry if: one party is male and the other female, neither party is already married, both parties are over the age of 16, parties are not related within the prohibited degrees of consanguinity or affinity.

1.2.1 Parties to be male and female

Corbett v Corbett (1971)
X and Y had participated in a marriage ceremony in 1963. In 1960, Y, born a male, had undergone so called sex-change surgery after which he had lived as a woman and had married X. During subsequent proceedings related to a decree of nullity of marriage, the court considered the problem of Y's sex.

Held: The so called marriage of X and Y was *void*. *Per* Ormrod J:

> Since marriage is essentially a relationship between man and woman, the validity of the marriage in this case, depends, in my judgment, on whether respondent [Y] is or is not a woman. The question then becomes what is meant by the word 'woman' in the context of a marriage, for I am not concerned to determine the 'legal sex' of the respondent at large. Having regard to the essentially heterosexual character of the relationship which is called marriage, the criteria must, in my judgment, be biological, for even the most extreme degree of transsexualism in a male or the most severe hormonal imbalance which can exist in a person with male chromosomes, male gonads and male genitalia cannot produce a person who is naturally capable of performing the essential role of a woman in marriage. My conclusion is that the respondent [Y] is not a woman for the purposes of marriage, but is a biological male and has been so, since birth.

Cossey v UK (1991)
C, a British citizen, had been born male and her birth certificate stated this fact. She developed psychologically as a female and received gender reassignment surgery. C's request for a change to her birth certificate was refused. C later married Mr X; the marriage was declared to be void because the parties were not male and female. C applied to the European Court of Human Rights, arguing that there had been a violation of article 8 (right to family life) and article 12 (right to marry).

Held (by a majority): the refusal to alter C's birth certificate was *not* a violation of article 8. The UK's birth registration certificate was a public record and respect for C's private life did not impose an obligation on the UK to alter existing records. There was no violation of article 12, which lays down that a person's right to marry is subject to domestic law. The

UK's restriction of the right to marry to persons of opposite biological sex did not affect article 12, which concerned traditional marriage between male and female. Judge Palm, and two colleagues, *in dissenting*, argued that there had been significant changes in public opinion as regards the full legal recognition of transsexualism which should be taken into account in the interpretation of article 12.

Re P and G (Transsexuals) (1996)

P and G, male-to-female transsexuals who had received gender reassignment surgical treatment, applied for judicial review of a refusal by the registrar to alter the birth register so as to show their sex at birth as female.

Held: the registrar was *correct* in considering the register as a historical record and not as a statement of the current sexual identity of P and G. Surgery undergone after registration was merely evidence of a pre-existing condition. Further, the registrar's refusal did not constitute a breach of the Sex Discrimination Act 1975: there was no evidence that either P or G had been treated less favourably than a male who had been registered at birth as a female would have been treated.

W v W (Physical Inter-Sex) (2000)

H and W had married in 1993. In 1997 a decree absolute had been granted following W's petition, and this was followed by ancillary relief proceedings. H did not contest the divorce but later sought a decree of nullity on the ground that at the time of the marriage the parties had not been male and female respectively. He contended that the marriage was void, in that W was not a woman but a physical inter-sex. Although W was registered at birth as a boy, and in spite of treatment with testosterone injections from an early age, her general appearance had been more female than male. From the time she was able to choose, she had lived as a female. In 1987, following oral oestrogen treatment, W had undergone gender reassignment surgery.

Held: H's application was dismissed. Charles J stated that the factors determining a person's sex for the purpose of marriage, as set out in *Corbett v Corbett* (1971), were biological, and, if the gonadal, chromosomal and genital tests were congruent, that was determinative of an individual's sex. W's genetic and gonadal sex was male but her genitalia were ambiguous and her body habitus and gender orientation appeared female. Partial androgen insensitivity caused her to be in a physical inter-sex state. Given such insensitivity, its cause and effect, evidence of W's final choice to live as a woman before the oestrogen treatment, her gender reassignment surgery, and her capacity to consummate the marriage, he was satisfied that this was sufficient to demonstrate that, for the purposes of the marriage, W was a woman.

Bellinger v Bellinger (2000)

W petitioned for a declaration that she was validly married to H within the terms of s 11 MCA 1973. Supported by H, W contended that she was female at the time of the marriage in 1981, and that the decision in *Corbett v Corbett* (1971) ought to be reconsidered in the light of medical advances and changed social conditions. The Attorney-General, intervening, argued that W's biological characteristics at birth were congruent, and she was male, despite having undergone medical treatment and an operation for gender reassignment.

Held: W's application for a declaration was *refused*. Johnson J stated that, while accepting that recent medical research suggested increasing medical recognition that sexual differences in the brain were an additional factor in determining an individual's gender, and that social attitudes had changed markedly since 1971, nevertheless, the law as it stood at present was quite clear: a marriage could be valid only where the sex of the applicant had been female at the time of birth, and, on the basis of the criteria set out in *Corbett*, that was not so in W's case. If any fundamental change to the law were to be introduced, this was a matter for the legislature, not for the judges.

1.2.2 Parties to be over 16 at the date of marriage

Pugh v Pugh (1951)

X, a British officer, domiciled in England, went through a civil marriage ceremony in Austria with Y, aged 15. Y was domiciled in Hungary, in which a marriage of that nature was recognised as valid. Later, Y presented a petition for nullity.

Held: the marriage was *void* since X lacked the capacity under English law to marry Y. (See s 2 MA 1949; s 11(a)(ii) MCA 1973.) *Per* Pearce J:

> According to modern thought it is considered socially and morally wrong that persons of an age at which we now believe them to be immature ... should have the stresses and responsibilities of marriage ... Child marriages by common consent are believed to be bad for the participants and bad for the institution of marriage.

Mohamed v Knott (1968)

X married Y, aged 13, in Nigeria; both were Nigerian Moslems and the marriage was valid under the Moslem law of Nigeria. The marriage was potentially polygamous. X and Y came to the UK where, on application to the juvenile court, it was held by the justices that the marriage was not recognised under English law. The Court of Appeal considered the validity of the marriage.

Held: the marriage was *valid* under English law, so that Y had the status of X's wife. Neither X nor Y was domiciled in the UK when the marriage took place; it would be recognised here unless there was strong reason to the contrary.

1.2.3 Neither party must be already married to some other person (see s 11(b) MCA 1973)

Baindail v Baindail (1946) CA

X, an Englishwoman, went through a marriage ceremony with Y in London in 1939. In the marriage certificate, Y was described as a bachelor. Eleven years earlier Y had married Z, a Hindu woman, at a Hindu marriage ceremony in India. The marriage was recognised in India and was potentially polygamous. It was recognised also by courts in British India. Z was alive when X married Y.

Held: X was married lawfully to Z at the time he purported to marry Y. His marriage to Z constituted an *effective bar* to his marriage to Y.

1.2.4 Parties must not be within the prohibited degrees (see Sched I MA 1949; Marriage (Prohibited Degrees of Relationship) Act 1986)

Cheni v Cheni (1965)

X and Y, who were uncle and niece, were married in Egypt in a ceremony based on Jewish rites. The marriage was valid under Egyptian and Jewish law and although it was, at the time of its celebration, potentially polygamous, it was rendered monogamous when a child of the marriage, Z, was born in 1926 (two years after the marriage). X and Y became domiciled in the UK in 1957. In 1961, Y, the wife, presented a petition praying that her marriage to X be declared void on the ground of consanguinity.

Held: the marriage of X and Y was *valid*. *Per* Simon P:

[The true test is] whether the marriage is so offensive to the conscience of the English court that it should refuse to recognise and give effect to the proper foreign law ... It would be altogether too queasy a judicial conscience which would recoil from a marriage acceptable to many peoples of deep religious convictions, lofty ethical standards and high civilisation. I must bear in mind that I am asked to declare unmarried the parents of [Z] who is unquestionably legitimate in the eyes of the law (*Re Bischoffsheim* (1948)). In my judgment, injustice would be perpetrated and conscience would be affronted if the English court were not to recognise and give effect to the law of the domicile in this case.

1.3　The significance of formalities

Note

Where persons have married in breach of certain specified formalities, that marriage may be void. (See ss 25, 49 MA 1949; s 11(a)(iii) MCA 1973.)

Small v Small (1923)

X was a deserter from the Royal Field Artillery. In order to avoid detection and prosecution he had assumed a false name which he used in relation to the publication of banns concerning his marriage to Y.

Held: X had a fraudulent intention to conceal his true identity and the banns had not been properly published. The marriage of X and Y was, therefore, *void*. (See the Marriage Act 1949, s 25(b).)

Chipchase v Chipchase (1939)

A woman named Matthews married Leetch in 1915; he deserted her in 1916. In 1928 she married the petitioner, following banns published in the name of Matthews. She was generally known by this name and had used it for two years before her marriage to the petitioner. Her motive was, apparently, a wish not to emphasise the fact of her marriage to Leetch. The justices held that the second marriage was void because there had been no due publication of the banns. She appealed to the Divisional Court.

Held: the appeal was *allowed* and the case was remitted to the justices for a determination of the question as to whether she had knowingly and wilfully concealed her identity in relation to the publication of the banns. *Per* Merriman P:

> I think it quite clear that the justices have not had their minds directed to the established interpretation of the Marriage Act 1823, s 22 ['Provided always, that if persons shall knowingly and wilfully intermarry without due publication of banns ... the marriage of such persons shall be null and void to all intents and purposes whatsoever.'] The object of this Act was to prevent clandestine marriages. There must be an element of intentional concealment of identity before it can be said that the marriage is void for undue publication of banns. I do not think that this element of the matter was considered sufficiently by the justices. *Small v Small* was cited. In that case unquestionably there was the element of deliberate concealment, and the motive was quite plain. It may be that this is such another case, but, at any rate, the wife must have the opportunity of establishing, as counsel says she is able to establish, that the name in which she was married was the name by which for years she had been commonly known, and that there was no intention to conceal her identity in the particular circumstances of this case.

Dancer v Dancer (1948)

Jessamine was the legitimate daughter of Mr and Mrs Knight. When Jessamine was aged three, Mrs Knight began to live with Mr Roberts, by whom she had children. All the children, including Jessamine, were known as Roberts. She did not discover that she was not Roberts' daughter until his death, when she was 17. She continued to be known as Roberts and was named in the banns as Jessamine Roberts. Later her husband petitioned for a decree of nullity, arguing undue publication of banns.

Held: there was *no undue publication* of banns. *Per* Ormrod J:

> She [Jessamine] had adopted the advice of the vicar, which was: 'If you give the name of Knight, no one will know anything about you. But if you give the name of Roberts, by which name you have always been known in this parish and everywhere else, then everyone will know who it is that is being married.' On that advice and with the intention of avoiding any form of concealment, she allowed her name to go forward in the banns as Roberts. I am satisfied that, in those circumstances, this is a case in which there was no undue publication of banns.

Puttick v AG (1979) CA

Astrid Proll, a German who had absconded to England from Germany where she was on bail for terrorist offences, entered the UK by use of a false passport. In England she married Robert Puttick by licence, using a false name and giving other false particulars. Following arrest on an extradition warrant she claimed registration as a British citizen and sought a declaration of the validity of her marriage.

Held: the declaration would be *refused*. The false details did not invalidate the marriage, but by obtaining residence in England by fraud, the petitioner was barred from obtaining a domicile of choice here, and, given the context of her conduct, it would not be just to make the declaration she sought. *Per* Baker P:

> A clear distinction has been recognised by the English courts between marriage by banns and marriage by licence. In the former, a misdescription of a party renders the marriage void because there has not been the required publicity. In the case of marriage by licence there is no such requirement and no such result follows, for the object of the licence is not publicity but identity.

Per Bankes LJ:

> It is unnecessary for me to repeat the Attorney-General's catalogue of evils which could flow from the grant of the application ... I do not think it would be just, indeed, in my opinion it would be utterly unjust, to grant a decree, even if she had proved an English domicile, which she has not. Perhaps I am back where I began with the maxim which I can now express as 'No woman can take advantage of her own wrong' ... This court should not and cannot further the criminal acts of this applicant and permit her to achieve her ends by the course of conduct which she has pursued. The petition fails and is dismissed.

Gereis v Yagoub (1997)

H and W were Coptic Orthodox Christians who had married in England in 1993. The ceremony was celebrated in accordance with the marriage rites of the Coptic Church, but without the formalities required under MA 1949. The church had not been registered, no notice had been given to the registrar, no licence or certificate to marry had been issued. H, W and others attending the ceremony assumed that they were participating in an ordinary marriage . Following the ceremony, H and W cohabited, and the marriage was consummated. W later petitioned for a decree of nullity on the ground that the marriage was void because it had not been carried out in accordance with the formalities required by MA 1949. H argued that there was never a marriage between him and W which was recognisable under English law.

Held: W's petition was granted. The ceremony involving H and W bore all the hallmarks of an ordinary Christian marriage recognisable to English law. It was, in the event, void because of the failure to give due notice to the registrar.

Chief Adjudication Officer v Bath (2000) CA

W, a widow aged 59, had at the age of 16 participated in a Sikh marriage ceremony at a Sikh temple in London in 1956, with H, then aged 19. They then lived together as man and wife for 37 years, until H's death in 1994. W then applied for widow's benefit, H having paid social security benefits as a married man. W's application was refused by an adjudication officer, and that decision was upheld by the Social Security Appeal Tribunal. W then appealed successfully to the Social Security Appeal Commissioner. The Commissioner now appealed on the ground that the temple at which the marriage ceremony took place was not registered for that purpose, so that it could not be presumed that a valid marriage existed under the terms of s 49 MA 1949.

Held: the appeal was dismissed. A presumption of marriage arose from the long period of cohabitation, and there appeared to be an absence of compelling evidence to rebut the presumption. A marriage was rendered void under s 49 if the parties had 'knowingly and wilfully' failed to comply with relevant statutory provisions. It was not possible to infer that in this case. There was no statutory provision that a marriage which was otherwise carried out in proper form by an authorised person at a place of worship eligible to be registered under the Act was invalid solely on the ground that the building had not been registered. *Collet v Collet* (1968) had emphasised the importance of upholding wherever possible the validity of a marriage entered into in good faith. In the present case, H and W were validly married in 1956 by reason of the ceremony at the London temple.

Q 'The time has come, surely, for Lord Penzance's moribund definition of marriage to disappear.' Do you agree?

2 Nullity: Void and Voidable Marriages

2.1 The significance of nullity

Note

The modern law concerning nullity of marriage is consolidated in MCA 1973. The effects of a decree of nullity will depend upon whether the marriage has been declared to be void or voidable.

2.2 The fundamental distinction between void and voidable marriages

De Reneville v De Reneville (1948) CA

Husband and wife were married in France; the husband was domiciled there, the wife in England. The wife petitioned on the ground of non-consummation of the marriage.

Held: the question of the marriage was to be determined according to *French law*, ie, the law of the country in which the parties intended to make the matrimonial home. Lord Greene considered the essential distinction between void and voidable marriage:

> The substance [of the distinction] may be expressed thus. A *void* marriage is one that will be regarded by every court in any case in which the existence of the marriage is in issue as never having taken place and can be so treated by both parties to it without the necessity of any decree annulling it. A *voidable* marriage is one that will be regarded by every court as a valid subsisting marriage until a decree annulling it has been pronounced by a court of competent jurisdiction.

2.3 The essence of the void marriage

Note

The grounds of nullity which make a marriage void are set out in s 11 MCA 1973: a party is under 16, parties are within prohibited degrees, the marriage is essentially bigamous; parties are not male and female; formalities have not been complied with. See 1.1 *et seq* above.

Re Spence (1990) CA

W married H in 1885 and gave birth to D in 1891. Later W left H to live with X and gave birth to two sons by him. In 1934 W went through a ceremony of marriage with X. H was alive at that time. In subsequent proceedings related to the grant of letters of administration to D, the question of D's legitimacy arose.

Held: the marriage of W to X was *void* (and, under s 1(1) Legitimacy Act 1976, persons born before their parents entered into a void marriage were not to be treated as legitimate). *Per* Nourse LJ:

> A void marriage, both as a matter of language and by definition, is a nullity ...
> It is only an idle ceremony, achieving no change in the status of the participants.
> It achieves nothing of substance.

Wicken v Wicken (1999)

W married H1, her first husband, in Gambia in 1989 in a Muslim ceremony. In 1990 they separated. W was convinced that the letter of divorce sent to her by H1 constituted a valid divorce under Islamic law. In 1992, W married H2, her second husband, and settled with him in the UK. In 1996 that marriage collapsed, and W applied for divorce. H2 cross petitioned for divorce and also applied for a decree of nullity on the ground that W had not been divorced from H1. Written evidence from H1 was tendered, but it did not establish whether or not a divorce had taken place.

Held: the application for nullity made by H2 was *dismissed*. Cross decrees of divorce were pronounced. The standard of proof in determining whether W lacked capacity when she went through the marriage ceremony with H2 was the balance of probabilities, and, under s 46(2) FLA 1986 (dealing with the validity of the recognition of overseas divorces), W's disputed divorce from H1 was 'otherwise than by means of proceedings' and would in those circumstances be recognised in English law, always provided that it was valid under Gambian law. The rules of evidence in English law had application in the circumstances, and, since the letter of divorce was genuine, it sufficed to constitute a divorce under the law of Gambia.

Rampal v Rampal (2000)

H and W were married in 1975, and W was pregnant at that time. Later, she discovered that H had been married at an earlier date in India, but he gave her an assurance that the Indian marriage had terminated in divorce before the marriage in 1975. H and W separated in 1997 and were divorced in 1999. H made an application for ancillary relief. W later found out that H's Indian divorce was not made absolute until 1983. W now applied for her divorce from H to be set aside, and for an order which would prevent H from seeking ancillary relief.

Held: W's application was *allowed* in part. A bigamous marriage was void *ab initio*. (The debarring of H from seeking ancillary relief was for the discretion of the court, and a further hearing might be necessary on this matter.)

2.4 The essence of the voidable marriage

Note

A marriage celebrated after 31 July 1971 is voidable: where it has not been consummated because of incapacity of either party or wilful refusal of respondent to consummate; where there was no valid consent to that marriage because of, eg, duress, mistake; where, at the date of the marriage either party was suffering from mental disorder; where respondent was suffering from venereal disease in a communicable form; where respondent was pregnant by some person other than the petitioner: s 12 MCA 1973.

P v P (1994) CA

The parties were married in 1992 and, three months later, H petitioned for annulment on grounds of non-consummation. A decree nisi was granted in June 1993. On 22 July 1993, W stated her intention to appeal against the decree nisi, and on 2 August 1993, H applied for an injunction. The judge ordered W to vacate the matrimonial home, given that the marriage of H and W did not subsist and, therefore, W had no remedy under MHA 1983.

Held: W's appeal would be *allowed*. A decree of nullity in relation to a voidable marriage operates only after the court has granted a decree absolute under s 16 MCA 1973, so that the judge did have jurisdiction to examine W's rights under s 1(3) MHA 1983.

2.4.1 Non-consummation of the marriage (s 12(a), (b))

D v A (1845)

The wife's physical defects made full intercourse impossible.

Held: mere incapability of conception was *not* considered to be a sufficient ground for declaring a marriage void. *Per* Dr Lushington (a celebrated 19th century judge of the London Consistory Court):

> Sexual intercourse in the proper meaning of the term is ordinary and complete intercourse; it does not mean partial and imperfect intercourse. ... The only question is whether the lady is or is not capable of full intercourse, or, if at present incapable, whether that incapacity could be removed ... If there be a reasonable probability that the lady can be made capable of *vera copula* – of the natural sort of coitus – though without power of conception, I cannot pronounce this marriage void ...

Napier v Napier (1915)

Following many years of marriage during which the husband's attempts at intercourse proved unsuccessful because of the wife's physical condition, he petitioned for nullity. A few days before the hearing, the wife underwent an operation designed to remedy her condition. The hearing was postponed in order to investigate the possibility of full consummation.

Held: the case would be *dismissed* because the wife's incapacity was curable.

Horton v Horton (1947) HL

The House of Lords considered the desirability of defining 'wilful refusal to consummate'. *Per* Lord Jowitt:

> I do not think it desirable to attempt any definition of the phrase 'wilful refusal to consummate the marriage'. The words connote, I think, a settled and definite decision come to without just excuse, and in determining whether there has been such a refusal, the judge should have regard to the whole history of the marriage.

Baxter v Baxter (1948) HL

H and W married in 1934; some 10 years later H left W. He petitioned for a decree of nullity on the ground of non-consummation due to W's wilful refusal. H stated that W refused sexual intercourse unless he used a contraceptive.

Held: consummation of the marriage was *not prevented* by the use of contraceptives. *Per* Lord Jowitt:

> I am unable to believe that Parliament, by using the word 'consummate' in connection with this new ground of nullity, intended that the courts should be involved in enquiries of this kind. Long before the passing of MCA 1937, it was common knowledge that reputable clinics had come into existence for the purpose of advising spouses on what is popularly called birth control and ... it is also a matter of common knowledge that many young married couples agree to take contraceptive precautions in the early days of married life. I take the view that in this legislation Parliament used the word 'consummate' as that word is understood in common parlance and in the light of social conditions known to exist, and that the proper occasion for considering the subjects raised by this particular appeal is when the sexual life of the spouses, and the responsibility of either or both for a childless home, form the background to some other claim for relief. On this basis I am constrained to say that, in my opinion, there is no warrant for the decision in *Cowen v Cowen* (1945) [in which the Court of Appeal had held that there had been no consummation where a husband had persisted in the use of a contraceptive]. The result is I would dismiss this appeal.

S v S (1962) CA

A wife's physical malformations made full intercourse impossible but evidence was given suggesting that an operation might solve the problem, although there would be no conception of children because of her lack of a uterus. Her husband petitioned for a decree nisi of nullity.

Held: a decree of nullity should be *refused* because the wife's incapacity was curable so that the marriage could be consummated. In considering whether Dr Lushington's test of *vera copula* could be satisfied, Willmer LJ stated:

> If it is to be held that a wife with an artificial vagina is incapable in all circumstances of consummating a marriage, it could be only on the basis that she was incapable of taking part in true sexual intercourse. If that were right, the strangest results would follow. It would involve, for example, that such a woman would be to a considerable extent beyond the protection of the criminal law, for it would seem to follow that she would be incapable in law of being the victim of a rape ... I should regard such a result as bordering on the fantastic, yet it is accepted as being the logical conclusion of the argument presented on behalf of the husband ...

W v W (1967)

The court considered a petition in which evidence was given suggesting that penetration had not led to ordinary, complete intercourse.

Held: a decree of nullity would be *granted*. *Per* Brandon J:

> There are binding decisions that the emission of seed, or possibility of procreation, are not necessary ingredients as a matter of law to ordinary and complete intercourse, and there are authorities which seem to me to be right, if not binding, that full and complete penetration is an essential ingredient to complete intercourse.

> I do not think that there is any authority which binds me to hold that any penetration amounts to consummation of a marriage, and in the absence of such authority I do not see why I should not make a finding of fact in accordance with what seem to me to be the realities of the case. On those grounds, in my judgment, this marriage has not been consummated and I am satisfied that the cause of that non-consummation is the impotence of the husband which existed at the date of the marriage and continued at all material times. There will, accordingly, be a decree of nullity of marriage on the ground of incapacity.

Singh v Singh (1971) CA

H and W, aged 21 and 17, were Sikhs who were married in a register office. W's parents had arranged the marriage and she had never seen H before the ceremony. It was intended that the civil ceremony would be followed by a religious ceremony. W took a dislike to H when she first saw him at the register office and she refused to participate in the religious ceremony or to live with him. W's subsequent petition for a decree of nullity was based upon duress and incapacity to consummate because of her 'invincible repugnance'. The petition was dismissed.

Held: W's appeal would be *dismissed*. *Per* Karminski LJ:

> There is the matter of repugnance. It is true that W never submitted herself to the physical embraces of H, because after the ceremony of marriage before the registrar it does not appear that she saw him again or went near him. Having taken the view which she did, that she did not want to be married to him, it is understandable that she did not want to have sexual intercourse with him: but that seems to be a very long way from an invincible repugnance ... Here W abandoned the idea of her marriage altogether, and there is nothing of a psychiatric or sexual aversion on her part which is in any way established. In my view that ground of nullity fails completely.

Potter v Potter (1975) CA

H married W in 1969. Because of a physical defect W was incapable of consummating the marriage, but an operation in 1970 cured this. W's emotional state led to her refusal to have intercourse. Later, H refused, although W now wished to have, intercourse. In 1973 W petitioned for annulment on the ground of H's 'wilful refusal to consummate'. The petition was dismissed on the ground that 'wilful' must have the meaning of 'without reasonable cause'. H's loss of sexual ardour for W occurred naturally and was in no sense deliberate.

Held: W's appeal against dismissal of her petition would be *dismissed*.

A v J (Nullity Proceedings) (1989)

Two Indian families arranged a marriage between H and W. They were to be married in a civil ceremony which would be followed four months later by a religious service. The religious service was necessary before any cohabitation. After the civil ceremony H went abroad for business reasons but returned for the planned religious ceremony. W insisted on the indefinite postponement of that ceremony because she was disappointed 'by H's cool and inconsiderate behaviour to her', evidenced by his going abroad. H's sincere apology was refused by W, who would not agree to any attempts at reconciliation. H petitioned for nullity on the basis of W's refusal to consummate the marriage.

Held: W's behaviour constituted a *wilful refusal* to consummate since a religious ceremony was absolutely essential to the cohabitation of H and W.

2.4.2   Lack of real consent to the marriage by either party (s 12(c))

Mehta v Mehta (1945)

The petitioner, P, who was domiciled in England, participated in a marriage ceremony in India with the respondent, R, an Indian. The rites of the ceremony were conducted in Hindustani, which P did not understand. P was under the impression that the ceremony was marking her conversion to the Hindu religion, a course on which she had agreed prior to that ceremony. P was informed later that, as a result of the ceremony, she had been converted to Hinduism and that she had been married to R in accordance with the ceremonies of a Hindu sect. P claimed that at no time had she ever intended to marry R and that she was never aware that the ceremony in which she had participated involved a marriage.

Held: it was clear that there was a lack of valid consent to the marriage, since P had never intended to marry R. It was clear that P had been totally unaware that the ceremony of conversion was also a marriage ceremony. P was *entitled* to the grant of a decree of nullity.

Park v Park (1953) CA

In proceedings which involved consideration of a will, evidence was given that the deceased had executed a will on 1 March 1948, in which he had favoured D, while on 30 May 1949 he had married P, and, on that same day, had executed a new will which favoured P. At the time of executing the new will he was old and suffering from physical and mental illness. Less than one month later he died. D claimed that on the date of the marriage to P, the deceased had been incapable of consenting, so that the marriage was null and void.

Held: the test to be applied in consideration of the validity of a marriage on the ground that a party was of unsound mind at the time of its celebration, is whether that party was capable of understanding the *essential nature* of the contract, and this involved his being mentally capable of understanding that it involved those responsibilities relating to marriage.

Per Birkett LJ:

> The marriage contract is essentially one of simplicity. There can be degrees of capacity apart from soundness of mind. It is understandable that a man who is illiterate, perfectly sound of mind, but not of high quality, might be able to understand the contract of marriage in its simplicity, but who, coming into wealth suddenly, might be incapable of making anything in the nature of a complicated will, but degrees of unsoundness of mind cannot have much relevance to the question whether it is shown that a person was not mentally capable of understanding the contract into which he had entered.

Per Singleton LJ:

> [The test to be applied is] was the person capable of understanding the nature of the contract into which he was entering, or was his mental condition such that he was incapable of understanding it? To ascertain the nature of the contract of marriage a man must be mentally incapable of appreciating that it involves the responsibilities normally attaching to marriage. Without that degree of mentality, it cannot be said that he understands the nature of the contract.

Silver v Silver (1955)

The petitioner, P, was a German national by birth who became engaged to be married to S, an Englishman, in 1919. Two years later she learned that S was married but estranged from his wife. P and S planned to live as husband and wife in Germany. In 1925, S decided to return to England and, so as to enable P to live in England, he planned the marriage of P to R, S's stepbrother. The marriage took place in November, 1925. Some six months later, P and R visited the Home Office where they declared six months' cohabitation, which would have made it unnecessary for P to have to return to Germany. She then lived with S as his wife until after S's death in 1948. Having met a German national whom she wished to marry, P discussed with R the possibility of divorce. She discovered later that, since 1940, R had been living with another woman; there were three children of that relationship. P petitioned for a decree of nullity on the ground of lack of valid consent, and, alternatively, for a decree of divorce on the ground of R's adultery.

Held: in the absence of fear or coercion, a mere ulterior motive *cannot* constitute duress which involves lack of consent. *Per* Collingwood J:

> The voluntary consent of both parties is necessary for a valid marriage and the marriage is void if such consent is lacking, as, for example, where it is procured by threats or duress; but mental reservations on the part of one or both of the parties to a marriage do not affect its validity … I hold that the parties here intended that they should become man and wife and went through the ceremony with that object. There being no element of duress, the prayer for a decree of nullity must be rejected. As to the prayer for dissolution, the court is asked to exercise its discretion in P's favour. I can see no social advantage in insisting on the maintenance of a union which has been a mere travesty from the beginning. Accordingly there will be a decree nisi in the exercise of the discretion of the court.

Kassim v Kassim (1962)

Respondent, R, a Moslem, belonged to the Mashona tribe in Southern Rhodesia. In July 1945 he married M, a member of his tribe, at a civil ceremony in Southern Rhodesia. In 1952 he participated in a marriage ceremony with the petitioner, P, in England. M was alive at that time. P later petitioned on the ground of R's cruelty. R argued that the 1952 marriage with P was bigamous and he produced an authenticated copy of a marriage certificate which was accepted as *prima facie* evidence of a valid marriage in Southern Rhodesia to M. R testified that he had believed, mistakenly, that his marriage in 1945 was a polygamous union.

Held: P's marriage to M in 1945 was valid. It was subsisting in June 1952, so that R's marriage to P was bigamous and *void*. *Per* Ormrod J:

In my view, the mistake of R in the present case should not be regarded as so fundamental as to vitiate his consent to marry M and so render the marriage at Rusape (Southern Rhodesia) void. The mistake in this case falls on the other side of the line and should be regarded as a mistake as to the nature of the mistake created by the ceremony. [Nevertheless] I am satisfied that the marriage certificate in the present case is *prima facie* evidence that the requirements ... were complied with in the present case and, accordingly, that the monogamous nature of the marriage created by the ceremony at Rusape was explained to R before that ceremony. Whether he understood the explanation is, of course, another matter. There is insufficient evidence before me to enable me to decide whether R's evidence on this point is reliable or not. I think, however, it would be wrong to regard his evidence as sufficient to displace the evidence of the marriage certificate which is *prima facie* proof of a valid marriage. I hold that the marriage in 1945 at Rusape was valid ... and it therefore follows that R's marriage to P was void.

Buckland v Buckland (1967)

The petitioner, P, while in Malta, was charged with the offence of 'corruption of a minor' and was advised by his Maltese solicitor that there would be no chance for him when confronted in the Maltese courts with a charge of this nature. Ultimately he was advised: 'You really have only one choice – marry the girl or go to prison.' P sought the advice of his superior who confirmed the lawyer's advice. P then decided that he would marry the girl, and did so. His petition was based on lack of valid consent.

Held: the marriage was null and void and a decree *would be granted*. *Per* Scarman J:

> The question I have to decide is whether the ceremony of marriage, to which P was a party, was invalid on the grounds that it lacked the reality of consent on his part. Such a question was considered by Karminski J in *H v H* (1953), where the wife was the petitioner. The headnote says: 'In the absence of consent there can be no valid marriage; and fear may vitiate consent.' The learned judge found that the petitioner's fears genuinely existed and were of sufficient degree to negative her consent to the marriage. He also found that they were reasonably entertained ... I understand that the effect of that judgment to be that in a case where it is alleged that the petitioner's consent to marriage has been vitiated by fear, it must be shown first that fear of a sufficient degree to vitiate consent was present; and secondly that the fear was reasonably entertained. In *Griffiths v Griffiths* (1944) [an Irish case] Haugh J added what may be a limitation; having said that duress or intimidation may well produce a fear that may lead a person to marriage, he stated: 'But, if fear is justly imposed, the resulting marriage, when contracted, is valid and binding.' Thus a third proposition may be stated to the effect that, even if the fear be reasonably entertained, it will not vitiate consent unless it arises from some external circumstances for which the petitioner is not himself responsible.

The conclusion I have reached, on the facts in the present case, is that P's fear was brought about by an unjust charge preferred against him. The fear which originated in this way was greatly strengthened by the advice given by the solicitor and his superior office. I am satisfied that, when he presented himself for the marriage ceremony, he believed himself to be in an inescapable dilemma – marriage or prison; and, fearing prison, he chose marriage. Basing myself on the judgment of Karminski J, in *H v H*, I have come to the conclusion that P agreed to his marriage because of his fears, and that his fears, which were reasonably entertained, arose from external circumstances for which he was in no way responsible ... P is entitled to a declaration that the marriage ceremony was null and void.

Szechter v Szechter (1971)

P, a Polish national, was arrested and imprisoned in Warsaw, having been charged with anti-state activities. R, an eminent Polish scholar, to whom the authorities had given permission to emigrate, assisted in effecting P's release by divorcing his wife and marrying P while she was in prison. P, R, and his former wife came to England. P petitioned for a decree of nullity on the ground of fear and duress, in order that R and his first wife might remarry.

Held: a decree *would be granted*. *Per* Simon P:

It is, in my view, insufficient to invalidate an otherwise good marriage that a party has entered into in order to escape from a disagreeable situation, such as penury or social degradation. In order for the impediment of duress to vitiate an otherwise valid marriage, it must, in my judgment, be proved that the will of one of the parties thereto has been overborne by genuine and reasonably-held fear caused by threat of immediate danger (for which the party is not himself responsible) to life, limb or liberty, so that the constraint destroys the reality of consent to ordinary wedlock.

Hirani v Hirani (1982) CA

P, aged 19, a Hindu, was living with her parents, also Hindu, in England. There she met X, an Indian Muslim. The parents opposed the friendship of P and X and arranged for P to marry a Hindu; neither P nor the parents had met him. P was threatened with expulsion from the family home unless she married in accordance with the parents' wishes. The marriage was not consummated and P left her husband after six weeks. She petitioned for nullity on the grounds of duress. The judge refused to grant a decree because there had been no threat to P's life, limb or liberty. P appealed.

Held: P's appeal was *allowed* and a decree nisi would be granted. *Per* Ormrod J:

It is clear that the judge was greatly influenced by the judgment of Simon P in *Szechter v Szechter* (1971) ... Reading that passage – and one can understand what the judge had in mind – he felt that he had to find a threat to life, limb, liberty in order to find duress. With respect, I do not for one moment think that the President intended that result. He was merely contrasting a disagreeable situation with one which constituted a real threat. The matter can be dealt with quite shortly by referring to *Pao On v Lau Liu Long* (1980) in which Lord Scarman said: 'Duress, whatever form it takes, is a coercion of the will so as to vitiate consent.'

The crucial question in these cases, particularly where a marriage is involved, is whether the threats, pressure or whatever it is, is such as to destroy the reality of consent and overbears the will of the individual. It seems to me that this case of a young girl, wholly dependent on her parents, being forced into a marriage with a man she has never seen in order to prevent her (reasonably from her parents' point of view) continuing in an association with a Muslim which they would regard with abhorrence. But it is as clear a case as one could want of the overbearance of the will of the petitioner and thus invalidating or vitiating her consent.

Militante v Ogunwomoju (1993)

H married W in 1991. At that time H was an illegal immigrant in the UK who had assumed the identity of a person living lawfully there. He gave W a false name. Because H had no right of abode in the UK he was deported in 1992. W petitioned for a decree of nullity.

Held: W's application would be *granted*. Where a person makes a false representation as to his identity, and another person marries him believing his misrepresentation, fraud of this nature will destroy consent. The marriage of H and W was declared null and void.

2.4.3   Mental disorder within the meaning of the Mental Health Act 1983 at the time of marriage (s 12(d))

Bennett v Bennett (1969)

H had married W in 1965, but they spent only very short periods of time with each other because H was abroad on active service. W had been admitted twice to a mental hospital before the marriage, once for a month and, later, for a fortnight during which she was given shock treatment. H was not aware of these facts when he married W. When he returned home in December 1965 he learned from a doctor that W had been receiving treatment in a mental hospital. Following another tour of duty abroad, he filed a petition of nullity.

Held: whilst accepting that W's behaviour was likely to be difficult over a relatively short period of time, it was clear that W was suffering from no more than a temporary neurosis. The marriage of H and W was *valid*.

Per Ormrod J:

> Concerning the definition of mental disorder [in the Mental Health Act 1959, s 4], the question is, what did Parliament mean by the phrase 'unfitted for marriage and the procreation of children', because they are conjunctive and not disjunctive. 'Unfitted' is a word which is not easily construed. It might be given a very wide interpretation or a very narrow one. It is quite plain to me, having regard to the context, with the background of mental deficiency in mind, that Parliament cannot possibly have intended to use the word 'unfitted' in an extensive sense. This must really mean something very much like the test of unsoundness of mind although perhaps not quite the same, it really must mean something in the nature of: 'Is this particular person capable of living in a married state and of carrying out the ordinary duties and obligations of marriage?' I do not think it could possibly be given any wider meaning than that.

2.4.4 At the time of the marriage respondent was suffering from a communicable venereal disease or was pregnant by some person other than the petitioner (s 12(e)(f))

Stocker v Stocker (1966)

H and W met in April 1963; sexual intercourse, during which H always used a contraceptive, followed regularly and in June W told H that she was pregnant. H was sure that he was the father and decided to marry W. He stated that he would have married her in any event. They married in August and a child was born in December. H petitioned for a decree of nullity on the ground of pregnancy by some other person.

Held: the petition ought to be *granted*. *Per* Karminski J:

> I have no doubt at all on the medical evidence that this child must have been conceived at a time before H and W had ever met each other, that is before 13 April 1963. On that finding the child cannot have been the child of H. That finding was reinforced. however, by very important evidence by Dr Grant on the subject of blood tests ... Dr Grant established to my complete satisfaction on the tests that H could not possibly have been the father, so that I am satisfied beyond any doubt that, at the time of marriage, W was pregnant by some person other than the husband ... The court has to be satisfied that, at the time of marriage, H was ignorant of the fact that W was pregnant by another person. I am perfectly satisfied that H was. He believed, and reasonably believed on the facts as he knew them, that he was the father of the child that was expected, and he believed that because W told him so. He told the doctor that the child was expected at a time which was consistent with the intercourse between H and W before marriage. So I am satisfied that H has established that he was ignorant at the time of the marriage of the facts alleged concerning W's pregnancy ... I find as a fact that no intercourse took place after H discovered that W was pregnant by a man other than himself.

2.5 Bars to the annulment of a voidable marriage

Note ───────────────────────────────────

Under s 13 MCA 1973, the following bars to relief of a voidable marriage exist: P, knowing that it was open to him to have the marriage voided, acted so as to lead R to believe reasonably that he would not seek to do so, and that it would be unjust to R to grant a decree; P had knowledge of the defect alleged; proceedings were not instituted within three years of the date of marriage (in the case of proceedings on the ground of lack of consent, allegation of venereal disease or allegation of pregnancy *per alium*).

Pettit v Pettit (1962) CA

H married W in 1939. The marriage was not consummated because of H's impotence. W continued to live with H, contributed to the purchase of the matrimonial home, worked during H's absence on active service, and paid life insurance and the mortgage interest. In 1945 W gave birth to a child which had been conceived following *fecundatio ab extra*. In 1953 H left W to live with another woman. In 1960 H presented a petition for a decree of nullity based upon his own impotence.

Held: it would *not* be fair and equitable to grant the decree to H. *Per* Davies LJ:

A passage from *Harthan v Harthan* (1949) [*per* Lord Merriman], as it seems to me, is a direct and authoritative statement that in a petition by an impotent spouse the whole of the circumstances, including the respondent's attitude and reaction to the situation created by the impotence of the petitioner must be looked at in order to see whether it is just or unjust that the impotent spouse should obtain a decree. With that view I respectfully agree …

Per Willmer LJ:

If, as I think, we are bound to take into consideration the reactions and interests of R's wife, there can be, in my judgment, but one answer to H's petition. Here is a wife who has given up her whole life to her husband. Yet H argues that he is entitled to relief against W without regard to what her wishes or interests may be. She has served her husband faithfully as a wife and mother to his child, as well as being of considerable financial help to him. To pronounce a decree of nullity would be a matter of serious prejudice to her. Having regard to her religious beliefs, such a decree would put her in an embarrassing position. On material grounds, even on the assumption that a most generous maintenance order were to be made in her favour, her future security might be gravely imperilled; for in the event of her husband predeceasing her she would no longer enjoy the rights of a widow. I can see no ground on which it could possibly he held that it was fair and equitable to grant relief to H … I concur in thinking that H's appeal should be dismissed.

D v D (Nullity: Statutory Bar) (1979)

The marriage of H and W was not consummated because of W's refusal to undergo an operation necessary to remove a physical impediment. Some months after they agreed to adopt two children, H left W to live with another woman. H petitioned for a decree of nullity on the ground of W's refusal to consummate. The court considered whether H's approbation of the marriage and the relevant provisions of MCA 1973 prevented the granting of a decree.

Held: a decree ought to be *granted*. Approbation of a marriage was no longer a bar to the grant of a decree of nullity. Public policy was no longer a relevant factor, and the bar in s 13 was absolute and not discretionary. The relevant considerations were the conduct of parties to each other and the possibility of injustice to the respondent. There was, in this case, no injustice to W so that, in all the circumstances, it would not be unjust to grant the decree and, hence, there was no statutory bar to such a grant.

Q Are there any advantages in the maintenance of the distinction between void and voidable marriages?

3 Divorce (1)

3.1 The contemporary significance of divorce

Note

Divorce involves the termination of a marriage on the ground of its irretrievable breakdown, by a decree of dissolution of the status of the marriage on the petition of either party. The law relating to divorce is consolidated largely in MCA 1973, as amended. Fundamental and far-reaching changes in the law relating to divorce would have been introduced by Part II Family Law Act 1996.

3.2 Procedural matters

Note

Procedural matters are of great importance in this area of family law. Family Law Act 1996 would have contained, in Part II, considerable revision of existing procedures and practices, had it been brought into force.

3.2.1 The staying of jurisdiction

De Dampierre v De Dampierre (1987) HL

H and W were French nationals and had married in France in 1977. In 1979 they moved to London where their child was born in 1982. W started a business in New York in 1984, moving with the child to New York one year later. H asked her to move back to London but she refused. H then commenced divorce proceedings in France and, at a later date, W petitioned in England for divorce. H made application to stay W's petition under s 5(6) and Sched 1, para 9(1) DMPA 1973. His application was refused on the ground that, under the French proceedings, W might be denied maintenance if she were found to have been solely responsible for the breakdown of the marriage (whereas under English law she might obtain financial relief even if her behaviour were to be taken into account).

H's appeal was dismissed by the Court of Appeal and he then appealed to the House of Lords.

Held: H's appeal would be *allowed*. When examining the general balance of convenience and fairness in order to determine whether proceedings of this nature ought to be stayed, the court should not be deterred from granting a stay merely because a plaintiff in this country might suffer the loss of legitimate personal benefit or other advantage, always provided that the court was satisfied that justice would be done in the court overseas. It could not be concluded, in the present case, that justice would not be done if W were to pursue her remedy in France. W had clearly severed her links with England when she went to New York, and the case appeared to have closer links with France than England. The natural forum for the dispute was, clearly, France. The proceedings in England, therefore, would be stayed.

3.2.2 Absolute bar on petitions within one year of marriage (see s 3(1) MCA 1973)

Butler v Butler (1990)

H and W were married in October 1986. In September 1987 W filed a petition for judicial separation on the ground of H's unreasonable behaviour. In January 1988 W's petition was amended so that she could seek a divorce. A decree nisi and decree absolute were pronounced, but it was then discovered that the decree had been granted on the basis of a petition which had been presented *less than one year* after the date of the marriage. At this point the Queen's Proctor intervened and asked for a declaration that the decree nisi and decree absolute were null and void.

Held: MCA 1973, s 3(1) states clearly that no petition for divorce shall be presented before the expiration of one year from the date of the marriage. This constitutes a clear, unambiguous statutory bar and the court has no discretion to avoid it on the ground of a genuine error. The petition and the subsequent divorce were *null and void*.

3.2.3 Granting of decree absolute

Torok v Torok (1973)

In 1956 H and W left Hungary and came to the UK where they were naturalised. They lived together until 1967 when H decided to settle abroad. In 1972 H commenced divorce proceedings in Hungary (where he was also a national) on the basis of five years' separation. A partial decree was issued by the Hungarian court. As soon as the English court recognised the Hungarian decree it would have no power to make any order under the Matrimonial Proceedings and Property Act 1970. W would be left, therefore, without an effective claim for financial provision. She petitioned in England for divorce.

Held: the decree would be *granted*. The court had jurisdiction to grant the decree and there were no grounds for refusing it.

Dackham v Dackham (1987) CA

The registrar had stated, in ancillary proceedings following the grant of a decree nisi, that he lacked jurisdiction because the decree had not been made absolute. He asked H and W whether they wished him to grant such a decree. He then purported to grant a decree absolute. Later, H died and W appealed against an order made by the registrar concerning her transfer of a share in the matrimonial home to H.

Held: prescribed formalities had been ignored and the marriage had *not* been dissolved. Neither H nor W had taken the necessary steps to apply for a decree absolute, there had been no endorsement on the decree nisi and the Court officials had not carried out their mandatory duty to search the court minutes. It was clear from the Matrimonial Cause Rules 1977 that the grant of a decree absolute necessitates total compliance with mandatory requirements: these rules were of vital importance since a decree absolute was binding on the parties and everyone else. The requirements had not been met and, therefore, there had been no valid decree absolute. Because the marriage had not been dissolved, H and W had remained married until H's death.

Smith v Smith (1990)

A decree nisi was granted and H applied for the decree to be made absolute. The registrar was satisfied concerning the requirements of r 65(2) Matrimonial Causes Rules 1977, but, because ancillary relief proceedings were pending, he refused H's application. H appealed, arguing that if the appropriate requirements were satisfied the registrar was obliged to make the order.

Held: H's appeal would be *dismissed*. Although it seemed as if the registrar had no discretion where the requirements of the rule had been satisfied, it was necessary to interpret that rule in the light of MCA 1973 and other rules, all of which allowed the registrar a variety of powers in considering an application such as H had made. H's appeal would be dismissed.

Callaghan v Hanson-Fox (1991)

W filed a petition for divorce after many years of marriage and H consented to the grant of the decree, which was made absolute in May 1977. In January 1986 W died and in May 1988 H issued a writ by which he sought to set aside the decree absolute on the ground of its having been obtained by a petition based essentially on fraud.

Held: H's action was *dismissed*. The decree absolute had been granted by a competent court following compliance with all the appropriate procedural requirements; it would therefore stand.

Manchanda v Manchanda (1995) CA

A decree of divorce was granted to W on 27 July 1994. On 16 September 1994 H applied for a decree absolute. On 20 September 1994 the decree was made absolute. W applied to set aside the decree absolute on the ground that, under s 9(2) MCA 1973, the necessary period of time had not elapsed before the application was made, and that no notice of it had been given to her. On 29 September 1994 H had gone through a ceremony of marriage with another woman. H argued that it was for W to show the mischief which the relevant legislation was designed to avoid, and that she had failed to show any such mischief as would necessitate holding the decree absolute void. Further, he submitted that, because the grant of the decree absolute was the result of a mistake, it should be held voidable rather than void.

Held: The decree absolute was a *nullity*, not merely voidable. *Per* Leggatt LJ:

> A distinction has to be drawn between cases in which the court lacked jurisdiction, because it had no power to grant a decree absolute in the circumstances in which it had purported to do so, and cases in which, though the court enjoyed jurisdiction, it had, through the inadvertence of one of the parties, failed to observe a statutory provision against the exercise of it, or there had been a procedural irregularity in the process of exercising it. The present case falls within the former category.

(Further, the failure to serve a summons on W, in accordance with r 2.50 of the Family Proceedings Rules (SI 1991/1247) rendered the decree absolute null and void, and W was entitled to have it set aside.)

3.2.4 The special procedure

Note

Following the Practice Direction (1977), undefended divorce petitions are considered by a district judge who examines a petition and a supporting affidavit, satisfies himself that the contents are proved, and issues and files a certificate. At a later date a decree nisi is issued in open court, neither party being required to be present. The petitioner is then entitled to apply for a decree absolute.

Day v Day (1979) CA

Following W's petitioning for divorce, H stated his intention to defend, but he failed to file an answer. Because the suit appeared to be undefended, the registrar gave directions under the Matrimonial Causes Rules 1977 and the cause was placed on the special procedure list. After W had given evidence, the registrar granted a certificate under r 48(1)(a), indicating that W had proved the essence of the petition and was entitled to a decree. Following H's application, the judge removed the case from the special procedure list. H was granted leave to file his answer out of time. W appealed.

Held: the judge was in error, and W's appeal would be *allowed*. Once the registrar issues a certificate under r 48 the court is obliged to grant a decree nisi. An application for a rehearing has to be dealt with as an application for rehearing after a decree nisi, so that it should be refused unless there existed clear grounds for believing that justice had not been done in all the circumstances. H had been given sufficient opportunity to file an answer; it was not essential that the case be heard again.

3.2.5   Agreement not to defend

N v N (Agreement Not To Defend) (1992)
H and W were married in 1973 and in 1990 W presented a petition for divorce. Later, she agreed with H that she would not continue her action for five months, during which time they would seek reconciliation. H agreed that, should the attempt fail, he would not defend the petition. After five months W decided that she would proceed with the petition. H applied (out of time) to defend, contending that the marriage had not broken down irretrievably. H's application was granted on the ground that divorce was essentially an inquisitorial process and the parties could not make an agreement to reject the jurisdiction of the court to enquire into the state of the marriage. W appealed.

Held: W's appeal would be *allowed*. The agreement not to defend was a proper agreement. H would not be allowed to present a defence. The court's duty involved its examining whether or not there was, in fact, a breakdown of the marriage.

3.3   The sole ground for divorce: irretrievable breakdown of the marriage, supported by one or more of the 'five facts'

Note ———————————————————————————————
A petition for divorce may be presented to the court by either party to a marriage on the ground that the marriage has broken down irretrievably (at the date of the hearing), *and* this involves the petitioner satisfying the court of one or more facts: s 1(1)(2) MCA 1973. Proof of one of the facts raises a presumption of irretrievable breakdown.

3.3.1   Failure to establish a fact

Richards v Richards (1972)
H and W married in 1963. In 1970 H began to suffer from mental illness, resulting in a change in his personality. He was 'moody and taciturn' and

suffered from insomnia. He assaulted W on several occasions, after which he and W accepted that he was mentally ill. W left him in 1971 and presented a petition for divorce under legislation which has now become s 1(2)(b) MCA 1973. The petition alleged that H's behaviour was of such a nature that she could not reasonably be expected to live with him.

Held: W's petition would be *dismissed*. She had not established to the satisfaction of the court that H's behaviour was such that she could not reasonably be expected to live with him. *Per* Rees J:

> What should be the correct approach to the undoubted fact that the whole of W's behaviour of which complaint is made stemmed from H's mental illness? In *Williams v Williams* (1964) HL, Lord Reid had said: 'In my judgment, a decree should be pronounced against an abnormal person, not because his conduct was aimed at his wife, not because a reasonable man would have realised his position, nor because he must be deemed to have foreseen or intended the harm he did, but simply because the facts are such that, after making all allowances for his disabilities and for the temperaments of H and W, it must be held that the character and gravity of his acts was such as to amount to cruelty. And if that is right for an abnormal person, I can see no good reason why the same should not apply to a person who is insane.'

> ... I am required to make a value judgment about the behaviour of H and its effect on W, the petitioner. In so doing, I take into account ... among all the other facts in the case the temperament of the parties and H's mental illness. Having done so, I conclude that W has failed to satisfy me that H has behaved in such a way that she cannot reasonably be expected to live with him. Accordingly, and notwithstanding that the marriage has broken down irretrievably, it is my duty to dismiss the petition.

Buffery v Buffery (1988) CA

H and W had been married for 20 years and had three children who, having grown up, had left the family home. W complained that, while the children were at home, she and H rarely went out together. Further, she complained of H's control of the family finances. H and W appeared to have moved apart and had lost the capacity to communicate with each other. W sought to divorce H on the ground of his behaviour under s 1(2)(b) MCA 1973. The recorder held that H and W had 'merely drifted apart'. W's petition was dismissed as she had failed to prove her case under s 1(2)(b). She appealed.

Held: W's appeal was *dismissed*. *Per* May LJ:

> Reading the judgment of the recorder in full, I conclude that in so far as any dissension over money matters was concerned, although H had been somewhat insensitive, nevertheless this did not constitute sufficient behaviour within the relevant statutory provision. In truth, what has happened in this marriage is the fault of neither party; they have just grown apart. They cannot communicate.

They have nothing in common, and there lies, as the recorder said, the crux of the matter.

It was submitted that if the matter went back to the recorder he could make various findings on the evidence about the sensitivity of W in relation to these matters and various further findings of fact about the nature and extent of H's behaviour complained of. I, for my part, do not think that he could. He heard all the evidence, and the conclusion to which he came was that nobody was really at fault here, except they both had grown apart. In these circumstances, in my judgment, W failed to make out her case under s 1(2)(b), although she satisfied the recorder that the marriage had broken down irretrievably. I do not think that any advantage would be gained by sending this matter back for a retrial. The matter was fully investigated and the recorder made the findings to which I have referred. In those circumstances I would reach the same conclusion as did the recorder, namely that the petition should be dismissed.

3.4 Fact 1: adultery plus intolerability (s 1(2)(a) MCA 1973)

Note ————————————————————————————————————

Adultery is described in this context as an act of voluntary sexual intercourse (which need not be completed) between two persons not married to each other, but one or more of whom are married at the time of the act to a third person. The petitioner must show that respondent has committed adultery *and* that she/he finds it intolerable to live with respondent.

3.4.1 Definition and proof of adultery

Redpath v Redpath (1950) CA

H and W were married in September 1938, In June 1944 W complained that she had been raped by X. X was charged with rape and was acquitted. In 1948 H filed a petition which alleged that, in June 1944, W committed adultery with X. The judge dismissed the allegation of adultery, stating that, given proof of an act of intercourse, the burden was on H to show that W had consented to the act. H appealed.

Held: the judge was *in error*. Once intercourse is established, the burden is on respondent to show that the intercourse was involuntary. *Per* Bucknill LJ:

Sexual intercourse is normally a consensual act, that is to say it requires the consenting minds and bodies of both parties. In my view once the act of intercourse is established, the burden rests on W to show that the act was one into which she was forced against her will. I do not think that H can be expected to prove the state of W's mind when the act of intercourse took place. On the other hand [under s 4(2) MCA 1937] the court must be satisfied that adultery was committed. Where, at the end of the case there is a doubt in the judge's mind as to whether adultery has taken place or whether it is a case of rape, it is his duty to dismiss the petition. In this present case the judge has placed an unnecessary burden of proof on H; that has, in part, led him to arrive at an incorrect decision. In the circumstances I am satisfied that W committed adultery and that the judge was in error in finding that adultery had not been proved.

A decree based on W's adultery would be *granted*.

Dennis v Dennis (1955) CA

H was impotent. He had spent a night in bed with a woman who was not his wife, thus creating an inference that he had committed an act of adultery. It was established that H had not penetrated the woman.

Held: there must be *some* penetration if an act of adultery is to be proved. *Per* Singleton LJ:

> Adultery cannot be proved unless there be some penetration. It is not necessary that the complete act of intercourse should take place. If there is penetration by the man of the woman, adultery may be found, but if there is not more than an attempt, I do not think that a finding of adultery would be right ... The inference of adultery is capable of being rebutted and on the findings of the commissioner in the present case it was rebutted, for he has found that at the time at which the two were together, H was impotent in regard to X at least ... That was the finding of the commissioner and I am satisfied that, on that finding of fact, he took the only course which he was entitled to take. He declined to find that adultery was proved.

Bastable v Bastable (1968) CA

H and W became very friendly with X and his wife, Y. During 1964 W and X appeared to have formed a close companionship while H and Y were working away from their homes. H began proceedings for divorce on grounds of desertion by W. He also alleged that W had committed adultery with X. The allegation was denied by W and X. The judge rejected evidence given by W and X and held that H had discharged the appropriate burden of proof and that W's adultery had been proved. W appealed.

Held: the appeal would be *allowed*. A high standard of proof was required for establishing adultery. In proportion as the offence is grave, so ought the proof to be clear. H had been unable to prove adultery between W and X, and his suspicion was insufficient. *Per* Willmer LJ:

> I confess that I have found the question raised by this appeal an exceedingly difficult one. It seems to me that much must depend on what is the appropriate standard of proof in relation to a charge such as that made here. If I may say so

with all possible respect, sitting in this court I do not find it altogether easy to follow the directions contained in various statements made by members of the House of Lords. In *Bater v Bater* (1951) CA, Denning LJ said: 'In civil cases, the case may be proved by a preponderance of probability, but there may be degrees of probability within that standard. The degree depends on the subject-matter. A civil court, when considering a charge of fraud, will naturally require a higher degree of probability than that which it would require when considering negligence. It does not adopt so high a degree as a criminal court, even when considering a charge of a criminal nature; but still it does require a degree of probability which is commensurate with the occasion. Likewise, a divorce court should require a degree of probability which is proportionate to the subject matter.' Until this matter has been considered by the House of Lords and further guidance received, I shall direct myself in accordance with that statement of principle.

In the present case what is charged is 'an offence' ... It is for H to satisfy the court that the offence has been committed. Whatever the popular view may be, it remains true to say that in the eyes of the law, adultery is a serious matrimonial offence. It follows that a high standard of proof is required in order to satisfy the court that the offence has been committed.

3.4.2 Intolerability

Goodrich v Goodrich (1971)

In 1970 W asked for the dissolution of her marriage to H, based on allegations of H's cruelty. She asked for the court's discretion in favour of her adultery. H denied the allegation of cruelty and sought a reconciliation which W refused. In 1971 H filed a petition alleging irretrievable breakdown of the marriage on the ground of W's adultery and that he found it intolerable to continue living with her, not as a result of her adultery, but because of her allegations of cruelty and her rejection of his attempts at reconciliation.

Held: H was *granted* a decree. The court may find that a marriage has broken down irretrievably where party A has committed adultery and party B then finds it intolerable to live with party A, even though the intolerability cannot be said to have arisen solely from the adultery. The approach must be a *subjective one*, so that the question to be determined is essentially not what a 'reasonable petitioner' would find intolerable, but what, in fact, the petitioner in a particular case finds intolerable.

Cleary v Cleary (1974) CA

H and W married in 1964. In 1971 W left H and went to live with another man. A month later she returned to H and stayed for six weeks, leaving to live with her mother. She petitioned in 1972 on the ground of irretrievable breakdown of the marriage, arguing that H had behaved in a manner making it intolerable for her to live with him. H admitted the breakdown of the marriage and asked for a dissolution on the ground of W's adultery. The court heard evidence showing that W's adultery was proved and H submitted that, because there was no longer any real basis for the marriage, he could no longer live with W. His petition was dismissed and he appealed.

Held: H's appeal should be *allowed*. *Per* Lord Denning:

> As a matter of interpretation I think that the two facts in the section [adultery and intolerability] are independent and should be so treated. Take this very case. H proved that W committed adultery and that he forgave her and took her back. That is one fact. He then proves that, after she comes back, she behaves in a way that makes it quite intolerable to live with her. She corresponds with the other man and goes out at night and finally leaves H, taking the children with her. That is another fact. It is in consequence of the second fact that he finds it intolerable – not in consequence of the previous adultery. On that evidence it is quite plain that the marriage has broken down irretrievably. He complies with the section by proving (a) her adultery which was forgiven; and (b) her subsequent conduct (not adultery) which makes it intolerable to live with her ...

> A judge in such cases as these should not accept the man's bare assertion that he finds it intolerable. He should inquire what conduct on W's part has made it intolerable. It may be her previous adultery. It may be something else. But whatever it is, the judge must be satisfied that H finds it intolerable to live with her. On the facts of this case I think that the judge could and should have found on the evidence the two elements required: (1) W's adultery, and (2) H found it intolerable to live with her.

3.5 Fact 2: respondent's behaviour makes it unreasonable to expect petitioner to live with respondent (s 1(2)(b) MCA 1973)

Note ———————————————————————————————
Petitioner must show that respondent's behaviour has been of a particular character, *and* that because of that behaviour it would be unreasonable to expect petitioner to live with respondent.
————————————————————————————————————

3.5.1 Interpretation of 'behaviour'

Carew-Hunt v Carew-Hunt (1973)
W, the petitioner, lived with H who denied that the marriage had broken down irretrievably. W's case was that H was totally 'self-preoccupied', that he did not require her even in the role of companion, and that he was becoming addicted to alcohol; nothing was left of the marriage, which was now empty of purpose.

Held: the facts pointed to irretrievable breakdown and there *should be* a decree. *Per* Ormrod J:

> The question here is not whether respondent has behaved unreasonably; and the court is no longer required, except in a marginal sense, to pass judgment on whether a person's behaviour is right or wrong, good or bad.

Ash v Ash (1972)

W filed a petition for divorce on the ground of irretrievable breakdown of the marriage, citing H's various acts of violence and drunkenness. H admitted this but denied irretrievable breakdown.

Held: W did not appear, clearly, to be of such a character that she could be expected to live with H. The marriage had broken down irretrievably and a decree *should be granted*. *Per* Bagnall J:

> In order to answer the question whether the petitioner can or cannot be reasonably expected to live with the respondent, in my judgment, I have to consider not only the behaviour of the respondent as alleged and established in the evidence, but the character, personality, disposition and behaviour of the petitioner. The general question may be expanded thus: can this petitioner, with his/her character and personality, with his/her faults and other attributes, good and bad, and having regard to his/her behaviour during the marriage, be reasonably expected to live with this respondent? It follows that if a respondent is seeking to resist a petition on the first ground on which the husband in this case relies, he must in his answer plead and in his evidence show the characteristics, faults, attributes, personality and behaviour on the part of the petitioner on which he relies. Then, if I may give a few examples, it seems to me that a violent petitioner can reasonably be expected to live with a violent respondent; a petitioner who is addicted to drink can reasonably be expected to live with a respondent similarly addicted ... and if each is equally bad, at any rate in similar respects, each can reasonably be expected to live with the other.

Bannister v Bannister (1980) CA

W alleged in an undefended petition that H rarely spoke to her, often spent nights away from the matrimonial home and was, in effect, living his own independent life. W failed: the county court judge decided that H's behaviour was not 'unreasonable'. W appealed.

Held: W's appeal would be *allowed*. *Per* Ormrod J:

> The learned judge, I am afraid, fell into the linguistic trap which is waiting for all of us when we speak of 'unreasonable behaviour' in relation to s 1(2)(b) cases. The basis of this subsection is not 'unreasonable behaviour', but behaving in such a way that the petitioner 'cannot reasonably be expected to live with the respondent' – a significantly different concept. It is difficult to find an alternative shorthand expression for this subsection, so we talk, inaccurately, of 'unreasonable behaviour'. It seems to me that W made out a clear case of

behaviour such that she could not reasonably be expected to live with H, and that she therefore proved irretrievable breakdown of the marriage.

3.5.2 'Positive' and 'negative' behaviour

Thurlow v Thurlow (1975)

W's epileptic fits, from which she suffered at the time of the marriage, meant that she was increasingly confined to her bed. She became very aggressive and damaged the home. It was obvious that she was in need of permanent institutional care. H petitioned for a decree of divorce on the ground that W's behaviour was such that he could not reasonably be expected to live with her. W contended that this did not amount to behaviour under s 1(2)(b).

Held: passive behaviour, eg, that caused by medical illness, *can* amount to 'behaviour' within s 1(2)(b), taking into account the strain undergone by H. A decree would be *granted*. *Per* Rees J:

> I am satisfied that by July 1972 the marriage had irretrievably broken down and since the wife, tragically, is to spend the rest of her life as a patient in a hospital, the husband cannot be expected to live with her. But the question remains as to whether the wife's behaviour has been such as to justify a finding by the court that it is unreasonable to expect him to do so.

> As to the distinction which has been made between 'positive' and 'negative' behaviour, I can find nothing in the statute to suggest that either form is excluded. The sole test prescribed as to the nature of the behaviour is that it must be such as to justify a finding that the petitioner cannot reasonably be expected to live with the respondent. It may well be that in practice such a finding will more readily be made in cases where the behaviour relied upon is positive than those where it is negative.

> In reaching a decision, the judge will have regard to all the circumstances including the disabilities and temperaments of both parties, the causes of the behaviour and whether the causes were or were not known to the petitioner, the presence or absence of intention, the impact of it upon the petitioner and the family unit, its duration and the prospect of cure or improvement in the future. If the judge decided that it would be unreasonable to expect the petitioner to live with the respondent then he must grant a decree of divorce unless he is satisfied that the marriage has not irretrievably broken down.

> Approaching the facts in the instant case upon the basis of these conclusions I feel bound to decide that a decree nisi should be granted. This husband has conscientiously and courageously suffered the behaviour of the wife for substantial periods of time between 1969 and 1972 until his powers of endurance were exhausted and his health was endangered. This behaviour stemmed from mental illness and disease and no blame of any kind can be attributed to the wife.

3.5.3 Behaviour involves conduct

Pheasant v Pheasant (1972)

H left W and petitioned under s 2(1)(b) of the Divorce Reform Act 1969, alleging that W was unable to give him the spontaneous affection which he sought and therefore, that he could not reasonably be expected to live with her. The marriage, he alleged, had broken down irretrievably. W stated that she wished for H's return. She did not believe that the marriage had broken down irretrievably, in any sense of that term.

Held: H been unable to establish the 'behaviour fact'; there was *no breach* on W's part of any of the obligations of marriage. *Per* Ormrod J:

> I have no hesitation in holding that there is nothing in W's behaviour which could be regarded as a breach on her part of any of the obligations of the married state or as effectively contributing to the break-up of the marriage. This, in my opinion, has been caused, if H's evidence is true, by a change in his personality and the development in him of a psychological condition which has made him totally egocentric ...

Katz v Katz (1972)

H and W married in 1954. In 1967 H was showing signs of mental instability: he had become obsessed with electrical recording equipment, and spent much time writing letters to distinguished persons. A period in a mental hospital produced some alleviation of his symptoms but subsequent conduct led to W's attempting suicide. She petitioned for divorce.

Held: W was *entitled* to a decree. *Per* Baker P:

> Behaviour is something more than a mere state of affairs or a state of mind ... Behaviour in this context is action or conduct by the one which affects the other. Such conduct may take either acts or the form of an act or omission or may be a course of conduct and, in my view, it must have some reference to the marriage. What is the standard of behaviour? It is for the judge, not the petitioner alone to decide whether the behaviour is sufficiently grave to fulfil the test, that is, to make it unreasonable to expect the petitioner to endure it, to live with the respondent ... On the whole of the evidence, I have come to the conclusion that H's behaviour was such that, making all the allowances that I should make, it was of that quality and reached the standard envisaged in s 2(1)(b) of the Divorce Reform Act 1969 so that W could not reasonably be expected to live with H. She has made out her case. There will be a decree nisi.

3.5.4 The 'right thinking person' test

Livingstone-Stallard v Livingstone-Stallard (1974)

H and W were married in 1969. A few months later, following violent harassment, W left H. In 1970 they were reunited, but, in 1972, W left after an argument which appeared to have been the culmination of a series of relatively trivial incidents. W petitioned on the ground of H's behaviour.

Held: W would be *granted* a decree nisi. *Per* Dunn J:

> I am quite satisfied that this marriage has broken down. W told me that in no circumstances would she continue to live with H ... I cannot, of course, dissolve this marriage unless I am satisfied that H has behaved in such a way that W cannot reasonably be expected to live with him. The question is, to my mind, a question of fact, and one approach is to suppose that the case is being tried by a judge and jury and to consider what the proper direction to the jury would be, and then to put oneself in the position of a properly directed jury in deciding the question of fact ... Taking the facts as I have found them in the round in relation to H's character, in my judgment, they amount to a situation in which this young wife was subjected to a constant atmosphere of criticism, disapproval and boorish behaviour on the part of the husband ... I think that any right-thinking person would come to the conclusion that this husband had behaved in such a way that this wife could not reasonably be expected to live with him. There will accordingly be a decree nisi under s 1(2)(b).

O'Neill v O'Neill (1975) CA

H had spent two years making extensive repairs to the matrimonial home, during which time the state of the home caused considerable discomfort and embarrassment to W and the children, who eventually left. During proceedings initiated by W, H wrote to W's solicitors questioning the paternity of the children. W's petition for unreasonable behaviour was rejected, the judge holding that W was merely complaining of aspects of H's personality. W appealed.

Held: W's appeal would be *allowed*. *Per* Roskill LJ:

> The judge appears to have thought that it was right to dismiss W's petition on the ground that H's conduct, such as he found it to have been, was based upon some defect of personality. Even if that were true, that does not excuse his conduct; nor does it make his conduct any less unreasonable. It may explain it, but it cannot possibly excuse it ... The judge does not mention H's letter. I entirely agree that that letter alone would justify the grant of a decree under s 1(2)(b), for to describe it as wicked is an understatement ... I think I would have granted W a decree on the strength of the letter alone.

3.5.5   Living together after the conduct in question

Bradley v Bradley (1973) CA

At the time of W marrying H, she had six children by a previous marriage. During the marriage to H, three more were born. W obtained a separation order against H on the ground of cruelty, but H returned to the matrimonial home. At the time of W's petition for divorce on grounds of

H's behaviour, he was living with W. The judge refused to hear further evidence. (Cohabitation for up to six months following the conduct in question is disregarded by the court.) W appealed.

Held: the case would be *remitted* for a full hearing by the judge. W had stated that she had no course of action except to live with H because of the children and the council's failure to rehouse her. She was not prevented in any way from alleging that she could not reasonably be expected to live with H. Denning LJ stated that the judge was wrong to dismiss the case: it was open to him to grant a decree nisi on the ground mentioned in the statute. The appeal should be allowed accordingly.

Q Can you support the reasoning behind the decision in *Richards v Richards* (1972)?

4 Divorce (2); Judicial Separation

4.1 Desertion and living apart

Note ───────────────────────────────────────

Facts 3, 4 and 5 are covered by s 1(2)(c), (d), (e) MCA 1973. Desertion involves the unjustifiable withdrawal by one spouse from the state of cohabitation without the consent of the other and with the intention of effecting a permanent separation of the spouses. It is based upon a continuous period of two years immediately prior to the presentation of the petition. Living apart involves periods of two or five years immediately preceding the petition.

──

4.2 Fact 3: the fact of desertion (s 1(2)(c) MCA 1973)

Hopes v Hopes (1949) CA

H and W were occupying separate bedrooms. H petitioned for divorce on the ground of desertion. He argued that W had moved into a separate bedroom, sexual intercourse had ended and she failed to look after him. Evidence was given, however, that W cooked for H and his meals were taken in a common dining room with W and his daughters.

Held: there was no *de facto* separation and, therefore, no desertion. H's petition *failed*. *Per* Lord Denning:

> One of the essential elements of desertion is the fact of separation. Can that exist while the parties are living under the same roof? My answer is, yes ... It is important to draw a clear line between desertion, which is a ground for divorce, and gross neglect or chronic discord, which is not. That line is drawn at the point where the parties are living separately and apart. In cases where they are living under the same roof, that point is reached when they cease to be one household and become two households, or, in other words, when H and W are no longer residing with one another or cohabiting with one another.

Naylor v Naylor (1961)

Following a series of quarrels, W indicated to H that she no longer considered herself as his wife. She symbolically removed her wedding ring and, from that time, their family life together ended. W performed no services for H and he then refused to give her money to meet household expenses. The magistrates dismissed W's complaint, holding that she was in desertion.

Held: W *was* in desertion. *Per* Lord Merriman:

> In the present case we think that the justices were right in their finding of desertion because we take the view that these two spouses were ... leading entirely separate lives, residing separately from each other, albeit under the same roof. We hold, therefore, that there is no ground for differing from their finding that the wife was guilty of desertion.

Le Brocq v Le Brocq (1964) CA

Following their marriage, H and W had a number of disagreements, often culminating in heated arguments. Following one such argument, W sought to shut out H from their shared bedroom by placing a bolt on the door, with the intention of excluding him. After this incident communication between H and W ceased almost entirely. Nevertheless, H continued to pay W for housekeeping; in return she continued to cook his meals. H later alleged that, in effect, W had deserted him.

Held: H was *unable* to establish the alleged desertion of W. *Per* Harman LJ:

> [There was] a separation of bedrooms, a separation of speaking, and a separation of hearts, but the evidence indicated clearly that H and W carried on in one household.

4.2.1   *Animus deserendi* (intention of deserting)

Crowther v Crowther (1951) HL

W filed a petition for divorce on the ground that H had deserted her in June 1948. H was detained in a mental hospital from 29 July 1948 to 10 October 1948, as a person of unsound mind. It was argued that, during H's detention, he lacked the capacity either to form or sustain the necessary *animus deserendi*, so that, effectively, he had not been in desertion of W for the necessary continuous period of three years immediately preceding W's presentation of her petition. The House of Lords heard the appeal.

Held: W had the right to be allowed to show that H was capable of possessing the appropriate *animus deserendi* throughout the appropriate period. She did not show this and her petition therefore *failed*. *Per* Lord Porter:

> I see no reason for imputing an irrebuttable inability on the part of a husband, who has been certified, to form or keep an intention. Persons who are abnormal in some respects may be quite normal in others; evidence can solve the question in which category an individual ought to be placed. A lunatic is capable of making a will in a lucid interval and, though a continuous intention is harder to establish, I cannot regard it as impossible ... If, in fact, a petitioner is

unsuccessful in proving that the lunatic was capable of forming an intention, or if no evidence is called, then, in my opinion, the court is not entitled to draw an inference of continued desertion from the intention shown in the pre- and post-certification periods. In accordance with these views, I would allow the appeal and send the case back in order that evidence, if offered, may be received and a conclusion reached in conformity with the principles set out above.

Per Lord Reid:

There are many degrees of mental incapacity and there appears to be no definition of that degree of mental incapacity which is necessary to justify a reception order. In the absence of such a definition it is not obvious to me that there cannot be a case where a reception order is justified, but where, nevertheless, the individual detained still possesses a mind capable of maintaining an *animus deserendi*. I am of opinion, therefore, that this wife ought to be allowed to prove, if she can, that this is such a case. I think that it can be taken to be common knowledge that persons so detained do not generally have such a mind, so, if it appears that the husband has been detained under a reception order, that does raise a presumption against the wife. I can see no ground for holding that it is more than a presumption.

Perry v Perry (1963)

Some 20 years after H and W had been married, W's mental state began to deteriorate: she accused H of seeking to kill her and was certified as suffering from paranoia. Following her leaving hospital, she left the matrimonial home, acting under the delusion that H had tried to murder her. Paranoid psychosis was again diagnosed. H petitioned for divorce on the ground of W's desertion.

Held: because of the intensity of W's delusions she was unable to form an appropriate *animus deserendi*. H's petition would, therefore, be *dismissed*. *Per* Lloyd-Jones J:

H, in my judgment, has failed to show to the satisfaction of the court that W had the mental ability or capacity to form an intention to desert when she left, or to show, as I believe he must, that that intention continued for a period of three years immediately preceding the presentation of the petition. I accept [counsel's] submissions that on the facts of this case it is impossible to separate the delusions from the decision to leave ... In my judgment the right view is that when something is genuinely believed to be true, albeit erroneously, the rights of the parties in relation to a charge of desertion are to be adjudicated as if that belief were true, and I have no doubt that this unfortunate woman did believe in her delusions and that she acted on them. I therefore reiterate my view that where a person's mind is dominated by a delusion which causes that person to leave the matrimonial home, it is impossible to say that that person had the necessary *animus deserendi* to constitute desertion. I accordingly dismiss the petition.

4.2.2 A reasonable offer of reconciliation must not be refused

Fletcher v Fletcher (1945)

H withdrew from the matrimonial home to live in a commune run by the Tramp Preachers' movement. This involved a complete withdrawal from married life, which affected W's health, leading to her having to go away. H later called upon W to live with him in or near the commune and she refused. She later petitioned for divorce on the ground of H's desertion.

Held: H's offer to W for her to return to him was, in the circumstances, unreasonable and did *not* end H's desertion. *Per* Denning J:

> I think that when H withdrew to the headquarters of the Tramp Preachers' movement, in circumstances in which he felt that he had to refuse all sexual intercourse ... that was a withdrawal from married life in any real sense of the term. Although W followed him in an attempt to keep the marriage together, I think his conduct ... was desertion on his part ... In law that desertion continues unless H can show that he has brought it to an end by reasonable offers on his part to set up home again in a proper married life ... W found that she could not bring herself to the way of life [of the commune]. I think that H was not entitled to call upon W to go and live with him in the commune or immediately adjoining it, when he was a member. It was an unreasonable demand for him to make. At all events, it was not such an offer as to terminate the pre-existing desertion ... H's desertion continued for the three years before the presentation of the petition and the result is that I pronounce a decree nisi on the ground of H's desertion.

Gallacher v Gallacher (1965) CA

Following a separation agreement, H and W had separated, but H had no wish for the separation to be permanent. He later wrote to W making a genuine offer to return and suggesting arrangements for W to live in a house which would be large enough to accommodate her and the children. W rejected the offer, stating that she had no wish to live with H ever again.

Held: W's rejection of H's genuine offer of a reconciliation was *unreasonable*. It ended the separation agreement, and put her *in desertion* of H. *Per* Willmer LJ:

> It may well be that the other party is entitled to say, 'I cannot accept this offer as it stands'; but what he or she cannot do, as I understand the law, is to ignore it altogether or refuse to entertain it ... While I am far from saying that W was bound, as a matter of law, to accept the proposal made in H's letter in its exact terms ... the fact is that she was presented with a concrete and reliable proposition, and the least she could do, as it appears to me, was to entertain it and consider it. Unless she was to make herself a deserter, she was bound in one form or another to show willingness to live once again with H, and that is precisely what she failed, and refused, to do. When, some weeks later, H called on W, she said in terms that she was not prepared to live with him ever again.

This being so, it seems to me that W has no real answer to H's contention that from the time of her refusal to entertain his offer, she has been in desertion.

4.2.3 There must be no just cause for the deserting spouse leaving

Quoraishi v Quoraishi (1985) CA

H and W, both Muslim citizens of Bangladesh, married in Karachi in 1964 and came to live in England. H went to work in Kuwait in 1979 and entered into a second marriage by proxy, according to Muslim law, with a Bangladeshi woman, hoping to have children. On his return to England, W asked H on several occasions to divorce his second wife. When he refused, W left him. Her complaint to the magistrates, alleging desertion, was dismissed on the ground that expert opinion, by which H and W had agreed to abide, stated that a Muslim wife had no cause of complaint regarding a second marriage. H petitioned in 1971 for divorce on the ground of W's desertion. His petition was dismissed and he appealed.

Held: it was the *personal circumstances* of H and W which were of significance. It is not necessarily the case in English law that a Muslim woman may not have a just cause for leaving her husband on the ground of a second marriage. H's appeal would be *dismissed*. *Per* Ewbank J:

> It is necessary to consider the particular husband and the particular wife, and the circumstances of their lives, the law under which they were married and their personal law. But, most importantly in most cases, it will be the personal circumstances of H and W which are of vital importance. The relevant circumstances in this case were the rights and obligations owed by each party to the other under their personal law, and the impact of their knowledge of that law upon the spouses in 1983, by which date they had been resident in England since the early 1970s. Both were doctors and were well-educated ... There are no reasonable grounds for interfering with the judge's decisions.

4.2.4 The concept of 'constructive desertion'

Marsden v Marsden (1967)

H believed, on unreasonable grounds, that W had committed adultery with X. W was not given any opportunity to answer H's allegations. Because of H's continuing allegations and his attitude, W left him.

Held: W *was not* in desertion because she had just cause for leaving H. H *was* in constructive desertion. *Per* Simon P:

> If a spouse reasonably believes that the other is committing adultery, the former is entitled to withdraw from cohabitation. It seems to me to follow that the former is equally entitled, without the use of any force, to expel the latter from cohabitation. On the other hand, an accusation of adultery which is unreasonable may afford the spouse against whom it is made good cause for

withdrawal from cohabitation, and, equally, it may constitute constructive desertion on the part of the spouse making such an unreasonable charge. That, I think follows from *Lang v Lang* (1954) PC. If a husband must know that his wife, if she acts like any reasonable woman in her position, would in all probability withdraw from cohabitation as a result of his conduct, he is guilty of constructive desertion if she does so. If, therefore, a reasonable wife, unreasonably accused of adultery, would, as a result, withdraw from cohabitation, it follows that, where a husband unreasonably makes an accusation of adultery, he may be guilty of constructive desertion ... I think that, here, W was entitled to treat herself as dismissed from the matrimonial home. I think that once the justices had found there was no adultery on the part of W and X, and that what H had 'discovered' called for an explanation, but that no explanation was given, they ought to have found that H was in desertion.

4.2.5   Resumption of cohabitation ends desertion

Mummery v Mummery (1942)

H, on active service in France, was evacuated in the retreat from Dunkirk (in May–June, 1940). The relevant period of desertion, upon which W's petition was based, would have terminated in April, 1941. In 1940, H called in to see W while on his way to stay at his grandmother's house. He spent one night with W, and the question arose as to whether the resumption of marital relations for that night was conclusive evidence of H and W having resumed cohabitation so as to bring the state of desertion to an end.

Held: termination of desertion depends on the intention of the parties. An act of sexual intercourse was not conclusive of the question of condonation, and W was *entitled* to her decree. *Per* Lord Merriman:

> It is clear beyond any possibility of argument that a resumption of cohabitation in the full sense of that phrase puts an end to a state of desertion, not merely because it condones a previous desertion for whatever period that offence has lasted, but also because a resumption of cohabitation is the precise negation of a state of desertion. The two things cannot exist together. In this case ... H had not the slightest intention of resuming cohabitation in the ordinary sense of the word ... It is plain that H resumed a state of desertion again the next day ... Does coming together for a single night raise an irrebuttable presumption that the parties have resumed cohabitation, even for that short time? Put in another way, does it raise an irrebuttable presumption that W, in consenting to that state of things, has condoned the previous desertion? I am bound to say that it would lead to an absurd state of things if one were bound to hold that it were so ... I think the law is that, as regards the wife at any rate, an act of sexual intercourse is not conclusive of condonation, and that it does not raise an irrebuttable presumption that cohabitation has been resumed.

Bartram v Bartram (1949) CA

W had deserted H, but after a period of five years she found it necessary to return to H, who was living in his mother's house, because the house in which she was living had been sold. W did no cooking for H and treated him like a lodger whom she disliked.

Held: the period of desertion *continued*, since W had no real intention of resuming cohabitation. *Per* Bucknill LJ:

> The question is: do the facts proved establish that [the period of desertion] was brought to an end? In my opinion it can only be brought to an end if the facts show an intention on W's part to set up a matrimonial home with H. If the facts do not establish any intention on W's part to set up a matrimonial home, the mere fact that W went to live under the same roof as H because she had nowhere else to go, does not remove the desertion which she had started and which continued to run ... I think that H has established desertion for the requisite three years and that a decree in his favour ought to be granted.

4.3 Fact 4: the parties have lived apart for a continuous period of two years preceding presentation of the petition (s 1(2)(d) MCA 1973)

Santos v Santos (1972) CA

H lived in Spain; W lived apart from him in England. Evidence showed that W had visited H and stayed with him on several occasions, so that the question arose as to whether, for the purposes of s 1(2)(d) MCA 1973, W and H were to be considered as 'living apart'.

Held: for purposes of the section, the phrase 'living apart' involves not only that H and W are living apart but *also* that H and/or W do recognise that the marriage has really come to an end. Where one party, say H, does recognise that the marriage has ended, he can make that decision unilaterally; he need not inform W of that decision, nor need W accept it. *Per* Sachs LJ:

> Authority to which we have been referred makes it abundantly clear that the phrase 'living apart' when used in a statute relating to matrimonial affairs normally imports something more than mere physical separation ... If these words import an element additional to physical separation, can that element depend on a unilateral decision or attitude of mind; if so, must its existence be communicated to the other spouse, and in any event how can it be identified so that, in practice, it is capable of judicial determination? ... In the end we have firmly concluded that communication by word or conduct is not a necessary ingredient of the new element. On the basis that a unilateral, uncommunicated ending of recognition that a marriage as subsisting can mark the moment when 'living apart' commences, the principal problem becomes one of proof of the time when the breakdown took place ...

'Living apart' [for purposes of the section] is a state of affairs to establish which it is in the vast generality of cases necessary to prove something more than that H and W are physically separated. For purposes of that generality, it suffices to say that the relevant state of affairs does not exist while both H and W do recognise the marriage as subsisting.

Mouncer v Mouncer (1972)

H and W were married in 1966. The relationship became unsatisfactory and from 1969 to mid-1971, they moved into separate bedrooms although they ate together and participated in keeping the house clean. H argued that he stayed in the house only in order to be involved in the upbringing of the children. H left in mid-1971 and petitioned on the ground of desertion.

Held: H and W had *not* been 'living apart'. Indeed, they had shared the same household. The fact that they did this from the 'wholly admirable motive' of caring properly for their children could not alter the result of what they did.

4.3.1 Respondent must indicate consent to grant of the decree

Mason v Mason (1972)

H was in a mental hospital and had lived apart from W while in the hospital and other institutions. W petitioned for divorce under s 1(2)(d). H signed a typed form of consent and his doctor maintained that he was capable of giving a valid consent.

Held: the question was whether H was capable of understanding the essence and effect of the matter to which he had indicated his consent. He was shown to have been capable and the decree would be *granted*. *Per* Baker P:

> The burden of establishing H's consent is, it seems to me, on the petitioner ... In the present case I am satisfied from the medical evidence presented to me that W has discharged the burden and I conclude that H was capable of understanding the nature of the consent, of expressing it, and appreciating the effects of so doing. The statutory requirements for the granting of a decree have been fulfilled.

4.4 Fact 5: the parties have lived apart for five years (but respondent's consent to the grant of a decree is not needed) (s 1(2)(e) MCA 1973)

Parsons v Parsons (1975)

W, in her petition for divorce on the ground of five years' separation, said that the marriage had broken down. She sought to show constructive desertion by H and the appropriate period of separation. H admitted irretrievable breakdown and five years' separation , but would not accept that his conduct had resulted in W's leaving the matrimonial home. He asked that the petition presented by W be refused and the marriage be dissolved.

Held: once the five years' separation is established by the petitioner, there remain *no grounds* upon which a cross-decree will be granted to the respondent.

4.5 Refusal of decree absolute

Note ———

Under s 5, respondent can oppose grant of a decree on the grounds that a dissolution of the marriage will result in grave financial or other hardship and that, in all the circumstances, it would be wrong to dissolve the marriage. Under s 10, the court may consider respondent's financial position on divorce and delay a decree unless satisfied that the financial provision is fair, reasonable, or the best in the circumstances.

Garcia v Garcia (1992) CA

H and W were married in 1974; H was Spanish, W was Scottish. The couple separated in 1982 and later concluded an agreement which was ratified by the Spanish court, under which H accepted his responsibility towards W's illegitimate son, who had been adopted by the couple, by promising to pay for his education for the next 10 years. The agreement was broken by H when he stopped the payments, having moved to England. His argument in favour of this course of action was based on five years' separation. W asked for an order under s 10(1), intended to delay the grant of a decree absolute until H had paid arrears arising from the agreement.

Held: the court *did* possess the jurisdiction necessary to effect a delay in making the decree absolute. It was essential that H remedy the injustice suffered by W, who had been placed at a financial disadvantage by H's actions.

4.5.1 The hardship involved must be 'grave'

Mathias v Mathias (1972) CA

H and W married in 1962; they separated in 1964. W had not done much work since that date, believing that her main responsibility was to look after their child. Her income was derived from maintenance and supplementary benefit. H petitioned for divorce, on the ground of five years' separation, in 1971. W argued that a decree would result in 'grave financial hardship', since her maintenance payments would be reduced and she stood to lose a widow's pension. A decree was granted and W appealed.

Held: W's appeal would be *dismissed*. In considering the matter of 'grave financial hardship', the court ought to consider the broader aspect, that is, whether it was not right in the public interest to end a marriage which had become a mere empty shell. *Per* Karminski LJ:

> So far as W is concerned, the fact that H has left her for many years and wishes to set up a home married to another woman is bound to cause W some degree of financial hardship. But on the other hand, what this court has to consider is whether in all the circumstances it would be wrong to dissolve the marriage ... One has to consider the broader aspect here: whether a marriage which has broken down hopelessly for so long should be preserved or whether it is not right in the public interest to put an end to it. W is still a young woman who may find a happy future with another man as husband. Having regard to all the circumstances of the case, I have come to the conclusion ... that this marriage should be dissolved ... I think that W's appeal should be dismissed.

Archer v Archer (1999) CA

H had petitioned for divorce following five years' separation from W. W opposed H's petition, arguing that, although H was paying maintenance, she would suffer 'grave financial hardship' through loss of her entitlement to H's occupational pension on his death. In such a case, maintenance payments would end, her income would be halved and she would have to use at least one half of her capital assets as a replacement, thus creating a substantial fall in her standard of living. The recorder did not accept the possibility of 'grave financial hardship', given the size of W's capital assets. H was granted a decree nisi and W appealed.

Held: W's appeal would be *dismissed*. W had substantial capital assets, but no income, while H had a substantial income, but relatively small capital assets. Although H's death would result in the ending of the maintenance payments, leading to W making use of her capital, this would not be an unusual state of affairs. The result of the recorder's exercise of discretion provided no reason for interference by the court. There was no 'grave hardship' in the state of affairs to which W had adverted in her appeal.

4.5.2   The word 'grave' in the phrase 'grave financial or other hardship' qualifies 'hardship' as well as 'financial'

Rukat v Rukat (1975) CA

H, a Pole, and W, a Sicilian, both Catholics, were married in Italy in 1946. They came to England where their daughter was born. W returned to Sicily and H told her not to return to England because he had fallen in love with another woman. W came back to England when the other woman died and sought to revive the marriage. In 1972 H petitioned for divorce, but W opposed the petition, contending that in Sicily she would suffer hardship on social grounds if she, a Catholic, were known to be a divorced woman. A decree was granted and W appealed.

Held: W's appeal would be *dismissed*. There was no evidence as to the reality of W's fears. *Per* Lawton LJ:

> The learned judge ... found that W was feeling at the time of the judgment that she could not go back to Sicily. That, if it was genuinely and deeply felt, would undoubtedly be a 'hardship' in one sense of that word. But one has to ask oneself whether sensible persons, knowing all the facts, would think it was a hardship. On the evidence, I have come to the conclusion that it would not ...

Per Ormrod LJ:

> The court has first to decide whether there was evidence on which it could properly come to the conclusion that W was suffering from grave financial or other hardship; and 'other hardship' in this context, in my judgment ... must mean other grave hardship. If hardship is found, the court then has to look at the second limb and decide whether, in all the circumstances, looking at everybody's interests, balancing respondent's hardship against the petitioner's interest in getting his or her freedom, it would be wrong to dissolve the marriage.

4.6 Judicial separation

Note

Judicial separation is based on a decree as a result of which it becomes no longer necessary for the petitioner to cohabit with the respondent: see s 17 MCA 1973.

4.6.1 Discharge of decree when cohabitation has been resumed

Haddon v Haddon (1887)

The question was whether an order that W shall no longer be bound to cohabit with H is avoided, or merely suspended, upon the parties subsequently renewing cohabitation.

Held: the effect of a resumption of cohabitation is to put an end to the legal existence of the order and to render it *no longer operative*.

Oram v Oram (1923)

An application was made by petitioner for discharge of a decree of judicial separation at the suit of W on the ground of H's adultery. W had subsequently petitioned for increased alimony, but during those proceedings, H had been taken ill and W had nursed him. A reconciliation followed and the parties lived together until H left W. Petitioner asked that the decree of judicial separation be discharged.

Held: the court *was able* to discharge a decree of judicial separation when the parties, by resuming cohabitation, appear to have put an end to it. The court has an inherent power to discharge an order which has become ineffective.

Q 'The technicalities which surround the concept of desertion have rendered it almost meaningless in practice.' Do you agree?

5 Occupation Orders Under FLA 1996, Part IV

Note ───

Domestic violence has not been defined in specific terms under statute. It appears, however, to cover aspects of physical, sexual and emotional abuse. Part I of FLA 1996, which came into force on 1 October 1997, is based largely on the recommendations of *Domestic Violence and the Occupation of the Family Home*, 1992, Law Com No 207. It repeals DVMPA 1976 in its entirety, ss 16–18 DPMCA 1978, and MHA 1983 in its entirety, and introduces a code of remedies available in those courts concerned with family proceedings. It provides for occupation orders (ss 33–41) and non-molestation orders (ss 42–49).

5.1 Order where applicant has estate or interest or has matrimonial home rights

Note ───

Under s 33, an applicant who is entitled to occupy the dwelling-house may apply for an order against anyone with whom he is associated, provided that the dwelling-house is, or was intended by both parties to be, their home.

Chalmers v Johns (1999) CA

Following a period of living together for 25 years, during which time they had occupied the family home as joint tenants for 20 years, H and W decided to separate. They had a seven year old daughter, D, and an adult son. The relationship of H and W, described as 'stormy', had involved assaults of a minor nature. W and D moved into a temporary council accommodation which was much further away from the school attended by D. D had regular staying contact with H. H and W made cross applications for a residence order for D, and W was granted an interim occupation order under s 33 FLA 1996 on the ground of H's violent conduct. H appealed against the occupation order.

Held: H's appeal was *allowed*. The court held that the judge had misdirected herself and that the application for occupation orders was to be dealt with at the substantive hearing. *Per* Thorpe LJ:

> In approaching its function under s 33, the court has first to consider whether the evidence does establish that the applicant or a relative child would be likely to suffer significant harm attributable to the conduct of the respondent if an order is not made. If the court answers that question in the affirmative, then it knows that it must make the order unless, balancing one harm against the other, the harm to the respondent or child is likely to be as great. If however, the court answers in the negative, then it enters the discretionary regime provided by s 3(6) and must exercise a broad discretion having regard to all the circumstances of the case and particularly those factors set out in the statutory checklist within sub-paras (a)–(d).

Given the facts of this case, a 'draconian' occupation order was not appropriate. A non-molestation order seemed to be the correct remedy.

B v B (Occupation Order) (1999) CA

H and W occupied a council house where they lived with S, who was H's six year old son from a previous relationship, and D, the two year old daughter of H and W. Following H's violent conduct towards W, W moved, with D, into bed and breakfast accommodation. H and S remained in the home. The court issued an occupation order under s 33, ordering him and S to leave the home. The tenancy of the home was transferred to W and a non-molestation order in W's favour was granted. H appealed against he occupation order, arguing that it would cause significant harm to S under the terms of s 33(7).

Held: H's appeal was *allowed*. Weighing the likelihood of harm in relation to D and S, it was clear that the balance moved in favour of S, if an occupation order were to be made. Indeed, if S were to move, a change of school would be necessary and, further, being removed from his father was in no way a solution to the resulting problems. *Per* Butler-Sloss LJ:

> For a child of D's age, the essential security is being where her mother is. Furthermore ... W's residence in bed and breakfast accommodation is likely to be temporary ... For S, the position is much more complex. His security depends not merely on being in his father's care, but on his other day to day support systems, of which his home and school are clearly the most important ... In our judgement if, on the facts of this case, the respective likelihood of harm are weighed as far as D and S are concerned, the balance comes down in favour of S suffering the greater harm if an occupation order is made ... We have no sympathy for H ... were it not for the fact that he is caring for S, and that S has particular needs which at present outweigh those of D, an occupation order would undoubtedly have been made.

G v G (Occupation Order: Conduct) (2000) CA

H and W, married with two teenage children, had begun divorce proceedings but were continuing to reside in the same house. The general atmosphere within the house was tense and strained, and this was attributed to the conduct of H. W made application for an occupation order under s 33 FLA 1996. The judge found out that the tensions within the household had resulted in harm to the children. But because H's conduct was not intentional, that harm could not be attributed to him. The application under s 33 was dismissed, and the court made a direction for a final hearing of an application for residence orders and ancillary relief by W. W then appealed.

Held: W's appeal was *dismissed*. Under s 33 an occupation order could be made under s 33(7) where there was a likelihood that the applicant or child would suffer 'significant harm' because of the alleged conduct, unless the making of an order would result in an even greater degree of harm. Intention was not material, in that the important factor was the effect of the alleged conduct, not the intention said to be behind it. Should an order not be made under s 33(7), the court retained a discretion under s 33(6) to make an order. The judge was in error in concentrating on the intentions of H, but nevertheless, in the circumstances, his conclusions would be supported. In this case there was no violence, and directions for final hearing involved a swift hearing of outstanding issues between H and W.

Re Y (Children) (Occupation Order) (2000) CA

H and W occupied the matrimonial home with their children X, aged 13, and Y, aged 16 (and expecting a child of her own). Life in the matrimonial home was characterised by continuous and acrimonious disputes. As a result, H made application for a non-molestation order and an occupation order. By the time the occupation order application fell to be heard, the parties had agreed and had undertaken to refrain from molesting each other. The recorder who heard the application for an occupation order decided that there was evidence of the family having divided into 'two warring camps': H and X, on the one hand, appeared to be in conflict with W and Y, on the other hand. The tense atmosphere in the family home was characterised in particular by antagonisms between H and Y. The recorder decided that maintenance of the status quo would cause greater harm than that which might result from its disappearance and, further, the local authority would be able to house W and Y more easily than in the case of H and X. Consequently, the recorder made an order for W to vacate the home. W argued that the order resulted from a misapplication of s 33(7) FLA 1996. W appealed.

Held: W's appeal was *allowed*. In finding that s 33(7) was applicable, the recorder had been in error. In order that the provision might have application, the court would have to be satisfied that applicant or child would be likely to suffer 'significant harm' which could be attributed directly to respondent's conduct if an application order was not made. In the case of H (who was registered as disabled) the court had not found that he or X was likely to have suffered any measure of 'significant harm'. Nor had there been a finding that any harm suffered by W could be attributed to H's conduct. Eviction from the home was a remedy of last resort. It was important to take into account the fact that H and W could be accommodated in the family home until a pending application for ancillary relief might be determined. Further, given the fact that the parties' undertaking appeared to be effective, the occupation order ought not to be dismissed.

5.2 Order where applicant (former spouse) is not entitled to occupy the dwelling house but respondent (former spouse) is so entitled

Note

Under s 35, an occupation order may be available if one former spouse is entitled to occupy a dwelling house by virtue of a beneficial estate or interest or contract, or by virtue of any enactment giving him the right to remain in occupation, and the other spouse is not so entitled, and the dwelling house was at any time their matrimonial home or was at any time intended by them to be their matrimonial home.

S v F (Occupation Order) (2000)

In 1994 H and W divorced. Their matrimonial home was in London; they had two children, S, a boy aged 17, and D, a girl aged 15, at the time of trial. H and W agreed that W would remain in the home in London with S and D in order that they might finish their education. H then moved to Kuala Lumpur, and argued that, because of his contributions, he had a beneficial interest in the London home. During a visit by S and D to H in Kuala Lumpur, W declared her intention to leave the London home and move to Somerset. S refused to move with W. D was taken by another relative to the country; S was taken in by H's sister. H was granted an order preventing the sale of the London home. He applied for an order permitting him to occupy the London home with S.

Held: H's application was *allowed*. He was instructed to proceed under s 35 because of a lack of firm evidence relating to his beneficial interest. Under s 35(6) consideration had to be given to an applicant's resources and housing needs. Additionally, attention had to be given to the effect of an order on the parties' health and well being. When the facts were balanced, the order for which H was applying would provide greater security when compared with any short term problems likely to involve W. It had to be remembered too, that W was responsible in some measure for the existing state of affairs. H would be allowed, therefore, to return to the London home for six months; W would be given leave to apply for discharge of the order if H failed at any time to comply with an undertaking which he had given to pay the mortgage.

5.3 Order where applicant is a cohabitant or former cohabitant

Note

An order may be available under s 36 where the applicant is a cohabitant or a former cohabitant who is not entitled to occupy the dwelling house and the respondent is a cohabitant or a former cohabitant who is so entitled.

Gay v Sheeran; Enfield LBC v Gay (1999) CA

S and his partner X, held the joint tenancy of a council flat in which they lived. X moved out and was replaced by G, but the tenancy continued. Some 18 months later, the council (ELBC) were made aware that S and X were no longer living in the flat, and they sought an order for possession. G, now the sole occupation, applied for a transfer of the tenancy, but ELBC refused. Then G applied under s 36 for an occupation order which would protect her against eviction. A six month order was granted, and this had the legal effect of enabling a transfer of tenancy. ELBC and G appealed.

Held: The appeal was *dismissed*. The court was entitled to make an occupation order under s 36, since the facts of the case appeared to suggest that S might return to the council flat, and the holding order was not made solely for the purposes of obtaining a transfer of a tenancy order, there was nothing irregular in its being made. Per Gibson LJ:

> For my part I cannot see any objection to the utilisation by a non-entitled cohabitant who obtains an occupation order for the purpose of seeking a transfer order ... There is nothing in the section or elsewhere in the 1996 Act to suggest that that is improper.

Q What do you consider to be the fundamental principle of the occupation order?

6 Non-Molestation Orders Under FLA 1996, Part IV

Note

Under s 42 FLA 1996, non-molestation orders (which may be made by the court of its own motion as well as upon application) include orders containing either or both of the following provisions – provision prohibiting the respondent from molesting another person who is associated with the respondent, and provision prohibiting respondent from molesting a relevant child. Applicants eligible for protection include (see s 63) former spouses, former cohabitants, relatives, parents of a child, parties to the same family proceedings. 'Relevant child' (see s 62) means one who is living with or might reasonably be expected to live with either party to the proceedings, any child in relation to whom an order under AA 1976 or Ch A 1989 is in question in the proceedings, and any other child whose interest the court considers relevant.

6.1 Meaning of 'molestation' under the Act

C v C (Application for Non-Molestation Order) (1998)

Following the divorce of H and W, W published articles in the national press in which she purported to give information concerning H's relations with her and his three former wives. The articles were couched in very unflattering terms. H complained that W's intention was to humiliate and embarrass him. He applied for a non-molestation order under s 42 so as to prevent W harassing him by publishing matter which might affect the determination of financial issues between H and W. W contended that the facts of the case did not justify the making of such an order.

Held: H's application was *refused*. Although the Act did not define 'molestation', the word seemed to imply conduct which was intended to result in a high degree of harassment of the other party, justifying the court's intervention. A mere invasion of privacy did not constitute harassment. H's concern to protect his privacy did not come within the scope of s 42. *Per* Brown P:

It is significant in my judgment that s 42 is to be found in FLA 1996 Part IV, which is concerned with the general topic of domestic violence ... The material complained of is some alleged revelations by the former wife of what she regarded as her former husband's misconduct. In my judgment it comes nowhere near 'molestation' as envisaged by s 42 FLA 1996.

6.2   Applications for non-molestation orders

Banks v Banks (1999)

H, aged 72, lived with W, aged 79, in the matrimonial home in which conditions had deteriorated, due in some measure to W's suffering from a mental disorder within the meaning of the Mental Health Act 1983. In July 1987 W was admitted to hospital and returned home after two months. Following a deterioration in her condition, during which she was considered to be a threat to J because of her physical and verbal abuse, she was re-admitted so as to avoid injury. H's mobility had deteriorated and he was considered to be physically and psychologically frail. Because of W's intensified abuse, H began divorce proceedings. W's threats led him to apply for a non-molestation order (and an occupation order). A medical consultant stated that W was no threat to H.

Held: A non-molestation order would *not* be granted. W's behaviour did not threaten H's health in significant manner, and should W become violent, she could be returned to hospital. Any injunction which ordered W to refrain from a particular pattern of behaviour would be unproductive even were she able to understand it.

Chechi v Bashier (1999) CA

Hostility and a family feud had erupted between the brothers B and C and their families, resident in the UK, because of a land dispute in Pakistan. A district judge made non-molestation orders against B and his six sons on *ex parte* applications under s 42. A county court judge considered later that the institution of civil proceedings might be more appropriate, and in the exercise of his discretion, he refused a further order against B. He decided that the family relationship was merely incidental to a civil dispute, and that the court would be obliged to attach a power of arrest to any order it might wish to make. C appealed against the judge's refusal to make a non-molestation order against B.

Held: C's appeal was *dismissed*. The judge was in error, since it was clear that the dispute between B and C had been exacerbated by the existence of a family relationship, and the protection afforded by Part IV FLA 1996 was available to any applicant associated with the defendant within the context of a family relationship. But if a case did come within s 47(2), because of the threat or use of violence, and it was considered essential for applicant's protection that a power of arrest should be attached to the order, such a power should be attached. It was within the power of the judge, therefore, to exercise his discretion under s 42 so as to reject the application for a non-molestation order since the power of arrest would give C an unacceptable degree of power over the defendants.

G v F (Non-Molestation Order: Jurisdiction) (2000)

The Wimbledon Family Proceedings Court had refused to hear an application for a non-molestation order under s 42, on the ground that the parties could not be considered as 'associate persons' within the meaning of s 62(3)(b) FLA 1996. The applicant appealed, appealed contending that the justices had misdirected themselves in making findings against the weight of the evidence and in refusing to hear oral evidence tendered by the applicant in relation to the question of cohabitation.

Held: the appeal would be *allowed*, and the case remitted for a rehearing. Wall J stated that the powers of the court were intended to provide swift and accessible protective remedies to persons who were the victims of domestic violence, provided that they were 'associated persons' within s 62(3). In spite of the fact that applicant had been granted previously a non-molestation order with power of arrest attached, in December 1999, the justices refused to hear the application; their reasons referred to the existence of separate households and applicant's statement that the parties did not, in reality, live together. But the evidence did support the proposition that the applicant and respondent were cohabitants within the meaning of s 62(3)(b). Three of the signposts set out in *Crake v Supplementary Benefits Commission* (1982) were present: a sexual relationship, a measure of financial support, and respondent's evidence suggesting that, from his perspective, the parties were cohabiting. It would be unfortunate if s 62 were to be narrowly construed so as to exclude borderline cases; the section demanded purposive construction. A fresh non-molestation order would be made in terms which were identical to the previous order, and which would last until the determination of the application or any further notice.

6.3   Breach of non-molestation order

Hale v Tanner (2000) CA

Under the terms of a non-molestation order, T had been restricted from harassing, pestering, or intimidating H or threatening to use violence against him. A power of arrest had been attached to the order. Subsequently she had harassed H and his partner by making a large number of abusive and threatening telephone calls to H. She was arrested and received a suspended sentence of six months' imprisonment. T appealed against the sentence, arguing, *inter alia*, that the sentence was excessive, given her early admission of a breach of the order. An admission of this nature, she contended, was equivalent to an early plea of guilty in criminal cases, and should be treated accordingly (see ss 2, 3 Criminal Justice Act 1991).

Held: T's appeal would be *allowed*. A sentence of 28 days' imprisonment, suspended for the full duration of the non-molestation order, would be substituted. There were no grounds for concluding that, in general, statutory provisions relating to sentencing in criminal proceedings could result in proceedings for contempt; but in relation to family proceedings it should be remembered that cases concerning contempt would come before the court only on application to commit. The fact that a person had breached an order for the first time would not preclude imprisonment (see *Thorpe v Thorpe* (1998)). Contempt proceedings were intended to mark the court's disapproval of a breach and to ensure compliance in the future. T had not had the benefit of any warning concerning the consequences of a breach of the non-molestation order, since she had not been in court when that order had been made. Additionally, she was the mother of a young child and hardship would result if the sentence were to be activated in full; that sentence was manifestly excessive.

Rafiq v Muse (2000) CA

M had been taken into care at the age of six, from the age of eight until he came out of care he had not seen his mother, R. On release from care he had threatened, terrorised and molested R. As a result of his conduct, R had attempted to commit suicide. Non-molestation orders had been made but M had not complied with them. In January 2000 (when M was aged 21), the court sentenced M for three breaches of the orders. The first breach concerned an incident in November 1999, the second and third breaches related to incidents in December 1999. M was sentenced to three months' imprisonment in relation to the first incident, and to two consecutive six month terms, to run concurrently, in relation to the second and third incidents. M appealed, arguing that the first breach had been proved in error, and that, given an absence of violence, or even a threat of violence, the consecutive terms were excessive.

Held: M's appeal was *allowed* in part. The sentence relating to November 1999 breach, having been proved in error, would be quashed. In relation to the other breaches, in spite of the fact that there had been no violence, they had resulted in the serious terrorising of R. If the continuing contempt of court were also taken into account, the total of six months' imprisonment was justified.

6.4 Power of arrest attached to order

Re B-J (A Child) (Non-Molestation Order: Power of Arrest) (2000) CA

F and M, parents of a child, B-J, were unmarried and had separated in 1995. F applied in 1999 for a parental responsibility order, which was granted. In addition, however, because of proof of a variety of incidents involving F and M, the judge also made a non-molestation order. That order was made for an indefinite period and had a power of arrest attached to it for a two year period, as provided for under s 47(2) FLA 1996. F, relying on *M v W (Non-Molestation Order: Duration)* (2000), appealed against the non-molestation order and the power of arrest, arguing that it was wrong for the duration of the power of arrest to be shorter than the duration of the order to which it was attached.

Held: F's appeal was *dismissed*. Non-molestation orders could be constructed for a wide range of purposes and could be flexible. *M v W* (2000) was overruled. The effect of placing limits on the duration of an order because of the power of arrest attached to it would be as unjust as extending the duration of a power of arrest so that an order might comply with a non-molestation order. In this case the order had been made for the benefit of B-J and M, in accordance with s 42(5), and its indefinite extent was justified because of the nature of the relationship between F and M.

Q 'It is not necessary to define "molestation" ... we all know what it is, and problems will multiply if an attempt is made to restrict the workings of section 42 by attempts at precise definition.' Do you agree?

7 Financial Provision on Breakdown of Marriage

7.1 Essence of ancillary relief

'Ancillary relief' refers to the incidental relief which is auxiliary to some other action or suit, eg, divorce. Orders available, in favour of a party to the marriage and/or a child of the family, include: maintenance pending suit; financial provision orders; property adjustment orders; and property sale orders.

7.2 Maintenance pending suit

Note ──

Under s 22 MCA 1973, the court can order such periodical payments for maintenance pending suit as it considers reasonable.

──

Peacock v Peacock (1984)

H and W were married in 1967 and separated in 1982. W petitioned for divorce in that year. She applied for interim maintenance. When she made her application she was living on supplementary benefit (now income support); the DHSS were paying mortgage interest relating to the matrimonial home. H was paying £20 weekly to DHSS towards the support of W and their two children. W's application was refused on the ground that, taking into account H's means, it would not be possible to make an order which would really increase the amount of money received by W. W appealed.

Held: W's appeal would be *allowed*. The court would act on the same principles when dealing with interim orders as when determining final orders. The amount of an order would be assessed on what H could reasonably afford to pay, taking into account his income, needs and obligations. Maintenance was ordered at £15 per week, pending suit.

7.3 Periodical payments

Note

Under s 23(1) MCA 1973, the court can make an order on granting a decree of divorce, nullity, judicial separation, that either party to the marriage shall make to the other periodical payments for a term specified in the order. Payments may be secured or unsecured.

Aggett v Aggett (1962) CA

H had maltreated W and seemed inconsiderate in relation to providing for her. There was a strong possibility of H's emigrating to the USA, thus leaving W penniless and without any means of support. Periodical payments had been ordered.

Held: the order for periodical payments by H to W would be *secured on H's house*, his sole asset of any value. The charge on the house would be cancelled only at the end of the payments period.

Stockford v Stockford (1982) CA

H and W were married in 1965, had separated in 1972 and had divorced in 1977. In 1979 an order was made which provided financial relief for W. In 1978 H remarried; his second wife was in full time employment. W remained responsible for the mortgage on the matrimonial home which she continued to occupy with the child of the marriage. She applied for an increase in the order for periodical payments. Her application was refused and she appealed.

Held: W's appeal would be *dismissed*. H's sole capital asset was in the home he had occupied with W. W could go out to work so as to increase her income. H's income had been reduced and the order for W would be reduced to enable him to support his second family.

H v H (Financial Provision) (1993)

Following ancillary relief proceedings, H was ordered to pay W periodical payments and to provide her with a car every three years during their joint lives, and continuing for 10 years after W's remarriage. Following H's remarriage he ceased making the periodical payments and providing for the car fund. W sought to enforce the outstanding arrears. H applied for the discharge of any future obligations to W. It was shown at the subsequent hearing that there was a marked difference between the capital position of H and W. H had no income and considerable liabilities whereas W was in a strong financial position. H was ordered by the district judge to pay periodical payments and W was given leave to enforce arrears. H appealed.

Held: H's appeal would be *allowed in part*. H was in difficulties and dispute between H and W should be ended. On payment of H's arrears, W's claim to periodical payments or other financial claims would be rejected.

Wachtel v Wachtel (1973) CA

The marriage of H and W was dissolved after 20 years on the ground that each had behaved in a manner which made it impossible to reasonably expect them to continue living together. Blame for the break-up of the marriage fell, according to the judge, equally on H and W. H was ordered to pay W, effectively, one-half of his capital and about one-half of his income. H contended that the judge had started from a presumption that equal division was right, and had allowed almost nothing for the fact that W had contributed to the break-up of the marriage.

Held: the fact that W had contributed to the break-up of the marriage was *not* a reason in this case to make a reduction in the financial provision to be made to her. The 'one-third rule' was a convenient starting point for the appropriate calculations to be made. (As an example, the one-third rule, as applied to income, would result in the husband being ordered to pay such sums as will result in bringing the wife's income up to one-third of the spouses' joint income.) *Per* Lord Denning:

> The one-third rule has been much criticised ... But it has retained its attraction for a very simple reason: those who have to assess maintenance must have some starting point. They cannot operate in a void. No better starting point has yet been suggested than the one-third rule ... But this so called rule is not a rule and must never be regarded as such. In any calculation the court has to have a starting point. If it is not to be one-third, should it be one-half or one-quarter? A starting point at one-third of the combined resources of the parties is as good and rational a starting point as any other, remembering that the essence of the legislation is to secure flexibility to meet the justice of particular cases, and not rigidity, forcing particular cases to be fitted into some so called principle within which they do not easily lie ... One-third as a flexible starting point is in general more likely to lead to the correct final result than a starting point of equality, or a quarter.

Slater v Slater (1982) CA

Following the divorce of H and W an order was made against H for periodical payments to W. H appealed against the level of payments.

Held: H would *not* be allowed to deduct heavy property maintenance expenses, involved in his living in a large country house, in working out the amount of his available income. The one-third calculation remained a useful guideline. *Per* Arnold P:

> The one-third guideline might not be very helpful in cases involving very large or very small sums of money, but in cases in between it remained useful, always provided that it was used on the understanding that it might be necessary to depart from it to an extent depending on the particular facts of a case. It was useful to have a starting guideline ... It was desirable to reduce to a minimum the number of cases involving a decree absolute in which financial disputes had

to be settled by the court. This could be achieved only where practitioners had a clear understanding of what principles were likely to apply and were confident that financial issues between spouses would not be determined by caprice.

Bullock v Bullock (1986) CA

Following the divorce of H and W, proceedings for financial provision resulted in W being granted an order which represented one-third of H's resources, based upon the judge's calculations. H appealed against the order, arguing that the one-third rule was no longer acceptable in the light of recent decisions.

Held: H's appeal would be *dismissed*. The adoption by the court of the one-third rule would not result in the judgment being overturned. There remained considerable authority for the use of the rule; the fact that it had not been followed (but not disapproved) in some recent cases did not constitute a direction to the court that its application be rejected.

7.4   Variation of order

Scott v Scott (1978) CA

H and W separated and W applied for periodical payments and a property adjustment. H appealed from the order of the registrar to a judge and the order was varied. H appealed further to the Court of Appeal.

Held: H's appeal would be *allowed in part*. *Per* Cumming-Bruce LJ:

> In respect of that part of the appeal concerned with periodical payments, I do not find in this case that the reference to the one-third rule is of any assistance, because in relation to the finances of this family, the dominating feature is the necessity of providing for the three young children of H and W and the necessity for providing a home for them by means of mortgage payments ... What I seek to do is to try to picture the reality of the standard of living in H's home and W's home, having regard to the needs of the adults and the children. For my part, I would hold that the registrar and judge are in error in failing to pay sufficient regard to the consequences of the order upon the comparable standards of living of H's and W's households. The order for periodical payments ought to be varied.

Garner v Garner (1992) CA

A periodical payments order had been made by consent of H and W. Later W applied for a variation of the order and it was increased by £3.50 per week. She was dissatisfied with the size of the variation and appealed to the circuit judge. The appeal was dismissed on the ground that once W had established a material change in her circumstances, the judge was not entitled to consider matters anew. W appealed.

Held: W's appeal would be *allowed*. Section 31(7) MCA 1973 required that the court should give first consideration to the welfare of any child of the marriage, having regard to all the circumstances, including those matters set out in s 25. Weight had to be given to the original order; the court did have power to consider anew all the matters involved.

Cornick v Cornick (No 2) (1995) CA

An order was made requiring H to make periodical payments to W and their children. The order had been varied as a result of a substantial increase in H's income. H was ordered to pay an amount which was halfway between W's reasonable needs and an amount which would be proportional to his increased income. He contended that the judge had acted well beyond her discretionary powers and that the amount ought to have been based on W's reasonable needs plus a small adjustment for inflation. H appealed.

Held: H's appeal would be *dismissed*. The discretion of the judge had been exercised correctly under MCA 1973 by her considering the circumstances of the case in their entirety. The argument that only W's reasonable needs should be considered was not based upon any authority.

Atkinson v Atkinson (1995)

An order requiring H to make periodical payments to W was varied. The initial settlement involved W's receiving the matrimonial home outright. The judge considered that W had no intention of marrying X, the partner with whom she was sharing the matrimonial home. Evidence was received concerning X's business. H contended that X's means ought to be taken into consideration, since X and W were cohabitants. H appealed.

Held: H's appeal would be *allowed*. It was necessary to assess X's means: cohabitation was not to be equated with marriage, but it was a factor which had to be taken into account. The weight, if any, to be given to the means of a partner would be determined by the facts of a case. W was giving support to X in the establishment of his business by providing him with a home. The business was proving very profitable. The level of H's payments would be reduced.

7.5 Lump sum orders

Note

On granting a decree of divorce, nullity or judicial separation, the court may order either party to the marriage to pay the other a lump sum or sums as may be specified: s 23(3)(c), (6)MCA 1973.

7.5.1 Amount of the lump sum

O'Donnell v O'Donnell (1975) CA

H and W were married in 1960; they had three children. In 1972 they were divorced after H left W. H was employed by his father, a successful businessman and held shares in family companies, including a hotel business, in the development of which W had played an important role. W applied for maintenance and the judge, applying the 'one-third rule' awarded W a lump sum payment. H appealed against the size of the sum.

Held: H's appeal would be *dismissed*. The award of a lump sum was quite appropriate in all the circumstances, and the order was fully within the judge's discretion. *Per* Ormrod LJ:

> The court must consider with great care the effect on H of any order which it has mind to make, because its purpose is to do justice to H and W, and the appropriate section requires the court to have regard to what is practicable. But the court is entitled to look at all the surrounding circumstances realistically. In many cases the difficulty of raising a large lump sum immediately may be very real, in which case arrangements for some kind of deferred payment may be appropriate … in other cases the court may be able to find that there are ways of complying with the order. In the present case one of the family companies has recently sold a hotel for £50,000, and has bought the building next door … It is legitimate, as the judge did, to take such matters into account when considering H's submission that the lump sum ought to be reduced owing to his difficulties in realising part of his assets … Moreover, the court cannot overlook that as periodical payments cease on remarriage, an order of this size must be a strong disincentive, if not a prohibition, for remarriage to this comparatively young woman … She requires an adequate capital sum over and above the house.

Preston v Preston (1981) CA

H and W married in 1954; W was a successful, well-paid fashion model, H worked for a travel agency for an average salary. For some 10 years W continued to work, helping H to start and build his own business. H left W in 1977; his assets were worth £2.5 million, and W's sole asset was a half-share in the matrimonial home worth about £50,000. The judge awarded W a lump sum of £600,000 payable by instalments. H contended that this was much too high and the judge must have misdirected himself in calculating the award. H appealed.

Held: H's appeal would be *dismissed*. In the normal course of events, W could have expected a very comfortable life had the marriage not broken down. It could not be said that the size of the lump sum was so excessive as to be based on an error in principle. There would be no interference with the exercise by the judge of his discretion.

Gojkovic v Gojkovic (1990) CA

H and W married in 1978 and were divorced in 1987. They built up a property and hotel business, W concentrating on administering the hotel side, and working exceptionally hard in the process. In ancillary relief proceedings H's assets were valued at £4 million; the wife had little in the form of a legal interest. W sought sufficient capital to buy her own hotel. The judge found that W had contributed in a very exceptional manner to the business and awarded her £1 million so as to enable her to buy a hotel. H appealed on the ground that the judge's award went well beyond making provision for W's reasonable needs.

Held: H's appeal would be *dismissed*. The judge was entitled to take W's work into account in assessing the lump sum and it was appropriate for the lump sum calculation not to be linked only to W's needs. *Per* Russell LJ:

> I detect nothing wrong with the approach [of the judge]. The husband has assets of about £4 million and there is no suggestion that he cannot raise the necessary finance. There has been no suggestion that there are circumstances in this case, for example, W's conduct, which can militate against her entitlement based, as the judge stated, on need and contribution, two important considerations set out in s 25 ... In my view the award in this case was right.

Clark v Clark (1999) CA

H, who had been infatuated with his wife, W, who was 36 years younger, had paid off her very large debts, had bought her several properties and had handed over a large part of his assets to her. The marriage was not consummated and, on some occasions, W had forced H to live in a caravan in the grounds of the matrimonial home, during which time she had cohabited with X. In a hearing for ancillary relief, H had offered to pay W a lump sum of £352,000. The judge had increased this figure to £552,00, although he had made a finding of severe misconduct on W's part. H and W then made cross appeals.

Held: W's appeal was *dismissed*; H's appeal was granted. It was held that it was not possible to justify the judge's award, given the nature of his finding. There was no doubt that W was guilty of serious misconduct of a marital nature with X, and of misconduct concerning her use of H's resources and, indeed, of the litigation itself. There would be a reduction in the size of the lump sum to £125,000, and W would transfer all the assets, but for £50,000, to H.

Purba v Purba (2000) CA

After a marriage which had lasted for 10 years, H and W separated in 1995. H petitioned in April 1996 for a dissolution of the marriage, and a decree absolute was granted in October 1996. H and W worked in the professions. W was almost entirely dependent on H because of a back injury. Immediately upon separation, H commenced the disposal of his capital and assets so as to diminish or extinguish his liabilities to W. The court ordered H to set aside a transfer of £65,000 to his uncle, and he was ordered also to repay arrears in periodical payments and to pay a lump sum of £82,500 to W. In H's appeal he contended, inter alia, that the judge was in error in taking his conduct into account in calculating the size of the lump sum payment to W.

Held: H's appeal was *allowed*, but only to a limited extent. The dominant criterion in estimating the size of the lump sum payable by H to W was not related to H's conduct but to the fact of W's need for housing accommodation. The calculation of the lump sum ought to start by noting how much capital was available to H and W. The lump sum payable to W would be reduced to £65,000, so as to take into account the extent by which W's deposit account would be restored by the enforcement of the maintenance arrears. The judge had made a realistic assessment of W's ability to continue in employment and had considered carefully the appropriate proportion of H's substantial income that ought to be employed in W's support.

7.6 Other matters relating to lump sum orders

Calderbank v Calderbank (1975) CA

H and W married in 1956. In 1973 W left home and brought divorce proceedings. A decree absolute was granted; W was granted custody of the three children. She had large capital assets and a good investment income; her second husband earned a reasonable salary. H continued to earn and his new wife was also in paid employment. H had no capital. W was ordered to make a lump sum payment of £10,000 to H. She appealed.

Held: W's appeal would be *dismissed*. The court has the power to treat husband and wife on an equal footing. While the award could be considered substantial, it was not so large as to require modification. *Per* Scarman LJ:

> Whatever be the position today as between husband and wife while they remain married, it is quite clear that fresh powers have been given to the court to make financial and property adjustment orders on divorce, nullity or judicial separation. There is nothing in the relevant sections of the Act to indicate that, for the purpose of these sections, husband and wife are not to be treated on an equal basis ... there is nothing [in ss 21–25] to suggest that only in exceptional circumstances may the court make a financial order by way of a periodical

payment of a lump sum in favour of the husband. The principle behind the sections is that the spouses come to the court on a basis of equality. But the court must have regard to s 25 and the particular circumstances of the case.

MT v MT (Financial Provision: Lump Sum) (1992)

H and W, German nationals, divorced after 20 years of marriage. Evidence was given which showed that they had been living well beyond their means, having been supported by the sale of gifts from H's grandmother and on loans secured on an expectation that H's very wealthy father might soon die. On that event, H stood, under German law, to inherit a portion of his father's estate. W had made application for a lump sum and now wished to adjourn that application until the death of H's father, since H had no immediately available assets from which the award could be satisfied.

Held: the court has a discretionary power allowing it to adjourn an application for a lump sum where there exists a real possibility of assets of a substantial nature becoming available in the future and where that event would provide the sole means of achieving justice between the parties. That power *would* be exercised by the court in this case.

L v L (Lump Sum: Interest) (1994)

H was ordered to pay W a lump sum, a large part of which was intended to be raised from the sale of property used in business operations. The market in property of this nature was severely depressed and H was unable to sell, so that he could not pay the lump sum. W applied for implementation of the order and payment was ordered for a fixed date. That payment was not made and interest began to run. W made application for interest to run from an earlier date. The judge held that s 23(6) MA 1973 allowed interest to be ordered for any time following the making of the original order. H appealed.

Held: H's appeal would be *allowed*. Interest on a late lump sum payment could run only from the date of the order which specifically made provision for the payment of interest.

Re C (A Minor) (Financial Provision) (1994)

Magistrates made an order for periodical payments and a lump sum order, for which W had not made application. The parties were given no warning that the magistrates had in mind the award of a lump sum; they learned of this only when the magistrates' decision was announced. H, against whom the lump sum order was issued, appealed.

Held: H's appeal would be *allowed*. The lump sum order was made in error because the magistrates had failed to warn the parties of the kind of order they were thinking of making. They had failed to pay attention to H's capital means and had given no reasons for making the order in the circumstances.

Baker v Baker (1995) CA

A lump sum order had been made in W's favour against H. He claimed that his principal company had collapsed and that he had been left with only a painting worth £10,000 and some furniture worth a few thousand pounds. (The lump sum order was for £160,000.) The judge did not believe H's evidence concerning his assets and found that there had been an important element of non-disclosure. He decided that H had assets from which the lump sum could be paid. H argued that the judge had acted in the absence of appropriate evidence and that he had misdirected himself as to the burden and standard of proof in deciding whether or not there had been non-disclosure. He contended, further, that the burden of proof was on W throughout and that the standard of proof was higher than a mere balance of probabilities.

Held: H's appeal would be *dismissed*. The burden of proof in ancillary proceedings was on the applicant, but it was for the respondent to make a complete disclosure of all the relevant facts. Further, the judge was correct in making an evaluation of H's assets on a balance of probabilities (see *Bater v Bater* (1951)), and there was sufficient evidence from which the judge might conclude that H had assets from which the order could be met.

7.7 The principle of 'the clean break'

Note

Under s 25A MCA 1973, inserted by s 3 MFPA 1984, it is the duty of the court to consider whether it would be appropriate so to exercise its powers that the financial obligations of each party towards the other will be terminated as soon after the grant of the decree of divorce or nullity as the court considers just and reasonable.

Minton v Minton (1979) HL

A consent order obliged H to convey the matrimonial home to W and to pay her maintenance until completion of the conveyance. Following completion and the cessation of maintenance, W sought to vary the periodical payments to her and the children. The judge varied the order in relation to the children, but not in relation to W. The decision was confirmed by the Court of Appeal. W appealed to the House of Lords.

Held: the consent order had made a 'clean break' between H and W. The court could *not* make a future order on a subsequent application by W following H's compliance with his obligations. *Per* Lord Scarman:

> There are *two principles* which inform the modern legislation. *One* is the public interest that spouses, to the extent that their means permit, should provide for themselves and their children. But *the other* – of equal importance – is the principle of 'the clean break'. The law now encourages spouses to avoid

bitterness after family breakdown and to settle their money and property problems. An object of the modern law is to encourage each to put the past behind them and to begin a new life which is not overshadowed by the relationship which has broken down. It would be inconsistent with this principle if the court could not make, as between the spouses, a genuinely final order unless it was prepared to dismiss the application. The present case is a good illustration. The court having made an order giving effect to a comprehensive settlement of all financial and property issues as between spouses, it would be a strange application of the principle of the 'clean break' if, notwithstanding the order, the court could make a future order on a subsequent application made by W after H had complied with all his obligations.

Seaton v Seaton (1986) CA

H and W were married in 1969. The financial burdens of the marriage were carried by W, who was a teacher. In 1983 W left H, who had developed problems related to drinking. She lived with another man in a house which she had bought on the basis of a heavy mortgage. In 1984 H and W were divorced and, later that year, H suffered a stroke which left him almost totally disabled. He made application for periodical payments from W. The judge refused to make the order and, intending to apply the 'clean break' principle, stated that H should not be entitled to make any future claim against W. H appealed, arguing that he had no resources although his wife continued to earn a salary, so that it was wrong to order a 'clean break'.

Held: H's appeal would be *dismissed*. H should be disentitled, under s 25A(3) MCA 1973 from making future claims against W. It would be quite unjust to make W support H out of an income which, after outgoings, merely enabled her to live a reasonable life.

M v M (Financial Provision) (1987)

Following the divorce of H and W, the matrimonial home was sold, the proceeds being divided equally between them. W's job prospects were not bright. H earned a high salary and had pension rights which would have passed to W had he predeceased her, had they not been divorced. It was agreed that W's reasonable needs would be met through an order for periodical payments. H argued that payments should end after five years, under s 25A MCA 1973. W asked for a lump sum payment.

Held: a termination of the order for periodical payments after five years would *not* be appropriate. W no longer had an opportunity of future security from H's pension rights and it was very doubtful that she would become self-supporting. Should H's position deteriorate he could apply for variation under s 31. It was appropriate in the circumstances to award W a lump sum. *Per* Heilbron J:

W was understandably apprehensive about the future and I do not think she was exaggerating ... She could be left in a very vulnerable position and financially distressed ... H, on the other hand, is in a very much better position. He has a high income and is in very secure employment ... I have come to the conclusion that it is not appropriate to terminate the payment of maintenance to W either in five years or at the end of any fixed period, nor would it be either just or reasonable to do so. To order termination of these payments, in my view, would be to cause undue hardship to W.

C v C (Financial Provision) (1989)

In ancillary proceedings related to the divorce of H and W, evidence was given showing that both possessed considerable capital assets. W wanted to keep the matrimonial home and asked also for a lump sum for periodical payments.

Held: there appeared to be no reason which would justify W's wanting to live in the very large matrimonial home. H was ordered to make periodical payments and to pay a large lump sum, which would take into account the needs of W and their two children. The concept of making periodical payments to a wealthy young or middle-aged woman was falling into disfavour. The court had a duty to consider, where the circumstances were appropriate, a cessation of parties' mutual obligations. H's periodical payments to W would *cease*, therefore, on a date which would be specified.

Barrett v Barrett (1988) CA

H and W were married in 1964, separated in 1979 and divorced in 1987. There were three children of the marriage. An order was made for W to be paid £25 weekly during the parties' joint lives or until remarriage or further order. Later, this order was varied on appeal to one by which W would be paid £25 weekly for a period of four years. The judge had concluded that there was a probability that W would be able to find employment during that period. He believed that s 25A(2) MCA 1973 required the imposition of a 'clean break'. W appealed.

Held: W's appeal would be *allowed* and the original order *restored*. Per Butler-Sloss LJ: 'It is desirable that people should not remain locked into matrimonial financial situations if justice to both sides can be brought by an order to end, either immediately on decree absolute or within as short a period thereafter as possible.' The judge had taken an approach which unduly restricted the exercise of his discretion. Section 25A had not prohibited the court, in the exercise of its discretion, from a consideration of all those matters set out in s 25, and arriving at a conclusion based on that consideration. It was important to note that W was aged 44, had restricted her employment opportunities by giving her time to looking after the children and, as a result, there were now few prospects of her finding suitable employment.

Ashley v Blackman (1988)

On the divorce of H and W, H was ordered to pay W maintenance. W, suffering from schizophrenia, lived on state benefits. H remarried and was obliged to support two children and his second wife. His income was small. Later, the order was varied on a number of occasions. H argued that the order ought to be terminated: no hardship would be caused to W because the state would make up any deficiency suffered by her. The order was reduced and H appealed.

Held: H's appeal would be *allowed*. The courts ought to keep in mind the policy of not throwing on the state the burden of maintaining a spouse and the policy of effecting a 'clean break' between parties by making a periodical payments order when that would not involve either party in suffering undue hardship. A balance between those policies in the interests of justice was required. It was not right that H and W should have to argue for variations in the order at public expense. H's liability to pay periodical payments was to be discharged immediately. *Per* Waite J: 'I do not think there is necessarily any legislative inconsistency in introducing, on the one hand, the clean break objective for mandatory consideration in variation cases, and preserving, on the other hand, a formula for the exercise of the discretion which perpetuates the principle in *Barnes v Barnes* (1972) [intended to protect public funds from feckless husbands seeking to throw on to the state the burden of their wives' maintenance].'

Fisher v Fisher (1989) CA

Under a consent order H made periodical payments to W and their child. Later, W had a second child by another man, and applied for a variation of the periodical payments. H made cross-application for a reduction or discharge of payments, basing the application on the 'clean break' principle. The registrar ordered an increase in H's payments and took into consideration W's second child as a matter related to her earning abilities. H appealed, contending that the birth of the second child was a voluntary act which ought not to have been taken into account by the registrar.

Held: H's appeal would be *dismissed*. It was necessary for the court to examine *all* the circumstances in considering whether it was appropriate to end the financial dependency of one spouse on the other. The argument that W's giving birth to a second child constituted a voluntary reduction of her earning capacities was not based upon any known authority.

Waterman v Waterman (1989) CA

H and W were divorced after a marriage which had lasted for 17 months. A five year old daughter, D, lived with them. H was ordered to pay maintenance to D, while W would receive a lump sum and maintenance for five years. The payments were to end after that period. The judge ordered that W should not be allowed to make an application for variation of the order. He had taken into account W's earning capacity. W appealed.

Held: W's application would be *allowed* in part. The judge had been in error in removing W's right to apply for a variation of the order, since D, who would require care, would be no more than 10 at the termination of the order. *Per* Brown P:

> I believe that [the judge] was fully entitled on the evidence before him to express his view that there ought to be a term for periodical payments, but having regard to the fact that there was still a child of tender years and to the uncertainty as to what the provision might be in five years' time, he was wrong to add a prohibition preventing W from applying for an extension under any circumstances.

Hewitson v Hewitson (1995) CA

Divorce proceedings were brought in the USA and a decree was granted. H and W agreed to a wide-ranging 'clean break' agreement. Later H and W resumed cohabitation for brief periods in the UK and the USA. When they parted finally W made an *ex parte* application under s 13 MFPA 1984, asking for leave to apply for financial relief against H. The judge granted the application and H appealed.

Held: H's appeal would be *allowed*. The court will not interfere with a 'clean break' order made by a foreign court with competent jurisdiction. The 1984 Act ought not to be extended to cover a case in which divorced parties later cohabit. A relationship which develops between parties after a marriage has ended is to be dealt with under the civil law but not as a matter which might extend the objectives of the 1984 Act.

J v J (1999) CA

H and W had been married for 27 years and had four children. H's commercial success had not continued and he was now beset by financial problems. W, a teacher, had been unemployed for several years. H's pension entitlement was the only asset. There were large debts to be settled and the matrimonial home had been repossessed. W's application for a nominal periodical payments order so as to achieve a clean break, and for a deferred lump sum order, had been rejected, and she now appealed on the ground that the lump sum order would make provision for her from H's pension, while the periodical payments order would allow her a measure of protection should H's business become profitable.

Held: W's appeal was *allowed* in part. A deferred lump sum order was inappropriate since it would not benefit W, given the pension's low value. A nominal periodical payments order could be made, since there was no presumption favouring a clean break because of the length of the marriage, and W's concentration on family rather than career. H's finances might improve, allowing W to make application for a variation in the order rather than living on state benefits.

7.8   A note on the *Duxbury* calculation'

Note

The '*Duxbury* calculation' is often used by the courts in the calculation of a lump sum. The calculation (which is now at the basis of a computer program) produces a figure which, if invested on the assumptions as to life expectancy, rates of inflation, return on investment, growth of capital, incidence of income tax, will produce enough to meet the recipient's needs for her life: *Gojkovic v Gojkovic* (1990).

Duxbury v Duxbury (1987) CA

H and W lived in a very expensive fashion. W had not brought any capital into the marriage and had not engaged in any paid employment. In pursuit of the 'clean break' principle, the judge had made an order involving a very large lump sum. H appealed, arguing that the judge had exercised his discretion incorrectly by not taking into account that the man with whom W was living would derive considerable financial benefit from the payment of the lump sum.

Held: H's appeal would be *dismissed*. On the facts the judge was correct, and the matter of cohabitation was not relevant. *Per* Ackner LJ:

> When one has to apply s 25, one is faced with what is essentially a financial and not a moral exercise, save only that the conduct of the parties is available to be considered and ought to be considered if it is such that in the opinion of the court it would be inequitable to disregard it ... It was common ground [in this case] that neither party wished the judge to have regard to the conduct of the other when considering the relevant figures ... It was essentially a mathematical operation which had to produce a fair and proper result ...

F v F (1996)

H and W had been married for 23 years. H possessed assets of some £3.5 million. W had not been in remunerative employment, had fulfilled her role as parent and home-maker but had not assisted in the running of H's business. She had no assets apart from her joint interest in the matrimonial home.

Held: an annual rate of 4.25% was to be assumed for purposes of calculation of the sum necessary to produce the settlement suggested by the court. *Per* Holman J:

> I stress that there may be from time to time cases whose particular facts justify a higher or lower assumed real rate of return and expert evidence in support thereof. An obvious example would be if a wife is going to live abroad and might, accordingly, reasonably be expected to invest there. Another example might be if a wife was so old or incapacitated that she could not reasonably be expected to give any management at all to her income producing fund. Another example might be if the wealth and security of the husband was so great that

the wife could indeed be expected to be free from all risk … But none of these calculations apply to this case. Evidence might be justifiable if there were a relevant change in economic or market conditions … Leaving aside special considerations, it is not, in my judgment, desirable that in case after case time should be taken up and expense incurred in having experts give evidence about an appropriate assumed real rate of return. This is all the more so when, as I cannot stress too strongly, a *Duxbury* calculation is merely a starting point or guide to one component of an overall lump sum award upon which all the s 25 considerations impact … In my view it is important that there should be indeed an 'industry standard' for the purpose of a *Duxbury* approach and in my experience that standard has already settled at around 4.25% (although as long ago as *B v B (Financial Provision)* (1990) Ward J in fact adopted the slightly lower real rate of return of 4%).

A v A (Duxbury Calculations) (1999)

H and W were married in 1955, and were divorced when H was 79 and W was 72. Both had contributed during the years of their marriage, but H's business had declined while W's had become very successful: W's assets were in excess of £1million, while H's were no more than £61,000. W was ordered to pay H a lump sum of £389,000 so that he could purchase a house, and so that he could be provided with an annual income of £16,000, with the income-producing fund being left intact. W appealed; she contended that sufficient income ought to be produced by a *Duxbury*-style fund of £87,000, given H's age and general needs; the lump sum ought to be reduced to £226,000.

Held: the award had been made *in error*, based on an assumption that the income-producing fund would remain intact and be used solely for income production, and that H's needs would be met by £16,000 per year. Having reached 79, there was now a distinct likelihood of H's living longer than suggested by the life expectancy tables used in *Duxbury* calculations, and those principles were, therefore, of limited assistance in this case. The lump sum would be reduced to £350,000.

Q Do you consider the reasoning behind the principle of the 'clean break' to be sound?

8 Property Adjustment Orders, Consent Orders, and Guidelines Under s 25 MCA 1973

8.1 Property adjustment orders

Note —————————————————————————————————————

Under s 24 MCA 1973, property adjustment orders may be made in favour of a spouse or child of the family, or any person for the benefit of such child, on the grant of a decree nisi or at any time following. Note the effect of the Trusts of Land and Appointment of Trustees Act 1996 on the concept of the 'trust for sale'.

Martin v Martin (1977) CA

H and W were married in 1957; the matrimonial home was bought in H's name. H left W in 1972 so as to live with another woman and W remained in occupation of the matrimonial home. Following divorce in 1974, W continued to reside in the matrimonial home, and sought a property adjustment order. The court ordered that the house be held upon trust for W for life or until remarriage or her voluntary departure. H appealed.

Held: H's appeal would be *dismissed*. The order was appropriate where there were no other available assets, where H was not in need of capital in order to provide accommodation for himself (the woman he intended to marry being the tenant of a council house) and where any share in the equity of the home awarded to W would not suffice to allow her to buy alternative accommodation. *Per* Stamp LJ:

> It is of primary concern that, in cases such as these, on the breakdown of the marriage, both parties should, if possible, each have a roof over his or her head, whether or not there are children of the marriage. This is perhaps the most important circumstance to be taken into account in applying MCA 1973 when the only available asset is the matrimonial home.

Mesher v Mesher (1980) CA

(*Note*: this case was decided in 1973, but first reported in All ER only in 1980.)

H and W were married in 1956; there was one child, and the matrimonial home was in the joint names of H and W. In 1970 , H left W to live with R. W continued to reside in the matrimonial home with the child, intending to marry the person with whom she was cohabiting. It appeared that the incomes of the two families were evenly balanced. The judge ordered that the home be transferred to W on her undertaking not to seek in future to recover arrears of maintenance due to her from H. H appealed.

Held: H's appeal would be *allowed*. Taking a broad approach, since the incomes of both families were equally balanced, it would be correct to order the home to be held on trust for sale until the child was older, the proceeds being held in equal shares for H and W. *Per* Davies LJ:

> It is submitted for H that it would be quite wrong to deprive H of the substantial asset which his half-interest in the house represents ... one must take a broad approach to the whole case. What is wanted here is to see that W and daughter, together, no doubt, in the future with the man she intends to marry, should have a home in which to live rather than that she should have a large sum of available capital. With that end in view I have come to the conclusion that counsel's submission for H is right. It would, in my judgment, be wrong to strip the husband entirely of any interest in the house. I would set aside the judge's order so far as concerns the house and substitute instead an order that the house is held by the parties in equal shares on trust for sale but that it is not to be sold until the child of the marriage reaches a specified age or with the leave of the court.

Harvey v Harvey (1982) CA

H and W were married in 1960. In 1981, after a divorce was granted, W moved out of the matrimonial home, taking three of the six children. H continued to reside in the home. He earned twice as much as W and, were the property to have been shared equally, it would have been unlikely that W would have been able to buy his share or any appropriate alternative accommodation. The court ordered that the matrimonial home be held equally in the joint names of H and W on trust for sale. W appealed.

Held: W's appeal would be *allowed*. *Per* Purchas J:

> I am of opinion that W is entitled to live in the matrimonial home as long as she chooses to do so ... on the basis that was adopted in *Martin v Martin* (1977) that, had the marriage not broken down, that is precisely what she would have been entitled to do. I would vary the judge's order, first of all, to say that the asset (the matrimonial home) be transferred into the joint names of W and H on trust for sale, in the shares two-thirds to W and one-third to H; and further that such sale

shall be postponed during W's lifetime, or her remarriage, or voluntary removal from the premises, or her becoming dependent on another man. I have in mind that if she begins to cohabit with another man in the premises, then obviously that man ought to take over the responsibility of providing accommodation for her. Until one or other of those events occur, W should be entitled to reside at the premises, but after the mortgage has been paid off, or the youngest child has reached the age of 18, whichever is the later, she should pay an accommodation rent to be assessed by the judge.

Carson v Carson (1983) CA

H and W were divorced in 1975. The judge ordered that the matrimonial home be transferred to trustees on trust for sale for H and W jointly, and that sale be postponed until the youngest child reached the age of 18 or completed full time education or until W asked for or consented to a sale. W later lost her job and applied for a property adjustment order to transfer the house to her absolutely. The judge held that he lacked jurisdiction to consider W's application and W appealed.

Held: W's appeal would be *dismissed*. Where a property adjustment order is made on a divorce, this constitutes a final order. It cannot be varied subsequently because of any changes in circumstances and leave to appeal would be given only in highly unusual conditions when the appeal was out of time. An end to litigation was essential and to grant W leave to appeal out of time would be to vitiate the very purpose of s 31 MCA 1973.

Harman v Glencross (1986) CA

W had asked for a property adjustment order on petitioning for divorce. A charging order absolute was obtained by H's business partner over H's interest in the matrimonial home; this order was varied and the partner appealed.

Held: the appeal would be *dismissed*. *Per* Balcombe LJ:

... An outright transfer of a husband's interest in the matrimonial home may be the appropriate way to protect fully the wife's right to have a roof over the heads of herself and the children, and it was, of course, such an order that the registrar made (and the judge affirmed) in the present case. Indeed, one of the points made in support of the wife's case, and accepted by the judge, was that if the charging order absolute stood, and was followed by a sale, she would not have enough money left to rehouse herself and the children. However, unless the transfer of the husband's share in the house to the wife is necessary to give her adequate protection so that she may have a home for herself and the children, it is difficult to see why the judgment creditor's undoubted rights should not take preference to the wife's claim to a transfer of property order. [See ss 1, 3(5) Charging Orders Act 1979.]

Clutton v Clutton (1991) CA

H and W were married in 1964; in 1985 they divorced. Their sole asset of any real value was the matrimonial home. W applied for ancillary relief and the registrar ordered that the home be transferred to her, subject to a charge in H's favour for £7,000, to be enforced in 1991. The judge held, on appeal by H, that there should, be a 'clean break' and that the home ought to be transferred, free of any charge, to W.

Held: the sale of the matrimonial home would be *postponed* until W died, or remarried or cohabited with another man; the proceeds would then be shared on the basis of two-thirds to W and one-third to H. *Per* Lloyd LJ:

> Where the judge went wrong, and plainly wrong in my opinion, was refusing to make a *Martin* order ... this is what the wife was originally content to accept. It is also what the husband was asking for. Why then did the judge not make a *Martin* order? We cannot tell, because we do not know his reasons. It cannot surely have been because a *Martin* order would offend against the principle of the 'clean break'. A charge which does not take effect until death or remarriage could only be said to offend against the principle of the 'clean break' in the most extended sense of that term ...

Per Ewbank J:

> It is of course important to retain flexibility to meet the circumstances of individual cases and changes in social conditions. On the other hand, justice and the provisions of the statute usually indicate that an asset acquired by the joint effort of the spouses should eventually be shared. Where the only asset is a jointly acquired home of modest value, it is often necessary to give its occupation to the parent with custody of children or to the spouse with the greater need. The 'clean break' principle does not mean, however, that the other spouse is to be deprived for all time of any share. Experience has shown that postponing such an interest until the children are grown up often merely postpones and exacerbates the problems in re-housing that the occupying spouse will have. This is why the *Mesher* type of order is regarded as unsuitable unless there is going to be sufficient capital available to provide a suitable alternative home. But postponement until death, remarriage or cohabitation does not produce the same problem and is not generally disadvantageous to the occupying spouse. It does ensure that either spouse will receive eventually an appropriate share in the jointly acquired asset.

Rust v Rust (1996) CA

An order was made under s 25 MCA 1973, which required W to charge the property purchased with proceeds of the sale of the matrimonial home. The object was to allow H to receive 35% of the proceeds eventually. H complained that the percentage was too low. He also disputed the nature of the events which would allow the sale of W's present house to be enforced. The completion of the children's full time education, he contended, should be an alternative event (to W's leaving the property, or on her death or remarriage) allowing for the sale of the house to take place. H appealed.

Held: H's appeal would be *allowed in part*. A *Mesher* order should be granted only in those cases where there were sufficient funds to enable W to purchase new accommodation for herself from the proceeds of the sale of the house. But in this case W was very unlikely to obtain employment and would eventually have to leave the house, with inadequate resources, when she was in her mid-50s. A *Mesher* order would be inappropriate in the circumstances of this case.

Jones v Jones (1997) CA

After 15 months of marriage, W petitioned for judicial separation in June 1995; divorce proceedings were pending. Both H and W were on income support and during the marriage they had lived as joint tenants in a council flat. H was disabled by emphysema and a heart condition, so that he required accommodation which did not necessitate his climbing stairs; the council flat had been modified for him. If made homeless as a result of a property transfer order, he would be near the head of the queue for rehousing. W would, if she lost her home, be at the end of the queue. The district judge had ordered that the flat be transferred to W on her undertaking that H would be permitted, pending rehousing, to have a wash and shower at the flat each day. The judge reversed the order, and W appealed.

Held: W's appeal would be *dismissed*. Phillips LJ stated that the reversal of the order of the district judge was wrong. Housing policy was of relevance in considering property transfer orders. The court must take into account what would happen to those deprived of the right to live in the matrimonial home. The court could not but have regard to the manner in which the performance by the housing authority of its functions was likely to affect the consequences of the court's decisions. Taking into account new evidence of a loan which was available to W, and the likelihood that she could obtain adequate accommodation in the private sector, the balance swung back to H, who ought to be permitted to retain the benefits of a tenancy which he had enjoyed and which was suited to the conditions arising from his disability.

Morritt LJ stated that Parliament evidently envisaged that the circumstances of security of tenure and its effects, and local authorities' housing policies ought to be matters which could be taken into account in determining whether orders should be made under s 24 MCA 1973.

Piglowská v Piglowskí (1999) HL

During the divorce proceedings relating to H and W, W made application for a property adjustment order which would allow her and two sons to continue living in the matrimonial home. For this purpose the district judge had made an order whereby she received 73% of the assets. H then appealed on the ground that his own housing needs had to be met and that it would be possible to accommodate W in a cheaper property. That appeal was dismissed by the High Court. H's further appeal was allowed by the Court of Appeal who awarded 40% of the assets to him. This would have involved selling the matrimonial home. W appealed to the House of Lords.

Held: W's appeal would be *allowed* in part. The original order was restored; s 25 gave no priority within the list of matters to be taken into account, and the weight to be given to each factor would vary with the circumstances of the case. There was no absolute rule entitling each party to purchase a dwelling. The Court of Appeal had been in error in altering the decision of the judge at first instance without having examined whether or not cheaper accommodation was available to W. *Per* Lord Hoffmann:

> There are many cases which involve value judgments about family life on which there are no generally held views. The present case provides a good example. Which should be given priority? W's desire to continue to live in the matrimonial home where she can conveniently carry on her business and accommodate her sons, or H's desire to return to England and establish himself here with his new family? In answering that question, what weight should be given to the history of the marriage and the respective contributions of the parties to the family assets? These are values on which reasonable people may differ ... The appellate court must be willing to permit a degree of pluralism in these matters. The judgment of Brennan J in *Norbis v Norbis* (1986) contains a valuable discussion of this question.

8.2   Consent orders

Note

'The law now encourages spouses to avoid bitterness after family breakdown and to settle their property and money problems': *per* Lord Scarman in *Minton v Minton* (1979). On an application for a consent order for financial relief the court may make an order in the terms agreed on the basis only of the information (eg, age of parties and children, parties' capital resources and estimated net income) furnished with the application: s 33A MCA 1973.

8.2.1 Duty of full disclosure

Jenkins v Livesey (1985) HL

W was granted a decree nisi on 1 March 1982, made absolute on 14 April. On 12 August 1982, solicitors for H and W agreed on a consent order for property adjustment and financial provision. H's half-share in the matrimonial home would be transferred to W, subject to her accepting future responsibility for the existing mortgage. On 18 August 1982, W became engaged to X, a matter which had not been disclosed to anyone. On 2 September 1982, a consent order was made by the registrar. On 22 September 1982, H conveyed his half-share. On 24 September 1982, W remarried. H became aware of this, and on 3 April 1983 made application for leave to appeal out of time and for the order to be set aside. H's appeal was dismissed, as was a further appeal to the Court of Appeal. H appealed to the House of Lords.

Held: H's appeal would be *allowed*. The discretion of the court could not be exercised properly under s 25(1) MCA 1973 unless it had been provided with information which was correct and up to date. H and W were under a clear duty to make a complete disclosure of all material facts to each other and to the court. Further, that principle applied also to any exchanges of information leading to consent orders. W's remarriage ought to have been disclosed: it was one of the 'circumstances' mentioned in s 25(1). Because it was not disclosed, the consent order would have to be set aside.

Cook v Cook (1988) CA

H and W became very friendly with Mr and Mrs X. Subsequently, Mr X lived in the matrimonial home with W; this relationship cooled but intensified later. Solicitors of H and W agreed on a consent order in which H transferred his share of the matrimonial home to W, this to be in settlement of any financial claims. In completing Form 91, W made no mention of her relationship with Mr X. As soon as H discovered this, he appealed against the consent order. His appeal was rejected. The judge held that although W had failed to disclose a change in her circumstances, this would have made no difference to the registrar's order. H appealed to the Court of Appeal.

Held: H's appeal would be *dismissed*. W's non-disclosure of her relationship with Mr X had been taken fully into account by the judge. This did not amount to a complete change of circumstances, rather it suggested the modification of a situation which was in existence. There would be no interference, therefore, with the exercise of the judge's discretion.

8.2.2 The situation where a fundamental assumption of the order is invalidated

Barder v Barder (1987) HL

During divorce proceedings, a consent order was made whereby H would transfer his interest in the matrimonial home to W absolutely, and periodical payments would be made to the children. Five weeks later, while the order was not yet in operation, W killed the children and then committed suicide. At this time the period for appealing had passed. The sole beneficiary of W's estate was X, W's mother. H's application for leave to appeal out of time was granted. His appeal was allowed and the consent order was set aside on the ground that it had been based on the underlying assumption that W and the children would need the home for some years ahead. An appeal by X, as intervener, was allowed by the Court of Appeal. H appealed to the House of Lords.

Held: H's appeal would be *allowed*. The judge's decision had been correct; he had jurisdiction to hear an application for leave to appeal out of time and he had made the right order. There had been an implicit and basic assumption by H and W, and their solicitors, that W and the children would require a house for several years after the making of the order, but this assumption had been invalidated totally. An order giving leave to appeal out of time ought to be made only where the appeal, if it were heard, had a strong likelihood of success, if the supervening event had happened within a short period after the making of the order, and if the application had been made promptly. But no application for grant of leave to appeal should be made where it would prejudice a third party who had obtained in good faith and for valuable consideration an interest in the property which was the subject of the order in question. These conditions had been fulfilled in this particular case.

8.2.3 Variation of consent order

Sandford v Sandford (1986) CA

Following the divorce of H and W, a consent order was based upon agreement concerning the transfer of the matrimonial home and its contents to W, and periodical payments for W and the children. Seven years later, in 1983, W applied for a variation in the level of periodical payments. In 1984, H decided to emigrate to Spain, bought a property there and sold his house in England. W discovered the fact of the sale and obtained an order restraining H from dealing with the house or removing any proceeds of the sale from the jurisdiction. H was not present and was not represented at the hearing of the application for variation by W. W was allowed to amend the application so as to include a lump sum (the registrar having heard of H's conduct). H did not comply with the terms of the order and W asked for a transfer of property order in relation to the property in Spain. An order was made and H appealed.

Held: H's appeal would be *allowed*. The agreement reached at the time of the divorce was a comprehensive settlement. It was not open, therefore, for W to apply for a further lump sum. The 1984 orders would be set aside.

Dinch v Dinch (1987) HL

Following the divorce of H and W, a consent order was made, based upon periodical payments to be made by H to W and the child of the marriage, and for the sale of the matrimonial home, proceeds to be divided equally, when the child reached 17 or ceased full time education, whichever was the later. H was soon in arrears on ceasing working and W was granted a charging order in relation to the arrears. H requested a variation of the order; W requested a transfer of property and a postponement order concerning the sale of the home. H's application was granted but the judge held that he had no jurisdiction in relation to W's application. W's appeal was allowed by the Court of Appeal: H's interest in the matrimonial home would be transferred to W, subject to a charge in favour of H. H then appealed to the House of Lords.

Held: H's appeal would be *allowed*. The consent order had determined the rights of H and W in relation to the matrimonial home in a manner which was final and conclusive. The judge was correct in concluding that he had no jurisdiction to make any further order. Once an order has been made by the court concerning particular property, under ss 23, 24 MCA 1973 no further order may be made, except in the few circumstances set out in s 31. *Per* Lord Oliver:

> This appeal is yet another example of the unhappy results flowing from the failure to which I drew attention in *Sandford v Sandford* (1986) to take sufficient care in the drafting of consent orders in matrimonial proceedings to define with precision exactly what the parties were intending to do in relation to the disposal of the petitioner's claims for ancillary relief so as to avoid any future misunderstanding as to whether those claims, or any of them were or were not to be kept alive. The hardship and injustice that such failure inevitably causes, particularly in cases where one or both parties are legally aided and the only substantial family asset consists of the matrimonial home, are so glaring in the instant case that I feel impelled once again to stress in the most emphatic terms that it is in all cases the imperative professional duty of those invested with the task of advising the parties to these unfortunate disputes to consider with due care the impact which any terms that they agree on behalf of clients have or are intended to have on any outstanding application for ancillary relief and to ensure that such appropriate provision is inserted in any consent order made as will leave room for any future doubt or misunderstanding or saddle the parties with the wasteful burden of wholly unnecessary costs ... In the instant case the consent order, on its face and in the light of the issues which were clearly before

the court, is not, in my judgment, capable of being construed in any other sense than as finally and conclusively determining the rights of the parties in the property.

Thompson v Thompson (1985) CA

H and W were divorced in 1980, W was granted custody of the two children. In 1981 a property adjustment order was made by consent which provided that the property was to be held on trust for sale until the youngest child reached the age of 17 or finished education, or grant of a further order. In 1983 W asked H whether he would sell the house as she wished to move elsewhere, but H refused. W applied for an order which would have compelled H to sell. The judge held that an early sale constituted a variation of the property adjustment order and was, therefore, prohibited by s 31 MCA 1973. W appealed.

Held: W's appeal would be *allowed*. The court, in making a property adjustment order, could make provision for the making of a further order in the future concerning the precise circumstances in which the property might be sold. Further, s 31 did not prevent any consideration by the court of the possibility of circumstances arising which rendered the postponement of sale until the agreed time unnecessary, The court had the power to compel H to concur in a sale by exercising its power under s 24A.

N v N (Consent Order: Variation) (1993) CA

H and W were married in 1980 and divorced in 1987; there was one child. W, rejecting legal advice, agreed that maintenance should end after five years; she accepted also that she would be bound by a letter stating that she would not seek, except in unforeseen circumstances, an extension of the five-year period. The terms of the agreement were set out in a consent order; the letter was not known to the district judge. Later, W, who wished to change the general direction of her career, applied for an extension of the maintenance period for three years, relying on s 31 MCA 1973. The judge held that he had no jurisdiction to effect an extension of the term. On appeal, the judge held that W could make the application but the terms of the consent order and the letter would bind her. W appealed.

Held: W's appeal would be *dismissed*. The very existence of the consent order was of importance, as was the ending of financial dependency. The letter could not be disregarded and it ought to have been shown to the judge who had made the consent order. Agreements freely entered into at arm's length by parties receiving proper advice would be upheld by the court.

Masefield v Alexander (Lump Sum: Extension of Time) (1995) CA

In ancillary proceedings a consent order was made: H was to pay a lump sum within a specified time enabling W to purchase a house. In default of payment, the matrimonial home would be sold and the proceeds divided.

H did not meet the fixed deadline and requested an extension of time in order to pay the lump sum, but the district judge refused his application on the grounds that he had no jurisdiction. Leave to appeal was refused by the High Court. H then tendered the lump sum plus interest some five weeks following the deadline. W refused it. H appealed.

Held: H's appeal would be *allowed*. The court did possess jurisdiction allowing it to extend time for the payment of a lump sum in circumstances where the party could not be blamed for the delay. The very purpose of the extension to the order should be looked at by the court to examine whether it affected the essence of the order. W was not prejudiced in any way by an extension of time, and, in this particular case, time was not of the essence.

B v B (Consent Order: Variation) (1995)

H and W, on the breakdown of their marriage, made a consent order in 1988, the terms of which provided for a lump sum payment to W and periodical payments which would fall over the following seven years, after which any claim for periodical payments was to be dismissed. H's earning capacity was high. W had been treated for depression, and in 1992 she applied for a variation of the 1988 order so as to extend the duration of the periodical payments.

Held: W's application would be *allowed* on its merits. W had received poor legal advice leading to the consent order. H's earning capacity seemed not to have been taken into account, and W's low earning capacity had not been given sufficient attention. It should have been obvious that W would require periodical payments for the remainder of her life.

8.3 Statutory guidelines for the exercise of the court's discretion

Note

In considering financial orders the court is directed under s 25(1) MCA 1973 to take into consideration *all* the circumstances and to have regard to a list of matters set out in the section. See *Trippas v Trippas* (1973): the court must make an investigation of circumstances past, present and, 'in so far as one can make a reliable estimate, future'.

J v S-T (1996) CA

Defendant (D), a transsexual male who had been born a female, had concealed his true gender from the registrar and his 'wife' (the plaintiff (P)) for some 17 years. The true facts became known to P only when she examined D's birth certificate. A decree of nullity was granted in 1994 and D applied for ancillary relief (periodical payments and a property adjustment order). P then challenged D's right to apply. In January 1996, the judge held that D was debarred from continuing the claim for ancillary relief on the ground that it was contrary to public policy. D appealed.

Held: D's claim would be *dismissed*. Sir Brian Neill stated that, in the exercise of the court's discretion under s 25(1) MCA 1973, it was legitimate to take into account principles of public policy. The applicant (D) had been guilty of a serious crime (perjury) and had practised deception of a grave nature on P; these matters constituted relevant circumstances which were to be taken into account. It was possible to make the necessary assumptions of hardship in D's favour – P was very rich, whereas D had nothing except assets given by P and, perhaps, an equitable interest in the sale of the matrimonial home. But no court could, in the proper exercise of its discretion, grant ancillary relief of the kind claimed by D. D's conduct at the time of the marriage ceremony (when he described himself as 'a bachelor'), when judged by principles of public policy, tipped the scales in decisive fashion against the grant of any relief.

8.3.1 The court must consider the parties' income, property, earning capacity, etc (see s 25(2)(a))

Schuller v Schuller (1990) CA

H and W were married in 1956 and separated in 1977 when W left the matrimonial home to keep house for an elderly friend, X. In 1987 a decree absolute was granted. On X's death, W inherited his flat, which was worth £130,000. She became a residuary beneficiary of X's estate, valued at £5,000. H remained in the matrimonial home, worth £127,500 with an outstanding mortgage of some £5,000. W contended that X's flat was an after-acquired asset which was not related to the marriage in any way and which ought not to be taken into account. W appealed against a lump sum order awarded on the basis of a 'clean break'; her appeal was dismissed. W appealed to the Court of Appeal.

Held: W's appeal would be *dismissed*. The word 'resources' in s 25 MCA 1973 was not qualified in any way; it could not, therefore, be limited in any way. The court had to approach the matter of parties' assets realistically; *all* available assets based on real figures must be taken into account. Neither the registrar nor the judge had been in error in treating W's after-acquired assets in the way they did; the flat was a highly relevant factor in their decision.

Delaney v Delaney (1990) CA

W made application for financial provision for herself and the three children of the marriage. Her income was £98 per week, her expenditure £112. H had left W so as to live with X, with whom he intended to have a family. H and X had joined a housing association scheme which allowed them to acquire a 50% interest in a three-bedroomed house for £30,000;

they paid some £80 weekly in relation to mortgage repayments and rent. The total weekly income of H and X amounted to £210; their expenditure was £180. H was ordered by the registrar to pay £10 for each child. H appealed. The judge found that H had deliberately entered into completely unnecessary financial commitments. The registrar's order was confirmed. H then appealed to the Court of Appeal.

Held: H's appeal would be *allowed*. The court ought to take into consideration a husband's general ability to meet the needs of his former family. H was entitled to seek to balance his hopes for the future against responsibilities to W and the children. H had not behaved as a spendthrift; he needed suitable accommodation, and the housing association scheme was of benefit to him. Given the reasonable financial commitments of H and X, H had insufficient left to maintain his former family. There were social benefits available to W, and H ought not to be damaged by orders. The 'clean break' principle would be observed by acknowledging that it was unrealistic to expect H to fulfil his obligations; nominal orders would be made for each of the three children. *Per* Ward J:

> In my judgment, the approach of this court must be, first, to have regard to the needs of W and the children for proper support. Having assessed that need, the court should then consider H's ability to meet it. Whilst this court deprecates any notion that a former husband and extant father may slough off the tight skin of familial responsibility and may slither into and lose himself in the greener grass on the other side, none the less this court has proclaimed and will proclaim that it looks to the realities of the world in which we live, and that among the realities of life is that there is life after divorce. H is entitled to order his life in such a way as will hold in reasonable balance the responsibilities to his existing family which he carries into his new life, as well as his proper aspirations for a new future. In all life, for those who are divorced and those who are not divorced, indulging one's whims or even reasonable desires must be held in check by the constraints imposed by limited resources and compelling obligations. But H's resources, even when added to the contribution made by X, are very limited indeed.

Van G v Van G (Financial Provision) (1995)

Following the separation of H and W, H transferred very valuable assets to W on the basis of previously-drawn up separation deeds. Later, W made an application for ancillary relief. In an affidavit of means H stated that his total net worth was in excess of £10 million; it was not necessary, he contended, to disclose his precise total net worth. He argued also that, because W was worth about £3.5 million, it was very unlikely that the court would order an adjustment of capital in ancillary relief. W then asked for a directions order in which she sought details of H's capital and income and of the pension rights which she had lost on grant of the decree absolute.

Held: the directions order sought by W *would be made*. Under s 25 MCA 1973, the court had the duty to take into account the property and financial resources available to H and W. Compliance with s 25 necessitated the court's receiving certain precise information. It would not suffice that H said that he was worth 'not less than £10 million' and that, as a consequence, he would be able to meet any order the court was likely to make. H would be ordered to make and provide the court with a summary of those of his assets worth more than £100,000, with an estimated value of each asset, together with an estimate of his income and the pension rights lost by W.

8.3.2 The court must consider actual or potential financial needs, obligations and responsibilities of the parties (see s 25(2)(b))

Furniss v Furniss (1982) CA

H and W were divorced, and H remarried. In ancillary relief proceedings the judge had used figures relating to the gross income of H and W and had arrived at new figures which took into account H's obligations in relation to his new home, but these should be ignored as H had chosen to remarry. As a result of the judge's order, H's financial obligations would exceed his income. H appealed.

Held: H's appeal would be *allowed*. The correct approach would be to look at the *net effect* of the joint income of H and W. This was the only appropriate way to resolve the problem presented by the varying needs of the parties.

8.3.3 The court must take into account the standard of living enjoyed by the family before the marriage breakdown, the parties' ages, duration of marriage, contributions of parties, conduct (see s 25(2)(c)–(g))

Kokosinski v Kokosinski (1980)

In 1947 H and W began cohabiting. In 1950 their son was born. They could not marry until 1971, when H was divorced by his first wife. During this period, W had assisted H in building up his business. After the breakdown of the marriage W and the son bought out H's share in the business. H then lived rent-free in the former matrimonial home. W lived in a bungalow with her mother and sister. She applied for a lump sum order so as to buy a flat which would be near the business.

Held: the court was obliged to have regard to both the conduct of the parties and the circumstances of the case. W's years of cohabitation with H would be considered. In all the circumstances H *would* be ordered to make a lump sum payment. *Per* Wood J:

Behaviour which has occurred outside the span of the marriage itself has been taken into account when exercising its discretion under s 25, at least in cases where such conduct has affected the finances of the other spouse. I find nothing in the authorities to suggest that a broad and general approach to the words 'conduct' and 'in all the circumstances of the case' are undesirable or wrong. W has given the best years of her life to H. She has been faithful, loving and hard-working. She has assisted him in building the family business. She has managed his home and been a mother to and helped him to bring up a son ... I believe that she has earned for herself some part of the value of the family business ...

Evans v Evans (1989) CA

H and W were divorced in 1953 and a periodical payments order was made in W's favour. H complied with all the terms of the order until 1985. In that year W was convicted of inciting other persons to murder H. H appealed to have the order discharged, and his appeal was successful. W appealed.

Held: W's appeal would be *dismissed*. W's behaviour had been such that it would be unjust and totally unrealistic to expect H to continue payments after 35 years, particularly as W had sought to have him killed.

R v R (Financial Provision) (1993)

H and W were married in 1985. The matrimonial home was bought in their joint names. H made the deposit from his savings. W paid for the wedding celebrations. In 1987 W left the matrimonial home and refused to return although protected by an injunction. Her financial contributions to the home were slight. In February 1988 she made application for financial provision and in August, she and her cohabitant bought a house which now had negative equity only. There were two young children of that relationship. H continued to reside in the family home. He had other capital of about £5,000. W asked for a lump sum of half the equity in the matrimonial home, less one-half of mortgage repayments made by H, and including one-half of a notional figure of an estimate of the rack rent for the property in relation to the period since the date of her leaving.

Held: W's delay in making application for financial provision had to be taken into account by the court. Further, W's payment for the wedding could not be considered as a real contribution to the welfare of the family within s 25(2)(f) but could be considered as conduct which might be taken into account under s 25(2)(g). The notional rack rent proposal was quite unrealistic in the circumstances. The *correct order in these circumstances was for a 'clean break'*, for a transfer of W's interest in the home to H upon H paying a lump sum equivalent to 10% of the gross value of the property less 10% of the capital repayments made.

L v L (Financial Provision) (1994)

After a 40-year marriage, W, aged 60, petitioned for divorce from H, aged 69. There were two children from the marriage who were financially independent. H and W had lived in a number of homes, placed solely, since 1967, in W's name. The family finances were under W's control, a state of affairs not unrelated to H's compulsive gambling; they had declined steadily. What assets existed were the fruit of W's management. H went to live abroad in 1988 after the breakdown of the marriage, living in one-half of a house owned by W. W had total capital assets of about £600,000, and £260,000 on the capital market. H had no assets of significant value. Both had state pensions. H made application for a lump sum.

Held: H's conduct throughout the marriage, as a compulsive gambler, had resulted in repeated financial crises within the family, and that constituted conduct which the court ought not to ignore. The children were grown-up and no longer dependent, and that had to be taken into account. It seemed, therefore, that H's needs were an important factor in assessing an appropriate lump sum. H was *awarded*, on the basis of a *Duxbury* calculation, a *lump sum* of £175,000.

Scheeres v Scheeres (1999) CA

H and W had divorced in 1993. H's business was affected by the recession, and he was earning annually £41,000. He paid £7,500 child maintenance under an assessment by the Child Support Agency. Following ancillary relief proceedings in 1997, H was ordered to transfer the matrimonial home to W and to pay her periodical payments of £18,000 annually. W's application for a lump sum was adjourned. W was unable to seek employment because one of the children for whom she had care had Down's Syndrome, requiring continuous attention within the home. H appealed.

Held: The application for a lump sum should have been *dismissed*. The periodical payments were reduced to £12,000 yearly. The recorder ought to have considered carefully all aspects of the test under s 25 MCA 1973. W's needs should have been balanced against the need for H to maintain his new family and to look after his business. Should the business pick up, then all the dependants of H would benefit; hence all should shoulder equally any burdens arising from difficulties experienced by H in his business.

White v White (2000) HL

H and W, who had divorced, had been considered by the court as 'equal partners' throughout their 33-year marriage, during which they had managed a very prosperous farming business. H's father had made a large contribution to the finances of the farm in its early years. In an application for ancillary relief, W had received 40% of all the total property. H had argued that this was an over-generous award because it represented much more than W's financial needs, within the meaning of s 25 MCA 1973, even if those words were to be interpreted as 'reasonable requirements' (see *Dart v Dart* (1996)). H appealed, and W cross appealed, contending that the resources ought to have been divided equally.

Held: The appeal and the cross appeal were dismissed by the House of Lords. Although there was no presumption of equal division, the principle of equality ought to be departed from only if and to the extent that there was good reason for doing so. A judge should be advised to check his tentative views against the yardstick of equal division, prior to reaching a decision. The financial needs of the parties, even when considered as 'reasonable requirements', were not to be considered determinative; they constituted only one of the factors to be taken into account. H and W had built up a sound business partnership in which W had looked after the family and the home and H had concentrated on business matters. Where, as in this case, assets exceeded financial needs of both parties, there could be no justification for considering W's share as reflecting her actual needs, while H was to be allowed to keep any surplus assets. Attention would be paid to the contribution made by H's father, and to W's express wish that she might be able to make appropriate provision in her will for the children. *Per* Lord Nicholls:

> Confusion might be avoided if the courts were to cease using the expression 'reasonable requirement' in cases of this type. There was much to be said for a return to the language of the statute. This would not deprive the courts of the necessary degree of flexibility. The end product of the court's assessment of financial needs should be seen and treated for what it was, namely, only one of the several factors to which the court was to have regard.

Q Do you consider the general criticisms of the *Mesher* order to have been justified?

9 The Child Support Act 1991

9.1 Essence of the CSA 1991

Note

The Child Support Act 1991 is intended to make provision for the assessment, collection and enforcement of periodical maintenance payable by certain parents with respect to children of theirs who are not in their care and for the collection and enforcement of certain other kinds of maintenance. CSA 1995 is concerned with modification of the application of the child support formula in prescribed cases. Modifications of CSA 1991, 1995 have been introduced under Part I Child Support, Pensions and Social Security Act 2000; it should be noted that under s 2, 'maintenance assessment' is to be known as 'maintenance calculation', and 'assessment' is to be known as 'calculation'.

9.1.1 Child support and 'the clean break'

Crozier v Crozier (1994)
H and W made a 'clean break' settlement whereby H transferred his interest (half-share) in the family home, which was valued at around £10,000, to W in settlement of her financial claims. A nominal maintenance order was made for the child of the family, X, who lived with W. W was to accept full responsibility for maintaining X. W was receiving income support. The DSS asked for and obtained an order from the magistrates ordering H to make a contribution to X's maintenance. H later became liable to pay child support for X and he asked for leave to appeal out of time in order to recover his half-share in the matrimonial home.

Held: H's application would be *dismissed*. A 'clean break' agreement between H and W on the break-up of a marriage does not represent a clean financial break between a parent and his child. It may not be set aside because of the bringing into force of a new statutory enforcement body (the Child Support Agency) which regulates the amount of maintenance payable to children. No 'new event' which suffices to invalidate the very basis of a consent order is constituted by either the magistrates' order or the assessment of H's financial responsibility under CSA 1991.

9.1.2 Disclosure of information and inquiries under the 1991 Act

Re C (A Minor) (Child Support Agency: Disclosure) (1995)

The court does not possess any powers allowing it to order the Secretary of State to disclose information in the possession of the Child Support Agency to a child concerning the address of a parent. There was an arrangement, however, under a Practice Direction (*Family Division: Disclosure of Addresses*, 1988) whereby the court may request that an address be disclosed where a custody order is sought.

R v Secretary of State for Social Security ex p Lloyd (1995)

Following a determination of liability made by the Agency under CSA 1991, H made application for judicial review of the decision. His argument was based on his view that no parent who had care of a child and who was receiving benefit ought to be required to authorise an action by the Secretary of State unless the Secretary had made prior inquiries of the absent parent.

Held: H's application for leave to move for judicial review would be *rejected*. Under s 6(2) CSA 1991, the Secretary of State should not require a person ('the parent') to give him authorisation, set out in s 6(1), if he considers that there are reasonable grounds for believing that if the parent were to be required to give that authorisation, or if she were to give it, there would be a risk of her, or any child living with her, suffering harm or undue distress as a result. However, under s 6(3), s 6(2) will have no application if the Secretary of State is requested by the parent to disregard it. H's argument received no support from CSA 1991.

9.1.3 Lump sum order and child support

Phillips v Peace (1996)

At the time of assessment of liability to child support maintenance concerning H's daughter, aged two, H was the owner of a house valued at £2.6m, and three cars worth £190,000. He was receiving *no remuneration* from the company. The assessment made by the Child Support Agency was based upon the Child Support (Maintenance Assessment and Special Cases) Regulations 1992 (SI 1992/1815), reg 7. It resulted in the decision that H had no assessable income, so that he was not liable to make any contribution to the support of C. However, C's mother then applied to the court for lump sum orders under s 15 and Sched 1 Ch A 1989, because, according to s 8(3) CSA 1981, she was not able to ask for periodical payments.

Held: the court's power to order lump sum payments could *not* be utilised so as to make provision for C's regular support. Where CSA 1991 had application, a lump sum order could be made solely in relation to a specific item involving capital expenditure.

9.2 Injunctions and revocation of orders

B v M (Child Support: Revocation of Order) (1994)

In 1985, H and W were divorced. H was ordered to pay child maintenance of £40 monthly for each child. W was given care of the three children. The Child Support Agency informed W in 1993 that she would be eligible to apply for child support assessment if and when the court order were revoked. W's application to revoke was granted by the district judge. H appealed.

Held: H's appeal would be *allowed*. Section 8(3) of the 1991 Act took away from the court its powers to make or vary an order concerning child maintenance. Under the transitional provisions (SI 1992/2644), where there was a maintenance order, a parent with care who was not in receipt of benefit could not apply to the Child Support Agency during the period of transition, and, under para 5, an existing order *could* be varied during that period. The court's powers to make or revoke a maintenance order during the transitional period were based upon s 25 MCA 1973, so that the court had to consider the welfare of the child as of prime significance when revocation was under examination. It had not been established, however, that the child's welfare required revocation of the order in this particular case.

Department of Social Security v Butler (1995) CA

In order to prevent H from disposing of his assets held by his solicitor before the DSS was able to obtain a liability order from the magistrates for maintenance collection, the DSS made a second application for a *Mareva* injunction (see *Mareva Compania Naviera SA v International Bulk Carriers SA* (1980)). H's arrears amounted to £4,000, based upon an assessment by the Child Support Agency. He had appealed against the assessment. The DSS contended that the court possessed a general power to issue an injunction when fairness demanded this; further, the High Court was able to grant interlocutory relief under s 37 SCA 1981.

Held: the application would be *dismissed*. The relevant issues fell for consideration in relation to CSA 1991, and it was this which controlled the power of the DSS to enforce maintenance collection and to bring proceedings concerning liability orders. Under the 1991 Act the Secretary of State was empowered to make deductions from earnings prior to the making of a liability order, but the Act did not give any ancillary jurisdiction to the High Court. Hence it would be unsuitable for the court to grant *Mareva* injunctions (now known as 'freezing injunctions') so as to lend weight to any statutory proceedings before magistrates.

9.3   Deductions from earnings

Note

Wide powers of collection and enforcement are given by the 1991 and 1995 Acts. Deductions from earnings orders may be made so as to ensure that 'liable persons' pay the amounts due under maintenance assessments made by the Child Support Agency.

Biggin v Secretary of State for Social Security (1995)

The Child Support Agency had issued a deduction of earnings order against B concerning two sons from his previous marriage. The magistrates had dismissed B's complaint. B's argument rested upon his belief that the Agency had not taken into account the welfare of the children as required by s 2 of the 1991 Act. B then appealed by way of case stated. That appeal concerned the construing of the term 'defective' which appeared in the Child Support (Collection and Enforcement) Regulations 1992, reg 22(3). The regulation allows an appeal to be made where an order for deduction of earnings is defective. B argued that it was essential that the word be construed in a wide sense.

Held: B's appeal would be *dismissed*. Section 2 of the 1991 Act was not concerned in any way with measuring liability resulting from assessment under the Act.

Secretary of State for Social Security v Shotton and Others (1996)

Five appeals were made by the Secretary of State against magistrates' decisions concerning deductions from earning orders and liability orders issued under the Child Support Act 1991.

First appeal: H had been assessed for child support maintenance. He assumed the everyday care of his child, and she ceased to be regarded under the Act as a 'qualifying child'. He complained against a deduction from earnings order made against him, rather than using the procedure involving asking for a review and cessation of the maintenance assessment. H's appeal was brought more than 28 days following the making of the order.

Second appeal: H made application for review of maintenance assessment on the ground that the child support officer had not taken into account the fact that there existed a court order for maintenance of the child. The Child Support Agency decided that the fact that the order existed would not have affected the assessment; they therefore made a deduction from earnings order. H complained to the magistrates and the order was quashed.

Third appeal: The Agency issued an interim maintenance assessment order and a deduction from earnings order. H argued that he had given the Agency all the information required for the making of a final assessment. The order was quashed by the magistrates.

Fourth appeal: H contended that he had complied with the requirements concerning the provision of information. An interim maintenance order, he argued, ought not to have been made. The Agency sought a liability order against H, but the magistrates held that he had no liability to pay the interim order once the required information had been provided. The deduction from earnings order was defective because it was based on an incorrect assessment.

Fifth appeal: Following an admission by the Agency that a deduction from earnings order was incorrect, H asked for the repayment of money deducted under it. The magistrates acted in the belief that they were empowered to require the Secretary of State to make restitution when they made an order of this nature.

Held: all five appeals would be *allowed*. In relation to the first four appeals, it was wrong for the magistrates to have questioned the validity of the assessments. Under ss 32, 33 CSA 1991 and the Child Support (Collection and Enforcement) Regulations 1992, the power of the magistrates was limited to determining whether reg 9 had been complied with. In relation to the making of a liability order, the role of the magistrates under s 33(3) is to discover whether payments have become payable by the liable party and remain unpaid. Should that be the case, a liability order *must* be made. Magistrates do *not* have the power to order the repayment of money which has been paid under an earnings order which is defective. Finally, the requirement that an appeal against a deduction from earnings order must be made within 28 days runs from the date of the making of the order, not from any subsequent date on which the liability to pay might have ended. It is essential that *all* appeals against assessment be made under the review and appeals structure established by the 1991 Act.

R v Secretary of State for Social Security ex p Singh (2000)

Before the making of a deductions from earnings order under s 31 CSA 1991, S had been overpaying. The amount he paid became insufficient and an increase in the amount required from him became necessary. S later fell into arrears and argued that any surplus from his overpayment ought to be set off against arrears. He sought judicial review of a deduction from earnings order.

Held: S's application would be *refused*. The overpayments had been made voluntarily by S; they could not be made available for deduction from subsequent arrears.

Dorney-Kingdom v Dorney-Kingdom (2000) CA

During ancillary relief proceedings, an order was made that H was to pay W £999 per month for the benefit of his children until they reached the age of 17 or ceased full time education, such sums to be reduced *pro tanto* by any sums payable as child support maintenance pursuant to CSA 1991, and that H should transfer to W absolutely his share in the matrimonial home. H appealed, contending that because there was neither consent between H and W nor any substantive entitlement to spousal maintenance, the judge lacked jurisdiction to make the order, and that the judge had erred in his consideration of the respective financial position of H and W in not giving H a deferred charge on the matrimonial home.

Held: H's appeal was *allowed*. The court lacked jurisdiction to make a maintenance order for the children in ancillary proceedings unless made under s 8(5) CSA 1991 and both parties consented to it. But it was now common practice to make an order for spousal maintenance under s 23(1)(a) MCA 1973 whereby that order incorporated some payment for the children as part of a global order, an important ingredient of the order being that it should reduce pro tanto by any sum payable under an assessment by the Child Support Agency by H to W. Further, in the present case, there were sufficient assets available to rehouse H and W, and the judge had been in error in refusing to grant a *Mesher* order (see *Mesher v Mesher* (1980)).

9.4 Determination of paternity and the 1991 Act

Re E (Child Support: Blood Tests) (1995) CA

X, the mother of E sought a child maintenance order for him from F through the Child Support Agency. F denied that he was E's father and the mother then applied to the court, under s 27 CSA 1991, for an order to determine E's paternity. She requested a direction under FLRA 1969 for the use of blood tests. An appropriate consent was signed by X. F opposed the direction sought by the mother.

Held: the mother's application would be *granted*. Blood tests concerned with the determination of paternity could be made by the court under s 20 FLRA 1969 and, in this case, should be made unless the court was convinced that tests of this nature would not be in E's best interests. There was, however, no evidence that the tests would go against those interests. An appropriate direction would, therefore, be made forthwith.

R v Secretary of State for Social Security ex p W (1999)

S had applied under s 4(1)(a) Ch A 1989 for a parental responsibility order; this was made in his favour by consent. At a later date S returned a form to the Child Support Agency, and denied paternity of the children involved in the order. That order was discharged. The Secretary of State made a decision not to make a maintenance assessment. W, mother of the children, made application for a review of that decision.

Held: W's application was *allowed*. The decision not to make an application was quashed. The making of a parental responsibility order did fulfil the requirements for a finding of paternity order under s 26(2) CSA 1991 (case F). The question of paternity was not mentioned in the application for a parental responsibility order, but it would have been *ultra vires* the children's interests to make an order of this nature unless the judge were convinced that S was the father of W's children. There was adequate evidence for this particular finding.

Q In what ways might the Child Support Act 1991, as amended by the 1995 Act, be made more effective?

10 Interests in the Matrimonial Home

10.1 Importance of protection of a spouse's interests

Note ————————————————————————————————

The rights of occupation enjoyed by a spouse may be threatened, eg, where the matrimonial home is to be sold against her wishes or without her knowledge. The significance of the protection of these rights emerges from the cases outlined below.

10.2 The spouse's beneficial interest and third parties

National Provincial Bank v Ainsworth (1965) HL

H deserted W; she remained in the matrimonial home which H owned. Later, H mortgaged the property to the National Provincial Bank. The question arose as to whether W had any proprietary interest in the matrimonial home which might be binding on the bank. The House of Lords discussed the nature of the deserted wife's rights.

Held: although W had a right to occupy H's property (the right commonly known as 'the deserted wife's equity'), such a right was essentially *personal and not proprietary*. *Per* Lord Wilberforce:

> Before a right or interest can be admitted into the category of property or of a right affecting property, it must be definable, capable of identification by third parties, capable in its nature of assumption by third parties, and have some degree of permanence or stability.

Per Lord Upjohn:

> I myself am unable to see how it is possible for a 'mere equity' to bind a purchaser unless that equity is ancillary to or dependent upon an equitable estate or interest in the land ... a 'mere equity' naked and alone is, in my opinion, incapable of binding successors in title even with notice; it is personal to the parties.

(The result of this case was that the bank was entitled to possession, W was without protection against a third party so that she could not stay in the home merely by virtue of her status as a wife. But registration of statutory rights of occupation has now effectively modified rights *in personam* to rights *in rem*, giving a degree of protection to the wife. This decision led directly to the Matrimonial Homes Act 1967. See also 'matrimonial home rights' under Part IV FLA 1996.)

Williams and Glyn's Bank v Boland (1981) HL

H purchased a house in his name and resided there with W and their son. W had contributed in substantial measure to the purchase price. At a later date the bank made a loan to H, who guaranteed it by a charge on the home. The land was registered land and the bank did not make any enquiry concerning W's possible interest. Proceedings for possession were brought by the bank subsequently. W claimed to possess rights which ought to prevail against those of the bank. She contended that she had a property interest in the matrimonial home by virtue of her contribution to the purchase. Further, she argued that she occupied the house and had a right to continued occupation. Her rights constituted, she claimed, an overriding interest under s 70(1)(g) LRA 1925. The court rejected her claim; its judgment was reversed by the Court of Appeal. The bank appealed to the House of Lords.

Held: the bank's appeal would be *dismissed*. W was a person 'in actual occupation' for purposes of s 70(1)(g), so that the bank's charge in relation to the matrimonial home was subject to W's overriding interest. *Per* Lord Wilberforce:

> There was a physical presence, with all the rights that occupiers have, including the right to exclude all others except those having similar rights. The house was a matrimonial home, intended to be occupied, and, in fact, occupied by both spouses, both of whom have an interest in it. It would require some special doctrine of law to avoid the result that each is in occupation ... A wife may, and everyone knows this, have rights of her own; particularly, many wives have a share in a matrimonial home. How can it be said that the presence of a wife in the house, as occupier, is consistent or inconsistent with the husband's rights until one knows what rights she has? ... The only solution which is consistent with s 70(1)(g) and with common sense is to read the paragraph for what it says. Occupation, existing as a fact, may protect rights if the person in occupation has rights. On this part of the case I have no difficulty in concluding that a spouse, living in a house, has an actual occupation capable of conferring protection, as an overriding interest, upon rights of that spouse.

Per Lord Scarman:

> The courts may not put aside, as irrelevant, the undoubted fact that if [W succeeds] the protection of the beneficial interest which English law now recognises that a married woman has in the matrimonial home will be strengthened whereas, [if W loses] this interest can be weakened, and even destroyed, by an unscrupulous husband ... The judicial responsibility remains – to interpret the statute truly according to its tenor. The social background is, therefore, to be kept in mind but can be decisive only if the particular statutory provision under review is reasonably capable of the meaning conducive to the

special purpose to which I have referred. If it is not, the remedy is to be found not by judicial distortion of the language used by Parliament but in amending legislation. Fortunately, [W's appeal] calls for no judicial ingenuity, let alone distortion. The ordinary meaning of the words used by Parliament meets the needs of social justice.

Kingsnorth Finance Co v Tizard (1986)

H and W married in 1968 and separated in 1982. W continued to stay in the matrimonial home when H was away, returning to it so as to look after the children. In 1983, H approached brokers so as to obtain a loan of £66,000 on the security of the house (which was unregistered land). In his application he declared that he was single. On the instruction of the brokers, a surveyor carried out a survey of the property at a time when H had ensured that W would be away. H told the surveyor that W was living elsewhere with someone else. The loan was made to H. Later, the brokers sought to enforce the charge and claimed possession.

Held: the claim of the brokers would be *dismissed*. W had a beneficial interest under s 199(1)(ii)(a) LPA 1925. The inspection made by the brokers was not within the category of 'such inspections ... as ought reasonably to have been made'. *Per* HH Judge Finlay:

> I would put it briefly thus. H appears to have been minded to conceal the true facts; he did not do so completely. The plaintiffs [the brokers] had, or are to be taken to have had, information which should have alerted them to the fact that the full facts were not in their possession and that they should make further inspections or enquiries. They did not do so and, in the circumstances, I find that they are fixed with notice of W's equitable interest.

Lloyds Bank v Rosset (1991) HL

H and W intended to buy as their home a house which required considerable repairs. The purchase was to be made with money from H's family trust and was in H's sole name. The vendors allowed H and W to enter the property with builders to do renovation work prior to exchange of contracts. The building work commenced on 7 November 1982. W carried out much of the work. Contracts were exchanged on 23 November. On 14 December, H drew £15,000 from his bank, without W's knowledge, to meet building costs and signed a legal charge, execution of the charge taking place on 17 December. Transfer and charge were registered on 7 February 1983 and the family moved in. In May 1984 H left W, who remained in the home with the children. Arrears increased and the bank claimed possession. W contended that she had an overriding interest under s 70(1)(g) LRA 1925 since she had been in actual occupation of the family home on the relevant date. Her argument was rejected by the judge, but her appeal was allowed by the Court of Appeal. The bank appealed to the House of Lords.

Held: the bank's appeal would be *allowed*. The appropriate date to be used in ascertaining whether an interest in land was protected by actual occupation in order to prevail against the holder of a legal estate as an overriding interest was that of the transfer of the estate and not its registration. Further, the House held unanimously that W did *not* possess a beneficial interest. *Per* Lord Bridge:

> The first and fundamental question which must always be resolved is whether, independently of any inference to be drawn from the conduct of the parties in the course of sharing the house as their home and managing their joint affairs, there has been at any time prior to acquisition, or exceptionally at some later date, any agreement, arrangement or understanding reached between them that the property is to be shared beneficially. The finding of an agreement or arrangement to share in this sense can only, I think, be based on evidence of express discussions between the partners, however imperfectly remembered and however imprecise their terms may have been. Once a finding to this effect is made it will only be necessary for the partner asserting a claim to a beneficial interest against the partner entitled to the legal estate to show that he or she has acted to his or her detriment or significantly altered his or her position in reliance on the agreement in order to give rise to a constructive trust or a proprietary estoppel … I cannot help thinking that the judge in the instant case would not have fallen into error if he had kept clearly in mind the distinction between the effect of evidence on the one hand which was capable of establishing an express agreement or an express representation that W was to have an interest in the property, and evidence on the other hand of conduct alone as a basis for an inference of the necessary common intention.

Abbey National Building Society v Cann (1990) HL

The appellants, A1 and A2, were living in a home provided for them by S, A1's son, in his own name, using a mortgage provided by the building society and a sum arising from the proceeds of sale of another house. S defaulted in paying the mortgage instalments and the building society brought an action against S, A1 and A2, claiming possession. A1 argued that she had an equitable interest in the property and that S had assured her that she would always have a roof over her head. Her interest, she claimed, constituted an overriding interest which, by virtue of her occupation at the date of registration took priority over the building society's charge, under s 70(1)(g) LRA 1925. A1's appeal was rejected and the decision was upheld by the Court of Appeal. The appellants then appealed to the House of Lords.

Held: the appeal would be *dismissed*. It was necessary to show actual occupation at the date on which the charge was created and not at the date on which registration was effected. *Per* Lord Oliver:

The relevant date for determining the existence of overriding interests which will affect the estate transferred or created is, the date of registration ... The question remains, however, whether the date of registration is also the relevant date for determining whether a claimant to a right is in actual occupation. It is to be noted that it is not the actual occupation which gives rise to the right or determines its existence. Actual operation merely operates as the trigger for the treatment of the right, whatever it may be, as an overriding interest. Nor does the actual quality of the right as an overriding interest alter the nature or quality of the right itself. If it is an equitable right, it will remain an equitable right ... I see no insuperable difficulty in holding that the actual occupation required to support such an interest as a subsisting interest must exist at the date of completion of the transaction giving rise to the right to be registered ... It is perhaps dangerous to suggest any test for what is essentially a question of fact, for 'occupation' is a concept which may have different connotations according to the nature and purpose of the property which is claimed to be occupied. It does not necessarily, I think, involve the personal presence of the person claiming to occupy ... I am unable to accept that acts of a preparatory character carried out by courtesy of the vendor prior to completion can constitute an actual occupation for the purposes of s 70(1)(g) ... [A1] fails, in my judgment, to establish the necessary condition for the assertion of an overriding interest.

Midland Bank v Cooke (1995) CA

H purchased a house in his sole name by a mortgage, a wedding gift, and by drawing on his savings. Later, the mortgage was replaced by a general mortgage in the bank's favour, so as to secure H's business overdraft. W signed a form of consent which effectively postponed any present or future rights she had in the property to the bank's security. The property was then transferred in the joint names of H and W. Proceedings were brought by the bank claiming payment of £52,000, with possession in default. W contended that her consent stemmed from H's undue influence. It was held by the judge that the bank had been aware of H's undue influence, so that W was not bound by the signed consent. Further, the judge held that W did possess an equitable interest in the house, based on her contribution to its purchase, which had taken the form of her share of the wedding gift. That interest was to be considered as approximating to some 6% of the house's value. W appealed.

Held: W's appeal would be *allowed*. When seeking to evaluate an equitable interest, the court should take into account the full history of dealings between parties and relevant to their ownership and occupation of the property and their sharing of burdens and advantages. It ought not to be bound, in arriving at a decision, by the monetary contributions of H and W where it was possible to infer some other arrangement relating to shares in the property. *Per* Waite J:

It will take into consideration all conduct which throws light on the question of what shares were intended. Only if that search proves inconclusive will the court fall back on the maxim 'equality is equity'.

The judge was wrong in considering W's share in the property as having been fixed according to her monetary contribution to the purchase price. Given all the evidence in the case, there appeared to be the presumed intention that H and W were to own equal shares in the house. A beneficial half interest would be granted, therefore, to W.

10.2.1 Problems arising from the overriding interest

Bristol and West Building Society v Henning (1985) CA

H cohabited with M as husband and wife. The property in which they lived was in H's sole name and he was the mortgagor. He left the property, and neither he nor M was able to make the mortgage repayments.

Held: the mortgagees (the building society) *were entitled* to possession since M could not show any beneficial interest under a constructive trust by establishing the existence of an intention on H's part that she should have such an interest. The mortgage was granted to the building society with the full knowledge and approval of M. The result of her claiming an overriding interest would be that she might be entitled to stay in the property indefinitely without making any payment. *Per* Browne-Wilkinson LJ:

> There was no way in which the house could have been purchased at all without the assistance of the mortgage and that mortgage could not have been properly granted without giving the building society a charge over the whole legal and equitable interest. Since the nature of [M's] interest has to be found in the imputed intention of the parties and that imputed intention must have been that her interest was to be subject to that of the building society, it is impossible for [M] to establish that she is entitled to some form of equitable interest which gives her rights in priority to those of the building society. I would hold, therefore, that, even on the assumption that [M] has some equitable interest or right in the house, such interest or right is subject to the building society's charge and provides no defence to that society's claim for possession.

Equity & Law Home Loans v Prestidge (1992) CA

X and Y cohabited in a home which they purchased with the assistance of a building society mortgage. Y made a contribution of some £10,000. Later, X remortgaged the house for a larger sum, but did not inform Y, nor did he ask for her consent. Following the collapse of the relationship, X left the house and did not make the necessary repayments. Possession proceedings were instituted by P; they were not contested by X. Y contended that her beneficial interest in the home had priority over P's rights arising under the mortgage. It was held, however, that P was entitled to enforce the security up to the amount of the original mortgage. Y appealed.

Held: Y's appeal would be *dismissed*. It was clear that the beneficial interest in the property did vest in Y, subject to the rights of mortgagees. It was necessary to impute consent by her to the transfer of the mortgage up to the original amount, although she did not know of it. Hence, the charge in P's favour must be considered as having priority over Y's beneficial interest up to the amount of the original mortgage. *Per* Mustill LJ:

> [Y] is being made homeless through a combination of P's dishonesty and Equity & Law's incompetence and, she might well add, some serious mistakes by her first solicitors. I am by no means convinced that this will be the result in practice of upholding the judgment, for it may be that a result can be negotiated which will keep her and her family in the house while giving recognition to the full mutual rights of the parties. I hope so. But in any event I am unable to see how Equity & Law could be regarded as owing towards her any duty of care which could alter the consequences of her initial imputed consent to the encumbering of the property ... The rights of the mortgagees are preferred, not because they override the equity, but because Y's beneficial interest was of a very special kind which, from the very outset, had carved out of it by anticipation a recognition of the rights of the mortgagees whose finance was intended to bring the purchase into being. In my view, once this is recognised, the problem disappears. I would therefore dismiss the appeal. Y has been cruelly deceived and suffered hardship, but this is not something to be placed to the account of Equity & Law.

10.2.2 Claim to beneficial interest

Pettitt v Pettitt (1970) HL

H and W were married in 1952 and lived for nine years in a home which W had inherited. H made a number of improvements to the property and in 1961 the house was sold and W acquired another. H and W lived for four years in the new home when W left H and obtained a divorce in 1967. H moved away from the home and commenced proceedings, seeking a declaration that he was beneficially interested in the proceeds of the sale of the home and seeking an order requiring W to pay. An order was made that W should pay. The Court of Appeal dismissed W's appeal and gave leave for an appeal to the House of Lords.

Held: the appeal would be *allowed*. It was not possible on the evidence to infer a common intention of H and W that H, by carrying out work and spending money on materials, should acquire a beneficial proprietary interest in the home. *Per* Lord Diplock:

It is common enough nowadays for husbands and wives to decorate and to make improvements to the family home themselves with no other intention than to indulge in what is now a popular hobby, and to make the home pleasanter for their common use and enjoyment. If the husband likes to occupy his leisure by laying a new lawn ... while the wife does the shopping, cooks the family dinner, bathes the children, I, for my part, find it quite impossible to impute to them as reasonable husband or wife any common intention that these domestic activities or any of them are to have any effect upon existing proprietary rights in the family home on which they are undertaken.

Per Lord Morris:

The mere fact that parties have made arrangements or conducted their affairs without giving any thought to questions as to where ownership of property lay does not mean that ownership was in suspense or did not lie anywhere. There will have been ownership somewhere and a court may have to decide where it lay. In reaching a decision the court does not, indeed, cannot, find that there was some thought in the mind of a person which was never there at all ... When an application is made under MWPA 1882, s 17, there is no power in the court to make a contract for the parties, which they themselves have not made. If there is a breakdown between spouses there will be a situation for which the parties cannot have provided. There may be a need for new adjustments ... The reported cases and the pattern of the situations which have given rise to them reflect problems of wide social consequence. Their solution must lie with those who decide policy and enact the law.

Gissing v Gissing (1971) HL

H and W were married in 1935; the matrimonial home was purchased by H in 1951 in his sole name. W obtained a decree absolute in 1966. Although W had made no direct contribution to the purchase of the matrimonial home, she had spent her own money on furniture, improvements to the premises and clothes for the family. W applied by originating summons for an order concerning her beneficial interest in the home; it was held by the judge that H was the sole beneficial owner and was entitled, therefore, to possession. The Court of Appeal reversed the decision and H appealed to the House of Lords.

Held: H's appeal would be *allowed*. It was not possible to draw from the evidence any inference that H and W had a common intention that W should have any beneficial interest in the matrimonial home. *Per* Lord Reid:

Why does the fact that H agreed to accept these contributions from his wife not impose a trust on him? There is a wide gulf between inferring from the entire conduct of the parties that there probably was an agreement, and imputing to the parties an intention to agree to share even where the evidence gives no ground for such an inference. If the evidence shows that there was no agreement in fact, then that will exclude any inference that there was an agreement. But it does not exclude an imputation of a deemed intention if the law permits such an imputation. If the law is to be that the court has the power to impute such an intention in proper cases, then I am content, although I would prefer to reach the same end in a rather different way. But if it were to be held to be the law that it must at least be possible to infer a contemporary agreement in the sense of holding that it is more probable than not there was in fact some such agreement, then I could not contemplate the future results of such a decision with equanimity.

Per Lord Diplock:

The picture presented by the evidence is one of husband and wife retaining their separate proprietary interests in real or personal property purchased with their separate savings and is inconsistent with any common intention at the time of purchase of the matrimonial home that the wife, who neither then nor thereafter contributed anything to its purchase price or assumed any liability for it, should nevertheless be entitled to a beneficial interest in it.

Re Nicholson (1974)

H and W purchased a house in 1938, in H's name for £900; W contributed £75, H £15, to the deposit. For five years H made the mortgage payments. W paid off the outstanding amount on the mortgage from a bequest and redeemed the mortgage; she also paid for the installation of central heating. The house was then worth £6,000; the increased value due directly to the improvement was £150. H died and left the house to W, then to D absolutely.

Held: the parties' common intention at the time of purchase of the house was that it would belong to them in equal shares. As a result, W was beneficially *entitled to a half-share*. The correct way to work out by how much W's beneficial interest in the matrimonial home should be enlarged as a direct result of improvements is to ascertain the value of the property at the date immediately before making the improvement, calculate the addition to the value due to the improvement, and increase the share of the responsible spouse by a proportionate amount.

Eves v Eves (1975) CA

X, a married man, met Y. They cohabited in X's house and two children were born. Following the sale of the house, another house was purchased in X's name; Y made no direct financial contribution. X told Y that the only reason it was not in their joint names was that she was under 21. Y, relying on her belief in a common intention, worked very hard in the renovation of the house (which was dilapidated). Some two years later, their divorces were effected. X then told Y that he intended to marry someone else and married the other woman. Y left X and applied to the county court for a declaration of an interest in the house. She then appealed to the Court of Appeal.

Held: X would hold the legal estate on *trust for sale* in the proportion one-quarter for Y and three-quarters for X. *Per* Lord Denning:

> X gained Y's confidence by telling her that he intended to put the property in their joint names but that it was not possible until she was 21. The judge described this as a trick. X never intended to put it in joint names. It seems to me that he should be judged by what he told her – by what he led her to believe – and not by his own intent ... It seems to me that this conduct by X amounted to a recognition by him that, in all fairness, Y was entitled to a share in the house, equivalent in some way to a declaration of trust; not for a particular share, but for such share as was fair in view of all Y had done and was doing for him and the children and would thereafter do ...

Burns v Burns (1984) CA

X, a married man, met Y. She was aware that X had no intention of marrying her. They lived together for 17 years, during which time two children were born. She changed her name to his by deed poll, stayed at home to bring up the children and performed all the domestic duties of a wife. When the children grew up, Y returned to work and used her earnings to buy furniture and fittings for the house. X left her and she appealed against a decision that she had no beneficial interest in the house.

Held: the judge had been correct in holding that Y had no beneficial interest in the home. The appeal would be *dismissed*. There was no evidence of any substantial payments by Y from which it could be inferred that they were relevant to the acquisition of the house. *Per* Fox LJ:

> ... There remains the question of housekeeping and domestic duties. So far as housekeeping expenses are concerned, I do not doubt that (the house being in X's name) if the woman goes out to work in order to provide money for the family expenses, as a result of which she spends her earnings on the housekeeping and the man is thus able to pay the mortgage instalments and other expenses out of his earnings, it can be inferred that there was a common intention that the woman should have an interest in the house since she will have made an indirect contribution to the mortgage instalments. But that is not this case.

> During the greater part of the period when X and Y were living together, she was not in employment, or, if she was, she was not earning amounts of any consequence and provided no money towards the family expenses ... The house was not bought in the contemplation that Y would, at some time, contribute to the cost of its acquisition. She worked to suit herself. Her money was in no sense 'joint money'; it was her own; she was not expected and was not asked to spend it on the household. I think that it would be quite unreal to say that, overall, she made a substantial financial contribution towards the family expenses. This is not in any way a criticism of her; it is simply the factual

position ... In my opinion, Y fails to demonstrate the existence of any trust in her favour.

Midland Bank v Dobson (1986) CA

H and W married in 1951 and lived with H's mother in her home. The home was sold by the mother in 1953 and the proceeds were used in the purchase of the matrimonial home, bought in the joint names of H and his mother; the balance was secured on a building society mortgage which was discharged in 1970. H became sole owner following his mother's death. W was not in employment, she had a separate bank account and paid for clothes and household expenses. In 1978 H secured the house to the bank (the plaintiffs) so as to buy shares in a company of which he was the director. W signed a letter of consent, postponing any interest she might have in the house in the bank's favour. W later claimed a beneficial interest in the property. The bank appealed.

Held: the bank's appeal would be *allowed*. Even if H and W had made an oral declaration that it was their common intention that the property should belong to them jointly, that would not act so as to create a trust because of s 53(1)(b) LPA 1925. An inference of the existence of a trust (constructive, resulting) would arise only if W were able to show that an agreement had been made under which W was obliged to do something to her detriment in relation to that agreement. It could not be shown here that W had acted to her detriment on the basis of some common intention of ownership of the house. *Per* Fox LJ:

In my view, W does not demonstrate that she was induced to act to her detriment upon the basis of a common intention of ownership of the house or that there was otherwise any nexus between the acquisition of the property and something provided or forgone by W.

I should add that I see no basis for any claim by W simply by way of resulting trust unaccompanied by a specific agreement. Thus, she made no direct contribution to the purchase price. There was no arrangement that she should go out to work and provide money which directly or indirectly would be used to pay off the mortgage. W, of course, performed various household duties and purchased household items, but those facts are quite consistent with H's absolute ownership of the house itself.

The result, in my opinion, is that W does not establish that she is entitled to any beneficial interest in [the house]. The result is that the case is one of a mortgage by the absolute owner of the fee simple (H). The bank is, under the legal charge, entitled to possession absolutely.

10.3 Rights of creditors and interests of companies

Re Citro (1990) CA

H1 and H2 were business partners. W1 was separated from H1; she occupied the matrimonial home together with three young children. H2 occupied the matrimonial home with W2 and their three young children. In 1985 H1 and H2 were adjudicated bankrupt. Their sole assets were half shares of the beneficial interests in the matrimonial homes. The trustee of the bankrupts' estates applied for orders under s 30 LPA 1925, for possession and sale of the homes. The judge made a declaration that the beneficial interest in each of the homes was held by the bankrupt husband and his wife in equal shares. Orders for possession and sale of the houses were made, but, taking into account the many problems that would affect the children of the two families, the orders for sale would be postponed until the youngest child reached the age of 16. The trustee appealed against the postponement provisos.

Held: the appeal would be *allowed* and a postponement period of six months maximum would be substituted. The creditors' interests prevailed over those of the spouses. Further, although the circumstances of W1, W2 and the children were distressing, they were not so very exceptional as to warrant a long term postponement. *Per* Nourse LJ:

> The broad effect of the authorities can be summarised thus: where a spouse who has a beneficial interest in the matrimonial home has become bankrupt under debts which cannot be paid without a realisation of that interest, the voice of the creditors will usually prevail over the voice of the other spouse and a sale of the property will be ordered within a short time. The voice of the other spouse will only prevail in exceptional circumstances. No distinction will be made between a case in which the property is still being enjoyed as the matrimonial home and one where it is not. What are exceptional circumstances? As the cases show, it is not uncommon for a wife with her young children to be faced with eviction in circumstances where the realisation of her beneficial interest will not produce enough to buy a comparable house in the neighbourhood, or indeed elsewhere. And if she has to move, there may be problems with schooling. Such circumstances, while engendering a natural sympathy in all who learn of them, cannot be described as exceptional. They are the melancholy consequences of debt and improvidence with which every civilised society has been familiar.

10.4 Proprietary estoppel and the matrimonial home

Note ───────────────────────────────

The doctrine of proprietary estoppel as applied to the matrimonial home means that where the owner of a title in land has given an assurance in express or implied terms in relation to present or future rights in that land, he cannot in conscience withdraw that assurance if the person to whom it was given had relied on it to his/her detriment. The principle relates to spouses and to cohabitants.

Pascoe v Turner (1979) CA

X and Y cohabited for 10 years in a house which X had bought in his own name. X left Y so as to live with another woman and told Y that the house and all its contents would be hers. Y relied on this statement and spent her money on improvements and repairs to the property. X did not convey the house to Y. X sought to evict Y and a possession action was dismissed by the county court. X appealed.

Held: X would be required to execute a conveyance. X had encouraged Y to believe that the house was hers and this had given rise to a *proprietary estoppel*. The mere bare licence under which Y occupied the house could be defeated by a sale. *Per* Cumming-Bruce LJ:

> We take the view that the equity here cannot be satisfied without granting a remedy which assures to Y security of tenure, quiet enjoyment, and freedom of action in respect of repairs and improvements without interference from X. The history of X's conduct ... in relation to these proceedings, leads to an irresistible inference that he is determined to pursue his purpose of evicting Y from the house by any legal means at his disposal with a ruthless disregard of the obligations binding upon conscience. The court must grant a remedy effective to protect Y against the future manifestations of X's ruthlessness. It was conceded that if Y is granted a licence, such a licence cannot be registered as a land charge, so that she may find herself ousted by a purchaser for value without notice ... Weighing such considerations, this court concludes that the equity to which the facts in this case give rise can only be satisfied by compelling X to give effect to his promise and Y's expectations. X has so acted that he must now perfect the gift.

Greasley v Cooke (1980) CA

Defendant (D), in her defence to a claim for possession of the house in which she resided, stated that she had moved to the house in 1936 as a domestic servant, and from 1946 until her employer died in 1975 she had cohabited there with the son of her employer and had looked after other members of the family. She then lived there alone after 1975. After 1948 she had received no remuneration, and had been reassured by the family in the belief that she could consider the house as hers for life. D contended that the plaintiffs were estopped from disputing her claim to occupation and sought an appropriate declaration. The judge refused to make such a declaration on the ground that he was not convinced that D had acted to her detriment. D appealed.

Held: D's appeal would be *allowed*. The court would be correct in inferring that she had acted to her detriment, in the absence of contrary evidence given by the plaintiffs. *Per* Lord Denning:

> It can be seen that the assurances given to D by two of the employer's children, leading her to believe that she would be allowed to stay in the house as long as she wished, raised an equity in her favour. There was no need for her to prove that she acted on the faith of those assurances. It is to be presumed that she did so. There is no need for her to prove that she acted to her detriment or to her prejudice. Suffice it that she stayed on in the house, looking after [two of the children], when otherwise she might have left and obtained a job elsewhere. The equity having thus been raised in her favour, it is for the courts of equity to decide in what way that equity ought to be satisfied, In this case it should be by allowing her to stay in the house for as long as she wishes. I would therefore allow the appeal and grant a declaration on the counterclaim that D is entitled to occupy the premises, rent free, for so long as she wishes to stay there.

Maharaj v Chand (1986) PC

P began associating with D who had two children. A child was born to P and D in 1970, two years after the association began. P built a house and D, acting on the basis of his representation that it would be a permanent home for her and her family, gave up her own flat and went to live with P in the house. She used her wages to care for the family. P left D in 1980 and began proceedings for possession. The action was dismissed; the Court of Appeal allowed P's appeal. D appealed to the Judicial Committee of the Privy Council. (The land in question was in Fiji, where P and D resided.)

Held: D's appeal would be *allowed*. The eviction of D by P would be inequitable. P had acted in a manner which would result in his being estopped from denying that D had been given permission to reside in the house permanently. There was no entitlement in this case to an order for vacant possession of the house. *Per* Sir Robin Cooke:

> In reasonable reliance on P's representations, D acted to her detriment by giving up the flat. She supported the application to the housing authority [for permission to build], used her earnings to pay for household needs, and looked after her *de facto* husband and the children as wife and mother. It is impossible to restore her to her former position. In these circumstances it would plainly be inequitable for P to evict D. It is right to hold that as against him she has, in effect, permission to reside permanently in the house, on the basis that the children may be with her for as long as they need a home … It is a personal right not amounting to a property interest diminishing the rights of P's lessor and mortgagee.

Coombes v Smith (1987)

P and D were both married to others when they decided to live together. D bought a house and P moved there when she became pregnant. D paid the mortgage instalments and provided financial assistance for the child. He did not move into the house permanently but visited P regularly. Later he offered P £10,000 if she would leave the house; she rejected the offer. P sought an order for the transfer of the house and its contents to her absolutely, or, in the alternative, that D allow her to occupy the property during her lifetime,

Held: P's action would be *dismissed*, subject to D's undertaking to provide accommodation for P and the child in the house until the child had reached the age of 17. It had not been possible to infer a contract between the parties that D would provide P with a house for the rest of her life. Further, P had not acted to her detriment in becoming pregnant, looking after the child and not seeking a job.

10.5   Charges over the matrimonial home

CIBC Mortgages v Pitt (1993) HL

H and W owned the matrimonial home which was valued at some £270,000. There was a relatively small mortgage debt outstanding. In order to obtain a loan which would have enabled him to buy shares, H coerced W into agreeing to his course of activity. P made a loan of £150,000 which was secured on the matrimonial home. H and W then executed a legal charge in P's favour. At no stage did W read the relevant documents concerning the transaction. H bought shares but found it impossible to maintain his repayment schedule, following the steep decline in equities in 1987. P commenced proceedings for possession of the matrimonial home, W pleaded undue influence; her claim was dismissed by the judge and the Court of Appeal, and she appealed to the House of Lords.

Held: W's appeal would be *dismissed*. She had proved H's undue influence, but this did not affect P since H was not acting in the capacity of an agent and P had no notice, real or constructive, of the undue influence. In the circumstances, therefore, the charge could be enforced. *Per* Lord Browne-Wilkinson:

> If third parties were to be fixed with constructive notice of undue influence in relation to every transaction between husband and wife, such transactions would become almost impossible. On every purchase of a home in joint names, the building society or bank which was financing the purchase would have to insist on meeting the wife separately from her husband, advise her concerning the nature of the transaction and make a recommendation to her to take legal advice separately from her husband. If that were not done, the financial institution would have to run the risk of a subsequent attempt by the wife to

avoid her liabilities under the mortgage on the grounds of misrepresentation or undue influence. To establish the law in that sense would not benefit the average married couple and would discourage financial institutions from making the advance.

Barclays Bank v O'Brien (1993) HL

Defendants, H and W, had entered an agreement to execute a second mortgage of the matrimonial home which would be security for an overdraft allowed by the bank, P, to a company in which H had the principal interest. P gave directions to the branch to which the appropriate documents were forwarded to ensure that both H and W were fully aware of the essential significance of the documents and that they had taken appropriate legal advice. The branch ignored P's directions. W signed the documents without reading them and relied on H's statements, which were untruthful. P later obtained an order for possession. W's appeal was dismissed and it was held that the mortgage could be enforced against her. Her appeal was allowed by the Court of Appeal. P then appealed to the House of Lords.

Held: P's appeal would be *dismissed*. Where misrepresentations had caused a wife to act as surety for the debts of her husband, the wife would then possess an equity against the husband, allowing the relevant transaction to be set aside. A right of that nature could be enforced against a third party who had notice, actual or constructive, of the events leading to the creation of the equity. In this case, the bank had constructive notice concerning the nature of the representations made to W. The charge on the matrimonial home could be set aside by W in these circumstances.

TSB Bank v Camfield (1995) CA

A decision of the court had granted TSB possession of the matrimonial home, and judgment for some £15,000. W had stood surety so as to assist in obtaining a series of loans for H's business. H had made an innocent misrepresentation to W that her total liability would be limited to the sum of £15,000; in reality, her liability was unlimited. TSB wished to enforce its security against W for the full sum of £15,000. The bank contended that the court was entitled to impose conditions upon W before it agreed to grant her a measure of equitable relief. W argued that she was entitled to set aside the agreement with H in full because of the misrepresentation made to her, of which the bank had constructive notice. W appealed.

Held: W's appeal would be *allowed*. W was entitled to have the charge set aside in its entirety as against H. The idea that a mortgagee might be allowed to enforce a charge in part against W was not supported by any rule or precedent.

Banco Exterior Internacional v Mann (1995) CA

A bank made a loan to a company secured by a second charge over the matrimonial home in which H and W resided. The bank's offer was conditional on the essence of the charge having been discussed with W by a solicitor, and the solicitor certifying that he had explained the transaction to W. The relevant documents were sent to the company solicitor who explained their content and effect to W. All the documents were signed in the presence of the solicitor who did certify to the bank that the contents had been made clear to W. Later, the company went into liquidation and the bank asked for an order of possession over the matrimonial home. The judge held that W was entitled to an equitable interest in the home and that there was a presumption of undue influence exerted by H. It was held, further, that the bank had to be considered as having constructive knowledge of H's undue influence over W. The bank appealed.

Held: the appeal was *allowed*; the bank had carried out its duty by insisting upon a certificate from the solicitor and was fully entitled to assume that independent advice had been given to W by the solicitor. In the circumstances there was nothing which could lead to an assumption that the bank had constructive notice of the undue influence exerted by H over W.

Massey v Midland Bank (1995) CA

X, who had a long-standing relationship with Y, owned a house in which she cohabited with him. Y made misrepresentations to X, asking her to charge the house to the bank as security for a loan made to Y's business partner. The bank insisted upon independent advice being tendered to X, and Y made provision for his own solicitor to advise her. The solicitor gave advice to X and she then signed the charge documents. The solicitor then confirmed to the bank that X had been advised and that an explanation of the nature of the charge had been given to her. After the loan was granted, the company went into liquidation. The bank sought possession of the home. It was held that the bank was not affected by Y's dishonesty. An order of possession was granted. X appealed.

Held: X's appeal would be *dismissed*. The bank had carried out its duty by making sure that X did receive advice from a solicitor. The bank had been put on enquiry by the specific circumstances in which X had agreed to give security; it was fully entitled, nonetheless, to assume that she had received appropriate and independent advice and that the solicitor had acted correctly and given that independent advice. The bank was not under any duty to find out what took place during the interview between X and the solicitor. The bank, therefore, could not be assumed to have had any constructive notice of the misrepresentations made by Y to X.

Dunbar Bank plc v Nadeem (1996)

H had used a bank loan to purchase property in the joint names of himself and W. The property was charged in order to secure H's personal borrowings from the bank. Of the joint loan facility of £260,000, £210,000 was used to purchase property, £50,000 was to be applied by the bank solely to meet H's personal liability to the bank. In effect, there had been a substitution of a joint debt for one for which H was solely liable. The bank brought an action for possession against H and W.

Held: the bank should have been put on notice of the possible existence of undue influence exerted by H on W. Steps had not been taken to ascertain whether W fully understood what she was doing. The right order, in the court's view, was to set aside the charge as against W *only* if she repaid to the bank one-half of the sum used by H to purchase the property. If, however, W was unable or unwilling to comply with this condition, the charge would stand.

Royal Bank of Scotland v Etridge (No 2) (1998) CA

The matrimonial home had been charged to a bank as a result, according to W's contention, of H's undue influence and misrepresentation. W made two appeals, arguing undue influence; the bank placed reliance on a record from the solicitors that they had provided W with a full explanation of the essence of the transaction. In fact, the solicitors had not done so.

Held: W's appeals were *dismissed*. Although she had established presumed undue influence in one appeal, she had not succeeded in establishing any measure of manifest disadvantage to herself which should have put the bank on inquiry. The bank was entitled to assume that the solicitors had discharged fully their professional duties to W. *Per* Stuart-Smith J:

> It is now settled law that the question of whether a bank can exercise its legal rights against the wife depends in the first instance on whether the wife has an equity to set aside the transaction and, in the second, on whether, at the time when it gave value, the bank had notice, actual, imputed or constructive, of the wife's equity. In relation to the first question, the issue is whether the advice actually given was sufficient to rebut the presumption of undue influence. In relation to the second, the issue is different; it is whether, in light of all the facts known to the bank, including the availability of legal advice, any risk of the wife having an equity appears to have been dispelled. The first question depends on what actually happened between the wife, her husband and the solicitor. The second question depends on how the transaction appeared to the bank ... It is highly undesirable that the validity of such transactions should depend on fine distinctions, particularly on distinctions in the wording of the instructions to the solicitors or the certificates they give.

National Westminster Bank v Leggatt (2000) CA

In 1972 H and W granted an unlimited second charge over their property to the bank so as to secure all their liabilities. In 1974 H entered a business partnership with J, and in 1976 W signed an unlimited guarantee in favour of the bank, guaranteeing all the partnership's liabilities to the bank. Additional overdraft facilities were granted to the partnership in 1990. Later in that year. H and W attended solicitors and, in the presence of H, W, following the solicitor's advice, executed, together with H, a charge form. Under that charge, the bank later obtained an order against H and W, ordering them to give possession of the matrimonial home to the bank. W appealed.

Held: W's appeal was *dismissed*. Where a wife provided security for her husband's debts, the creditor would be put on inquiry if the transaction was on its face not to the wife's financial advantage, with the consequence that unless the creditor took reasonable steps to satisfy himself that the wife's agreement to enter into the transaction had been properly obtained, he would have constructive notice of her rights. In this case, if it was not on its face financially disadvantageous to W to enter into the 1990 charge, the bank was not put on inquiry and no question of constructive notice arose in the circumstances. Additionally, the 1972 charge was expressed to secure 'all other liabilities whatsoever' of H and W to the bank. There was, therefore, no basis for implying any limitation on the scope of those words. The charge was not on its face disadvantageous in any way to W.

National Westminster Bank v Breeds (2001)

H, husband of the appellant, W, owned a business enterprise with S which they operated through a limited company, the secretary of which was also their solicitor. H made misleading representations to R, an officer of the company's bank, so as to obtain a continuation of funding for the company. H also made several misrepresentations to W and applied pressure so as to induce her to grant the bank a mortgage over their home with the object of securing the funding. As a result of later proceedings the county court judge granted possession of the home to the bank. W appealed, raising as an issue whether the bank was entitled to rely on a statement by the solicitor that he had explained the transaction to her when he was acting for borrower and lender, and was also the company secretary and, as such, interested in the company's need for finance facilities.

Held: W's appeal would be *allowed*. W had argued that the bank was put on inquiry as to her equity, and that it failed to take sufficient steps to satisfy itself that she had entered freely into the transaction and with knowledge of the real facts. The bank would not appeal against the judge's finding that W was entitled to set aside the transaction as against H, and that the solicitor's advice was not sufficient to ensure that she really was free from undue influence. It argued, however, that it was not put on inquiry because, as the judge had found, R had been misled by H, and had no reason to believe that W was learning about the mortgage for the first time at her meeting with the solicitor.

The bank had been aware that the statements of H and S could not always be relied on, and that the company had a serious cash flow problem. It knew, too, of the solicitor's role in the company. All the circumstances pointed to a strong probability of a real conflict of interest. That, together with the fact that the bank did have constructive notice of H's undue influence, strengthened the basis of W's appeal.

Q Do you agree with the suggestion that '*Midland Bank v Cooke* marks a retreat from the orthodoxy of *Lloyds Bank v Rosset*'?

11   Legal Aspects of Parentage

11.1   The term 'parent'

Note ──

The term 'parent' is used in family law in a variety of ways. See, eg, Sched 1, para 16(2) Ch A 1989 ('parent' includes any party to a marriage, whether or not subsisting, in relation to whom the child concerned is a child of the family); s 54 CSA 1991 ('parent', in relation to any child, means any person who is in law the mother or father of the child).

J v J (A Minor: Property Transfer) (1993)

X and Y were unmarried, but X's child had been treated as a member of the family for the 10 years during which X and Y cohabited. They were joint tenants of the council house which they occupied. Following the ending of the relationship, X applied for a transfer of the tenancy to herself for the benefit of the child, under the terms of s 15(1) Ch A 1989.

Held: X's application would be *dismissed*. The tenancy of the council house could be classed as 'property' within Sched 1 only if Y fell within the definition of 'parent' as set out in Sched 1. But Y had never been married to X and, therefore, could not in those specific circumstances be considered as a 'parent' under Sched 1, para 16(2).

Re W (Minors) (Surrogacy) (1991)

Twins had been born after a surrogacy arrangement. The genetic mother lacked a womb but was able to produce eggs, some of which were taken from her and fertilised with sperm *in vitro* from the husband and then implanted in the host mother who produced the twins. The twins lived with the genetic parents and were made wards of court. The local authority applied for a declaration as to the persons who were the legal parents of the twins.

Held: the local authority's application for a declaration would *remain adjourned generally* on an undertaking by the genetic parents to make an application for a parental order under s 30 HFEA 1990, requesting that they were to be declared the legal parents of the twins. The public interest did not require that either the names of the wards or the identity of the families be published.

11.2   The significance of legitimacy

The Ampthill Peerage (1977) HL

In 1921, Christobel, who was married to H, who later became the third Baron Ampthill, gave birth to Geoffrey, who had been conceived by the process of external fertilisation. H petitioned for divorce on the grounds of Christobel's alleged adultery. A subsequent divorce decree was rescinded and a declaration made, stating that Geoffrey was the legitimate child of Christobel and H. Geoffrey and John put forward competing claims to succeed H and the matter fell to be resolved by the Committee of Privileges of the House of Lords.

Held: Geoffrey *was entitled* to the benefit of the presumption of legitimacy, ie, a child born to a married woman is presumed to be her husband's child. *Per* Lord Simon:

> There is one status for which Parliament, in the wisdom of experience, has made special provision. This is the status of legitimacy. Status means the condition of belonging to a class in society to which the law ascribes peculiar rights and duties, capacities and incapacities. Such, for example, is the status of a married person or minor. Legitimacy is a status: it is the condition of belonging to a class in society, the members of which are regarded as having been begotten in lawful matrimony by the men whom the law regards as their fathers. Motherhood, although also a legal relationship, is based on a fact, being proved demonstrably by parturition. Fatherhood, by contrast, is a presumption. A woman can have sexual intercourse with a number of men, any of whom may be the father of her child; though it is true that modern serology can sometimes enable the presumption to be rebutted as regards some of these men. The status of legitimacy gives the child certain rights both against the man whom the law regards as his father and generally in society. Since the legitimate child, by virtue of his legal relationship with the man whom the law regards as his father, is entitled to certain rights both as against the father and generally in society, it is desirable that the legal relationship between the father and child should be decisively concluded.

Per Lord Wilberforce:

> There can hardly be anything of greater concern to a person than his status as the legitimate child of his parents ... It is vitally necessary that the law should provide a means for any doubts which may be raised to be resolved, and resolved at a time when witnesses and records are available. It is vitally necessary that any such doubts once disposed of should be resolved once and for all.

11.2.1 Presumption of legitimacy: standard of proof

Serio v Serio (1983) CA

H and W married in 1976. In 1980 they separated and W left the matrimonial home, giving birth to a child in 1981. H denied W's claim that he was the father of the child. Following blood tests, a report was made, stating that there was an 88% probability that H was the father. The report stated, further, that the statistical finding was not useful as a significant guide to paternity. The test was disregarded by the county court judge, who stated that it was of no value to him. He found that the evidence concerning paternity was evenly balanced, but that it could be considered as having discharged the burden of establishing on a balance of probabilities that H was not the father. That was all that was required of him under s 26 FLRA 1969. W appealed.

Held: W's appeal would be *allowed*. Although the purpose of s 26 had been to dispose of the principle that proof beyond reasonable doubt was required in order to rebut the principle of legitimacy, it did not state that the standard of proof ought to be merely the standard that would have application to a commercial action, for example. The proper standard must be that appropriate to the seriousness of the issue involved and, where paternity was involved, that was an issue of gravity.

W v K (1988)

Two married couples, H1 and W1, and H2 and W2, decided to change partners. W1 became pregnant and alleged that H2 was the father of the child. At the material time W1 had intercourse with both H1 and H2. Blood tests indicated that H2's paternity index was 97%. Evidence indicated that H1 was infertile. The magistrates, following s 26 FLRA 1969, found that H2 was the father. A maintenance order was made against him and he appealed.

Held: the appeal of H2 would be *dismissed*. The standard of proof was heavy: it was greater than the ordinary civil standard of proof, but not as great as that which was applied in criminal cases. All the available evidence in this case suggested a strong probability, almost a certainty, that H2 was the father of W1's child. *Per* Latey J:

> It seems very likely that after hearing the submissions of counsel, the justices did apply the appropriate high standard. Counsel has not argued the contrary. But I have thought it right to approach this case on the footing that they may have applied a lower standard. If they did, there would be two courses open to this court: either to remit the case for rehearing, or for this court to apply the correct standard and make its own decision if it is able to safely do so. None of the relevant primary facts as found by the magistrates are challenged, nor can they be. Accordingly, the court can safely adopt the second course ... In my judgment, the evidence establishes that there is so strong a possibility as to amount to a virtual certainty that the father of the child is the appellant.

11.2.2 Blood tests, DNA tests, and paternity

Re F (A Minor: Blood Tests) (1993) CA

W conceived a child during a period when she was having sexual intercourse with H (her husband) and X; the association with X came to an end before the child was born. The child was considered as a child of the family by H and W. There was no contact between the child and X. Later, X applied for parental responsibility and contact orders concerning the child, and asserted that he was the father, which was denied by W. The application was transferred to the High Court so as to determine whether blood tests could be ordered under s 20(1) FLRA 1969 in order to establish whether X was the father. The application was dismissed. The judge held that the tests would be of no value where the parental control and custody orders were very unlikely to be made. X appealed.

Held: X's appeal would be *dismissed*. When considering whether blood tests should be ordered under s 20(1), the court ought to take into account the likely outcome of the proceedings. In general, a series of blood tests ought not to be carried out against the will of the parent who has exercised sole parental responsibility for the child since its birth. No real benefit could be shown which would persuade the court that the order should be made.

Re T (A Minor: Blood Tests) (1993) CA

H and W separated and, later, H expressed doubts concerning the paternity of a child, following W's admission of a liaison with another man during the period in which the child was conceived. H applied for a DNA test, but his application was rejected. H appealed.

Held: H's appeal would be *allowed*. The judge had been correct in his refusal of H's application on the evidence presented to him, but the situation had now changed. W had expressed willingness for the tests to be administered, so that it was now clearly in the interests of the child for the court to intervene and order a test.

Re GW (A Minor: Blood Tests) (1994) CA

Following the birth of a child to X, she commenced proceedings to establish that Y, one of three men with whom she had intercourse around the time of the child's conception, was the father. Y denied paternity and argued that it would not be just if he were singled out from the other men. The judge held that Y was aware that he could be the father, and that explained his refusal of a blood test, but he was unable to infer from Y's refusal that he was the father of X's child. X appealed.

Held: X's appeal would be *allowed*. It was possible to establish certainty of paternity through the use of genetic testing, and a man who doubted his paternity could resolve the matter by undergoing the test. There were no very sound reasons as to why Y ought not to be tested. Y had no real excuse. It was reasonable to infer that he had fathered X's child.

Re CB (A Minor: Blood Tests) (1994)

Around the time of the conception of W's child, she was having sexual liaisons with H (her husband) and X. W persuaded both X and H separately to believe that each was the father. W prevented X seeing the child and he applied for contact and parental responsibility orders. W said that she would refuse to follow any direction for a blood test and would refuse to allow the child to participate in such tests. X applied for a direction for a paternity blood test.

Held: X's application would be *dismissed*. The court ought to permit the blood testing of a young child unless satisfied that it would be against the child's interests. But W's repeated refusal to allow the test was important and the court ought not to exercise its discretion to order a test following such refusals. X was unlikely to succeed in his application for a contact order, but this was not certain in the case of his other application. In all the circumstances, and weighing up the factors which had emerged, the court would, in the exercise of its discretion, refuse to order the blood test.

Re CG (A Minor: Blood Tests) (1994)

H and W married in August 1982. There was some question as to the date of their separation: W claimed that it was in early September, H that it was in November 1992. A child was born to W in April 1993; she contended that her new partner was the father. H and his mother applied for directions under s 20, for paternity blood tests to be administered.

Held: the court would seek to exercise its discretion *in favour of H and the grandmother*, although W had stated that she would not agree to the taking of blood samples from the child. H would have parental responsibility (given the presumption of legitimacy) and it was not in the interests of the child that the question of paternity remain in doubt. W's lack of consent was no more than one factor to be kept in mind: it was in no way determinative.

O v L (Blood Tests) (1995) CA

Following their separation, W informed H that he (H) was not the father of their child, C. H was granted an interim contact order. W argued that contact was meaningless if H was not C's father. She appealed against the judge's refusal to order blood tests to determine paternity.

Held: W's appeal would be *dismissed*. Tests were not necessary for the time being in relation to the matter of contact because C was a 'child of the family' within s 52 MCA 1973. Further, s 20 FLRA 1969 did not indicate how the court's discretion to order blood tests ought to be exercised.

Re H (A Minor) (Blood Tests: Parental Rights) (1996) CA

W had admitted to having a sexual relationship with her husband, H, and the applicant, X, at about the time the child was conceived. She disputed that X was the father. In 1990, H had undergone a vasectomy, but did not visit hospital in order to check the success of the operation. In March 1994, W became pregnant and, in the early months of the pregnancy, there was a clear understanding that she and X would live together, which happened when H left her in May 1994. In July she changed her mind and a reconciliation of H and W followed. X applied for a direction under s 20 FLRA 1969. W refused her consent to undergo blood testing for herself and C. The court ordered that W, C and X should provide blood samples. W appealed.

Held: W's appeal would be *dismissed*. An inference adverse to the refusing party could be drawn irrespective of whether the refusal was made before or after a direction by the court. Ward LJ stated that whereas refusal was a factor to take into account, it could not be determinative of the application. Common sense seemed to dictate that if the truth could be established with certainty, a refusal to produce certainty justified some inference that the refusal was made to hide the truth, even if the inference were not as strong as when a court's direction had been flouted. Welfare of the child was paramount in deciding applications for parental responsibility and contact orders; it did *not* dominate the blood testing decision. Every child has a right to know the truth unless his welfare clearly justified a cover-up. If the child had such a right, then the sooner it was told the truth, the better. The issue of biological parentage should be divorced from psychological parentage.

F v Child Support Agency (1999)

W, wife of H, gave birth to a child, the putative father of whom was F. The question was whether the presumption of legitimacy, arising out of W's marriage, might be rebutted by the refusal of F to comply with a court order to submit to a blood test, and hearsay evidence from W relating to the content of a previous DNA test report which excluded the possibility of H's being the father of the child. F appealed by way of case stated against a declaration that he was the father of the child.

Held: F's appeal would be *dismissed*. The court had the right to draw an adverse inference from F's unjustified refusal to take the blood test. That, together with the hearsay evidence presented by W, would suffice to rebut the presumption of legitimacy arising from the marriage of H and W.

Re O and J (Children) (Blood Tests: Constraint) (2000)

A had obtained a county court order under s 20(1) FLRA 1969, under which a sample of blood was to be taken from both O and J, minors, for the purpose of determining the issue of their paternity. M, the mother of O and J, had care and control, and she had voiced her opposition to the taking of any blood samples from the children. A made application for the enforcement of compliance with the county court order.

Held: A's application for an enforcement order would be *dismissed*. The court could not enforce compliance with the county court order. From s 21(1), (3) FLRA 1969, there was no doubt that a parent with care and control of a child could refuse a blood sample being taken from a child for purposes of establishing paternity. The court lacked the power or inherent jurisdiction which would allow the overriding of a parent's decision relating to s 20. It might indeed be in the best interests of a child that issues of paternity be settled swiftly, but this would necessitate a change in the law, and that was a matter for the legislature and not for the courts.

11.3　Artificially assisted pregnancy: a legal problem

Note

Recent advances in the techniques of human-assisted reproduction have resulted in the enactment of measures controlling the use of such techniques. The measures have, in turn, created further legal problems, of which some are noted below.

R v Human Fertilisation and Embryology Authority ex p Blood (1996)

W, the applicant, wished to use sperm taken from her unconscious husband in order to produce a child. The husband, H, died suddenly from bacterial meningitis. The sperm was stored by the Infertility Research Trust pending resolution of the legal issues, but continued storage and release for use were forbidden in the absence of written consent by the donor (H) unless H and W were undergoing treatment together within the terms of HFEA 1990. W made application for judicial review of the decision of the Human Fertilisation and Embryology Authority.

Held: W's application would be *refused*. The Authority had acted within the scope of its powers. Three matters arose.

First, the applicant was required to have treatment in the UK and a licence for the storage and use of gametes would be granted only where the donor had given written consent, after proper counselling, unless the couple were having treatment together. The 1990 Act permitted no discretion on the part of the Authority on this matter, so that W's application must *fail*.

Secondly, the Authority had refused to authorise the export of the gametes for use in a country (eg, Belgium, Greece) where written consent was not a prerequisite of treatment. The Authority's *General Directions* (1991) expressly prohibited such export if the gametes could not be used lawfully for the relevant purpose in the UK. Further, the donor's specific consent to export was required.

Thirdly, it was submitted that the EC Treaty, Arts 50 and 60, give an individual the right to obtain medical services in another member state and that extended to freedom from restriction on the export of those resources considered necessary to secure the services. But it was well established that European law could not be used so as to evade the application of national legislation, particularly in matters of public policy.

W's application *failed*, therefore, on all three grounds. *Per* Sir Stephen Brown:

> It is not for the court to make the decision on the fundamental matter in question. Parliament has entrusted that responsibility to the Human Fertilisation and Embryology Authority. The Authority must act within the powers given it by Parliament.

> The duty of this court is to see whether the Authority has acted properly within the scope of that discretion. It cannot assist the applicant for the court to express the view that it might itself have made a different decision if it had the authority to do so. I have found this to be a most anxious and moving case ... Nevertheless, for the reasons of law that I have endeavoured to explain, I am unable to accede to this application for relief by way of judicial review and I must, therefore, dismiss the application.

Re B (Parentage) (1996)

Following the ending of a three-year relationship between F and M, M was artificially inseminated through the use of sperm donated for the purpose by F. F fully accepted that he was the biological father of the twins who were born later, and he was so named on their birth certificates. Following M's application for financial provision for the twins, F questioned whether he was a parent within Sched 1, para 1(2) Ch A 1989.

Held: following Sched 3 HFEA 1990, a biological father is to be considered in law as a parent *only* if he has given his consent to the use and storage of gametes. Where there was no express consent, the biological father would be deemed to have given that consent if he and the mother, as in the instant case, were receiving treatment (including artificial insemination) together. For purposes of Ch A 1989, F was, therefore, the parent of the twins.

11.4 Parental responsibility

Note

Where a child's father and mother were married to each other at the time of his birth, they each have parental responsibility for the child: s 2(1) Ch A 1989. But where they are not married at the time of the child's birth, the mother has parental responsibility, but the father has not, unless he acquires it in accordance with the Act: s 2(2).

Re A (Minor) (Parental Responsibility) (1993)

X and Y were not married to each other, but had cohabited for three months. Y's name was recorded on their child's birth certificate. The relationship between X and Y collapsed. Y had not seen the child for over a year and he applied for parental responsibility and contact orders.

Held: Y's application would be *granted* in spite of X's objection. Y had displayed a high level of commitment to the child and his feelings towards the child did not appear to differ from those he would have had in the event of his having married X.

Re G (Minor) (Parental Responsibility) (1994) CA

X and Y were not married to each other. Their child was aged six. X had drug related problems. The judge had ordered that the child was to remain in care and that contact between her and Y should be at the discretion of the local authority. Y's application for a parental responsibility order was rejected and he appealed.

Held: Y's appeal would be *allowed*. The Court of Appeal held that where it was shown that there was some degree of regard between a father and his child and where the father's reasons for applying for an order were not obviously wrong or improper, it would be, *prima facie*, in the interests of the child that a parental responsibility order be made. Y had been difficult and not easy to deal with, but this did not constitute a reason to refuse the order for which he asked. It was obviously in the child's interests that Y be allowed to participate positively in her upbringing.

Re P (Minor) (Parental Responsibility) (1994)

X and Y were not married to each other. Their child was aged five. A relatively short period of cohabitation had come to an end in much bitterness. Y had been granted a contact order and, for a period when X was working, he had taken care of the child. When further hostility developed, Y applied for orders including a parental responsibility order. The order was refused and Y appealed.

Held: Y's appeal was *allowed*. The magistrates had been wrong to reject Y's application on the ground that the antagonism of Y and the mother would result in his questioning matters concerning the child's upbringing. Y would have no rights under a parental responsibility order to interfere with X's bringing up the child. It was certainly in the child's best interests that a parental responsibility order be made. An order would be granted that a parental responsibility order be made. *Per* Wilson J:

> It is to be noted that on any view an order for parental responsibility gives the father no power to override the decision of the mother, who already has such responsibility; in the event of their disagreeing on a specific issue relating to the child, the court will have to resolve it. Should the father seek to misuse the rights given him under s 4, such misuse could be controlled by the court under a prohibited steps order against him and/or a specific issue order. The last resort of all would presumably be the discharge of the parental responsibility order. But on the evidence before the magistrates, and indeed on the basis of

their conclusions concerning the father's fitness to continue to care responsibly for the child during regular contact periods in the future, there seems to be no basis for such pessimistic hypotheses, which I mention solely for the sake of completeness.

Re L (Contact: Transsexual Applicant) (1995)

Y was a transsexual who had undergone gender transition from male to female, following his separation from X. Y made application for a contact order and a parental responsibility order concerning his young child. X made cross-application for an interim contact order to be discharged.

Held: Y's application for a parental responsibility order would be *granted*; the contact order application was *adjourned*. Important evidence was tendered showing that X and Y were intelligent people and their differences on the matter of the applications were few. Y had demonstrated concern for the child and the court considered that, after therapy from a child psychiatrist, the relationship between Y and the child would be normalised.

D v S (Parental Responsibility) (1995)

X had denied Y access to their child, C, for a year, although access had recommenced by the date of the hearing. There was bitterness between X and Y, and a refusal to discuss any matters relating to C. Later, Y applied for a parental responsibility order in relation to C. Welfare reports suggested that such an order would be impracticable; magistrates found that, in fact, Y was committed to C and that previous contact had been to the benefit of C. Y appealed against the magistrates' order of 'no order' in relation to parental responsibility.

Held: Y's appeal would be *allowed*. Y had demonstrated the necessary qualities (see *Re H (Rights of Putative Fathers)* (1991)): appropriate degree of commitment, firm bond between applicant and child, genuine reason for making application. Hostility between father and mother did not constitute an appropriate bar. Y had demonstrated that he recognised his responsibilities to the child he loved. The magistrates were clearly in error, and a parental responsibility order would be made.

Re P (Terminating Parental Responsibility) (1995)

On the day on which a nine week old child, C, was admitted to hospital suffering from severe injuries, including fractures to her skull and ribs, the parents, X and Y, made a *parental responsibility agreement*, denying responsibility for C's injuries. Y was charged later with causing C's injuries and was imprisoned. X asked for termination of the agreement (and requested an order forbidding Y to apply for contact without leave of the court).

Held: X's application would be *granted*. A parental responsibility agreement should not be terminated on other than important grounds. C's welfare was paramount. There seemed no way in which Y might exercise his parental responsibilities in a manner which could benefit C.

Re H (Minors: Parental Responsibility: Maintenance) (1996) CA

Y's application for a parental responsibility order under s 4(1) Ch A 1989, concerning his two children, was adjourned until he had demonstrated his commitment to them by paying maintenance. Y appealed.

Held: Y's appeal would be *allowed*. The judge ought not to have postponed the order indefinitely so as to compel Y to pay maintenance. Criticism of Y might be justified in relation to his failure to pay maintenance, but it was important that adequate weight be given to his efforts to keep contact with his children. Further, the best interests of the children had to be given due consideration.

Re G (A Minor) (1996)

Y, the father of a young child, had made an application to the court for leave to appeal out of time against orders refusing residence and contact orders, and revoking a *parental responsibility agreement* between X (the mother) and Y. There was a history of X's involvement with crack cocaine, and Y had alleged that X punished her children with unusual severity. The judge had initially dismissed Y's allegations, but their truth had been established later.

Held: Y's appeal against revocation of the agreement would be *allowed*. Applications for leave to appeal out of time were rarely successful, but in this case the father had been advised erroneously against appealing at an earlier date. Y, the father, might have a significant role to play in the child's future; he had cared for the child and had shown a commitment to it. Recognition of Y's status would be advantageous to the child.

Re M (Contact: Parental Responsibility) (1999)

M, mother of three children, would not allow any contact between them and the father, F, because she feared his violence towards her. A supervised contact order appeared to have worked satisfactorily, but the children's behaviour seemed to have deteriorated on their return home to M. Indirect contact was ordered and F's applications for parental responsibility and family assistance orders were refused. F appealed.

Held: F's appeal was *allowed*. *Per* Ward LJ:

> A fundamental aspect of a parental responsibility order is that it is a matter of status. It was essential for the well-being of F's children, particularly when they had been denied face-to-face contact with him, to realise that their father was concerned enough to make an application to be recognised as such, and that his status as their father had the approval of the court.

Re X (Minors) (Care Proceedings: Parental Responsibility) (2000)

F and M, parents of two boys who were the subject of interim care orders to be followed by the local authority placing them for adoption, were unmarried, separated, and F was in prison. M wished to give F parental responsibility for the boys, realising that they were very unlikely to return to her care. The local authority were opposed to this course of action. Havering Family Proceedings Court refused to grant F parental responsibility, F appealed.

Held: F and M were at liberty to enter a parental responsibility agreement and there was, therefore, *no need* to proceed to hear F's appeal. To create a parental responsibility agreement. both parents had to act in unison and identically. The facility under s 4(1)(b) Ch A 1989, allowing the parents of a non-marital child to enter into such an agreement, was self-contained and did not depend upon the exercise of parental responsibility. A local authority had no power to prevent a parent entering such an agreement.

11.5   Problems of parents' and children's responsibilities

Gillick v West Norfolk and Wisbech Area Health Authority (1986) HL

Plaintiff, a Roman Catholic mother of five daughters, who were under 16, asked for a declaration that guidance given by the DHSS to doctors, which stated that in exceptional circumstances a doctor might give advice and treatment relating to contraception to a girl under 16, without her mother's consent, was unlawful. Mrs G's application for the declaration failed. Her appeal was allowed by the Court of Appeal. DHSS appealed to the House of Lords.

Held: the appeal would be *allowed*. *Per* Lord Fraser:

> Once the rule of parents' absolute authority over minor children is abandoned, the solution to the problem in this appeal can no longer be found by referring to rigid parental requirements at any particular age ... The solution depends on a judgment of what is best for the welfare of the particular child ... Mrs G has to go further if she is to obtain [the declaration]. She has to justify the absolute right of veto in a parent. But there may be circumstances in which a doctor is a better judge of the medical advice and treatment which will conduce to a girl's welfare than her parents. The only practicable course is, in my opinion, to entrust the doctor with a discretion to act in accordance with his view of what is best in the interests of the girl who is his patient ...

Per Lord Scarman:

> Parental rights clearly do exist, and they do not wholly disappear until the age of majority. Parental rights relate to both the person and the property of the child. But the common law has never treated such rights as sovereign or beyond

review or control. Nor has our law ever treated the child as other than a person with capacities and rights recognised by law. The principle of law ... is that parental rights are derived from parental duty and exist only so long as they are needed for the protection of the person and property of the child. The principle has been subjected to certain age limits set by statute for certain purposes; and in some cases the courts have declared an age of discretion at which a child acquires before the age of majority the right to make his/her own decision. But these limitations in no way undermine the principle of the law, and should not be allowed to obscure it ...

The underlying principle of the law was exposed by Blackstone and can be seen to have been acknowledged in case law. It is that parental right yields to the child's right to make his own decisions when he reaches a sufficient understanding and intelligence to be capable of making up his own mind on the matter requiring decision ...

I would hold that as a matter of law the parental right to determine whether or not their minor child below the age of 16 will have medical treatment terminates if and when the child achieves a sufficient understanding and intelligence to enable him or her to fully understand what is proposed. It will be a question of fact whether a child seeking advice has sufficient understanding of what is involved to give a consent valid in law. Until the child achieves the capacity to consent, the parental right to make the decision continues save only in exceptional circumstances. Emergency, parental neglect, abandonment of the child or inability to find the parent are examples of exceptional situations justifying the doctor proceeding to treat the child without parental knowledge and consent; but there will arise, no doubt, other exceptional situations in which it will be reasonable for the doctor to proceed without the parents' consent.

Re R (A Minor) (Wardship: Consent To Treatment) (1991) CA

R, aged 15, suffered from a mental illness which resulted in severely violent and suicidal behaviour. She required medication which she often refused, on which occasions it had to be administered without her consent. Medical evidence showed that, without drugs, R rapidly became violent and had to be restrained. She was made a ward of court so that the medication could be administered with or without her consent. The judge held that he could not override the decision of a competent minor to refuse medication, but it was clear that R was *not* competent. The application to administer the medication with or without R's consent was granted as being in her best interests. The Official Solicitor appealed on R's behalf in order that the relevant law might be clarified.

Held: the appeal of the Official Solicitor would be *dismissed*. The court was entitled, in the exercise of its wardship jurisdiction, to override the decision of a minor in relation to the giving of medication, and this was irrespective of the minor's general competence. R seemed not '*Gillick* competent' and, even if R had been, the judge was right to consent to her undergoing treatment which might involve compulsory medication. The judge's order had been made correctly.

Re J (A Minor: Consent To Medical Treatment) (1992) CA

J, aged 16, was diagnosed as suffering from anorexia nervosa (a psychological disorder in which a person refuses to eat adequately and becomes emaciated). The local authority asked for leave to place her in an institution where she could be treated, and to treat her even when she refused to give her consent.

Held: leave would be *granted*. Section 8 FLRA 1969 makes consent to medical treatment by a person aged 16 as effective as if he/she were an adult, The court, in the exercise of its inherent jurisdiction, had the capacity to override a minor's refusal of medical treatment, and this refusal had to be considered by the court in deciding finally whether to direct that treatment be given. Where a minor is competent in the *Gillick* sense, the parent could not generally override his/her wishes, but the court could do so.

Re K, W and H (Minors) (Medical Treatment) (1993)

A hospital unit which specialised in the treatment of adolescents, made three applications concerning three adolescents who had complained in relation to the use of emergency medication. The guardian ad litem gave evidence which suggested that the three complainants did not have the necessary understanding to take any part in the proceedings without a guardian or next friend. The applications of K, W and H had been rejected and they continued to be represented by the Official Solicitor.

Held: the applications, which had been made under s 8 Ch A 1989, were *refused*. In relation to the law concerning the consent of minors to medical treatment, the situation was quite clear: the minors were either *Gillick* competent or consent could be given by some other person with parental rights and responsibilities. The applications under s 8 were not necessary. The doctors involved in the treatment of the adolescents would not have been subjected to proceedings, criminal or civil, since they had parental support, and no criticisms were made of the method of treatment used.

Re E (A Minor) (Wardship: Medical Treatment) (1993)

E was almost 16. He and his family were members of Jehovah's Witnesses. He was suffering from leukaemia, the treatment for which involved blood transfusions. E and his family refused to consent to treatment of this nature. Because E's condition was very critical, the local authority had made him a ward of court, and asked for leave of the court to treat him. E's parents contended that, because he would soon be 16, his agreement to the proposed course of treatment was essential under s 8 FLRA 1969. In the alternative, they argued, under the *Gillick* test, he had the competence to enable him to decide upon a course of medical treatment. It was wrong, therefore, for the court to intervene.

Held: the consent of E and his parents would be *dispensed with*. E had no understanding of what would be the effect of his rejecting the treatment, and, because he was not yet 16, s 8 had no application. E's welfare was the paramount consideration; the objective standards of the ordinary father and mother would be decisive. His welfare demanded, therefore, that treatment involving blood transfusions ought to be administered.

Re M (A Child) (Medical Treatment: Consent) (1999)

Doctors treating M, aged 15, concluded that unless she received a heart transplant within a week, she would die. M would not consent, stating that she did not want to receive another person's heart and that she did not want to be on medication for the rest of her life. She also stated that she did not want to die. These views were expressed after the Official Solicitor had appointed a local agent to visit M and ascertain her views. Application was made for leave to carry out the appropriate emergency operation.

Held: the application would be *allowed*. M was mature and intelligent and weight would be given to her expressed views, but it had to be remembered that she had experienced much trauma. The risks of the operation and M's likely resentment in the future could not override the need to preserve her life. The desire to achieve what was best for M required authority to be given for the transplant operation.

Re A (Minors) (Conjoined Twins: Medical Treatment) (2000) CA

Twins had been born, joined at the lower abdomen and having four limbs. Evidence was given to show that the weaker twin, M, was living only because a common artery enabled the stronger twin, J, to circulate life-sustaining oxygenated blood for both of them, that it was possible to operate successfully so as to separate M and J, and that both M and J would die unless separation was effected within six months, even though M would die as a result of the operation. Parents of the twins, devoutly religious, could not consent to kill one child even to save the other. They appealed against a judgment given in the Family Division, granting the hospital a declaration that the operation would be lawful.

Held: the parents' appeal would be dismissed. Ward LJ stated that in the current law the right and duty to give consent to medical treatment was an incident of parental responsibility vested in the parent, under s 3(1) Ch A 1989, and that the peremptory terms of s 1(1)(a) placed the court under a duty, in overriding a refusal to consent, to do what was dictated by the child's welfare. The question of what was in the child's best interests was a discrete question from whether what was proposed was unlawful. M was clearly beyond help, and the scales came down heavily in J's favour. The best interests of the twins was to give the chance of continued life to the child whose actual bodily condition was capable of accepting that chance to her advantage, even if that had to be at the cost of sacrificing the life which was supported so unnaturally. The least detrimental choice, balancing the interests of M and J, was to allow the proposed operation to be performed, always provided that what was proposed to be done could be done lawfully. This operation could be carried out lawfully, and the decision in this case – unique in the particular circumstances – was no authority for a wider proposition that a doctor could kill a patient, having established that he would not survive. Brooke LJ stated that, given that the principles of modern family law pointed irresistably to the conclusion that J's interests were to be preferred to the conflicting interests of M, the three essential requirements for the application of the doctrine of necessity were satisfied in this case. Those requirements were: the act was necessary so as to avoid inevitable and irreparable evil; no more ought to be done than was reasonably necessary for the achievement of the purpose; the evil inflicted must not be disproportionate to the evil avoided.

Q Does the concept of 'legitimacy' retain any significance in family law today?

12 Orders Under s 8 Children Act 1989

12.1 Essence of s 8

Note ─────────────────────────────────

Part II of the 1989 Act contains the 'menu' of orders under s 8, designed to provide for a unified system of orders which may be made in any family proceeding. The orders include contact orders, prohibited steps orders, specific issue orders, residence orders. The court is empowered to issue directions as to how an order shall be carried out, and to impose conditions: s 11(7)(a), (b).

12.2 The 'welfare principle'

Note ─────────────────────────────────

A fundamental principle of the 1989 legislation is that the child's welfare is to be the court's paramount consideration where a court determines any question relating to the child's upbringing or the administration of his/her property and the application of any income arising from it: s 1(1).

12.2.1 The concept of 'welfare'

Goldsmith v Sands (1907)

'Welfare' does not mean merely financial or social or religious welfare, but includes as an important element the happiness of the child.

Walker v Walker and Harrison (1981)

Per Hardie Boys J:

[Welfare] is an all encompassing word. It includes material welfare, both in the sense of adequacy of resources to provide a pleasant home and a comfortable standard of living and in the sense of adequacy of care to ensure that good health and due personal pride are maintained. However, while material considerations have their place, they are secondary matters. More important are the stability and security, the loving and understanding care and guidance, the warm and compassionate relationships that are essential for the full development of the child's own character, personality and talents.

12.2.2 The essence of 'paramountcy'

J v C (1969) HL

The infant respondent, aged 10 at the time of the proceedings, had lived in England continuously since 1961 with the foster parents. The appellants, the child's natural parents, were Spaniards residing in Madrid. Orders concerning the child's future custody were the subject of appeal by the parents and were dismissed. The parents appealed to the House of Lords, who were being asked to grant them the custody, care and control of the boy, with the right to take him out of the jurisdiction.

Held: the appeal would be *dismissed*. *Per* Lord MacDermott:

> Reading these words [s 1 Guardianship of Infants Act 1925, later s 1 Guardianship of Minors Act 1971] in their ordinary significance ... it seems to me that they must mean something more than that the child's welfare is to be treated as the top item in a list of items relevant to the matter in question. I think they connote a process whereby, when all the relevant facts, relationships, claims and wishes of parents, risks, choices and other circumstances are taken into account and weighed, the course to be followed will be that which is most in the interests of the child's welfare as that term has now to be understood. That is the first consideration because it is of first importance and the paramount consideration because it rules on or determines the course to be followed ...

Per Lord Donovan:

> ... I also would dismiss the appeal. This is not a case where parents are being deprived for the time being of the custody and upbringing of their son simply to pander to the wishes of foster parents who have grown to love him. It is simply a case of the courts obeying the command of Parliament that the son's welfare is to be the first and paramount consideration ...

12.2.3 Restriction of the paramountcy principle

Re A and Others (Minors) (Residence Order) (1992) CA

Four emotionally disturbed children were placed with a foster mother in 1989 and were removed and placed elsewhere in 1991. They had kept in contact with their natural mother. The foster mother made application under s 10(9) Ch A 1989 for leave to apply for residence orders for the children. The children's natural mother was not informed of the foster mother's application. Leave to apply was granted, the judge stating that the children's welfare was the paramount consideration in deciding whether or not to grant leave. The local authority appealed.

Held: the appeal of the local authority would be *allowed*. Balcombe LJ stated that the judge was wrong in holding that on an application for leave to apply for a s 8 order by a person other than the child concerned, the child's welfare was paramount. In granting or refusing an application of this type, the court was not determining a question with regard to the child's upbringing. That question only arose when the court heard the substantive application. Some of the provisions of s 10(9) as to matters to which the court was to have particular regard in deciding such an application would be futile if the whole application were to be subject to the overriding provisions of s 1(1). There would have been little point in Parliament providing that the court was to have particular regard to the wishes and feelings of the child's parents, if the decision was to be subject to the overriding consideration of the child's welfare. The judge had applied the wrong test.

12.3 The 'no-delay principle'

Note

Section 1(2) Ch A 1989 provides that in any proceedings in which the question of a *child's upbringing* arises, the court shall have regard to the principle that any delay in determining that question is likely to prejudice the child's welfare.

Re B (A Minor) (Contact: Interim Order) (1994)

X, the father of a daughter aged three, applied for orders concerning contact and parental responsibility. The welfare officer had suggested a contact order, the effects of which would be monitored and reviewed in four months' time. These proposals were not accepted by the magistrates who suggested a final order by consent or following a full hearing, or a withdrawal of X's application because of delay in bringing the proceedings to a conclusion. X appealed.

Held: X's appeal would be *allowed*. An order involving a monitored programme intended to reintroduce contact between X and the child was not inimical in any way to the interests of the child and would not contradict the 'no delay principle' of s 1(2).

Re S (Care Order: Criminal Proceedings) (1995) CA

The parents of a young child were charged with murdering his sister. Care proceedings by the local authority were to be heard after the trial of the parents in the Crown Court. It became necessary to postpone the trial. The care proceedings judge would not allow the hearing to be postponed.

Held: in a serious case such as murder, it was desirable that the criminal trial *be concluded first*, to be followed by the care proceedings, unless unusual circumstances emerged which clearly demand that the child's long term future is to be decided immediately.

12.4 The 'non-intervention principle'

Note

By s 1(5), where a court is considering whether or not to make an order under the Act with respect to a child, it shall not make the order unless it considers that doing so would be better for the child than making no order at all.

Re S (Minors) (Access) (1990) CA

H and W married in 1980 and separated in 1986. There were two children, aged six and nine. An interim custody order had been issued but access proved difficult because W was terrified of H, who, she alleged, had beaten her. In 1988 one of the children, X, was handed over to H. He then applied for custody of X and the other child, Y. The judge refused an application for transfer of care and control of Y to H because of the possible upset of the child's life. No access order was made. H appealed.

Held: H's appeal would be *allowed*. Access was the right of the child, not of the parent. The judge had, in effect, denied this right to X and Y. It was wrong for the judge to have refused to make an order. Although he seemed to have considered that access was impracticable in the circumstances, the welfare of the child, X, required that the desirability of access be examined objectively, as far as possible. Orders for reasonable access would be issued.

B v B (A Minor) (Residence Order) (1992)

Application was made for a residence order by the grandmother, with the agreement of the mother, concerning a child who had lived with the grandmother for almost all her life, in the context of s 1(5). The magistrates would not make the order. The grandmother appealed.

Held: the grandmother's appeal would be *allowed*. The magistrates had been justified in not making an order on the evidence given before them, but, on appeal, more evidence had been given. In particular, the child showed anxiety because of the mother's inconsistencies and very unreliable habits. It would be better for the child if a residence order were made which would result in the conferring of parental responsibility on the grandmother.

12.5 Who may apply for a s 8 order

Note

Any parent or guardian of the child, and persons with a residence order, may apply for any order under s 8: s 10(4). Other persons, including the child himself, or organisations may seek leave to apply for a s 8 order: s 10(1). The court may make an order at its own motion: s 10(1)(b).

G v Kirklees Metropolitan Borough Council (1993)

A child was born to a mother who was aged 15. Foster placements for mother and child were not successful and a decision was taken by the local authority that the best interests of the child would be served by adoption. Appropriate care proceedings were commenced. An aunt applied for leave to be joined as a party to the care proceedings in order to apply for a s 8 residence order. The application was dismissed. The aunt appealed.

Held: the aunt's appeal would be *allowed*, but since there were no reasonable chances of her obtaining a s 8 order, there was no point in joining her as a party. Further, the magistrates had applied an incorrect test: in considering whether leave should be granted, the child's welfare was not paramount. The real purpose of seeking leave was in order that the aunt might obtain a s 8 order.

Re SC (A Minor) (Leave to Seek Residence Order) (1994)

S, aged 14, had been living in a children's home for some eight years, having been placed in care. She applied for a residence order, wishing to live with Mrs X, a longtime friend who supported the application. Mrs X had been rejected earlier as a foster carer by the local authority.

Held: S *would be given leave* to apply for a residence order. Even where a child showed sufficient comprehension to make an application for a s 8 order, the court retained its discretion on the question of whether or not to grant leave. There was no problem as to the child's upbringing, and the child's welfare was not the paramount consideration. Although it was not possible to make a residence order in favour of S herself, the 1989 Act allowed her to make application for a s 8 order. It would be wrong, therefore, to require S to be the very person in whose favour the order was to be made. The fact that Mrs X would not be likely to succeed if she applied for leave to make a residence order had to be taken into account.

Re C (A Minor) (Leave to Seek s 8 Order) (1994)

C, aged almost 15, had argued acrimoniously with her parents and refused to return to them at the end of a holiday during which she had stayed at a friend's house. C made application for leave to apply for a residence order so as to permit her to live away from her parents, and for a specific issue order which would allow her to travel abroad for a short vacation. The parents were opposed to both applications.

Held: leave to apply for a specific issue order would be *refused*; application for leave to apply for a residence order would be *adjourned*. The court would not obstruct the exercise by C of her statutory rights under Ch A 1989. C's welfare was the paramount consideration in deciding whether or not to grant leave. But the jurisdiction was to be utilised for important matters only. If leave were granted it could be construed as meaning that the court was ready to intervene in any matter based upon disagreement between parents and child, and this was not so.

12.6   Restriction power concerning applications

Note

On disposing of any application for an order under the 1989 Act, the court may order that no application for an order under the Act of any specified kind may be made with respect to the child concerned by any person named in the order without the leave of the court: s 91(14).

F v Kent County Council (1993)

The mother of four children who were subject to care orders made application to discharge the orders, but was unsuccessful. The father later applied for a variation of contact. Evidence given suggested that the father was kind and considerate and had behaved well towards the children during periods of contact. Contact, in this case, seemed to be of benefit to the children. The magistrates decided to give effect to the contact agreement between mother and father, but considered, additionally, that no further application concerning contact or the discharge of the care order was to be made without the leave of the court. The magistrates mentioned the likelihood of a disturbing effect on the children of further court proceedings. Father and guardian appealed.

Held: the appeals would be *allowed*. The exercise of the court's discretion under s 91(14) would be rare and considered only where the children were suffering or were likely to suffer, or where the parties were extremely hostile. The magistrates seemed to have exercised their discretion incorrectly in this case: there was no evidence that mother and father had behaved in a manner which could be described as less than reasonable.

Re F (Minors) (Contact Restraint Order) (1996) CA

The case involved two girls aged six and seven. Their father (F) had attempted unsuccessfully to achieve contact with them, but the mother was extremely hostile. A direction that the children should have the help of a psychiatrist had been accompanied by an order under s 91(14), prohibiting F from making any further application without leave. F argued that the judge had been wrong in reaching, on very limited evidence, a conclusion of his own on an issue of the utmost gravity, concerning a father being deprived of contact with his children. F appealed.

Held: F's appeal would be *allowed*. This case was not at all one in which an order under s 91(14) would be appropriate: F was neither vexatious nor in any way oppressive in his genuine attempts to extend his daughters' welfare by maintaining contact with them. The starting point in a case of this nature should always be that a child has a right to be brought up with a knowledge of his non-custodial parent. Save in the most exceptional circumstances a custodial parent would not be allowed to deprive the child of his/her right through a stubborn attitude or by adopting an attitude which resulted in the child becoming hostile to any contact with its non-custodial parent. Allowing F's application for leave to apply, the substantive hearing would proceed in the High Court as soon as was possible, the children should be joined and represented by the Official Solicitor, and leave should be given to the guardian ad litem to consult a child psychiatrist.

B v B (Child Orders: Restricting Applications) (1996) CA

A direction, tied to a residence order, ordered that a father should not be allowed, under s 91(14), to make an application relating to his son, aged 10, without leave of the court. The father appealed.

Held: the father's appeal would be *allowed in part*. Butler-Sloss LJ cited her statement in *Re H (Child Orders: Restricting Applications)* (1991):

> Section 91(14) is a very useful weapon in the court's arsenal to keep litigants in family matters, who are carried away by an excessive view of the case or by excessive bitterness, from taking up the time of the court and upsetting [others] ... It is not ... a run-of-the-mill type of order, nor should it be generally used in that fortunately a minority, but, nevertheless, substantial minority, of cases where the bitterness between the parties inevitably is detrimental to the child.

The instant case was one where bitterness between the parties was clearly detrimental to the child, but that was no reason for making use of the sub-section. The power of the court in this area ought not to be used unless the parent had crossed the line from making applications which it was his right to make, to making applications which were oppressive or vexatious. The father in this case could not possibly be said to be a 'vexatious litigant'. There were no grounds upon which the judge could have made the order. Accordingly, it would be set aside.

Waite LJ, agreeing with Butler-Sloss LJ, said that the power under s 91(14) represented 'a substantial interference with the fundamental principle of public policy enshrined in our written constitution that all citizens enjoyed a right of unrestricted access to the Queen's courts'. So jealously guarded was that principle that orders restricting rights of future applicants were normally reserved as a weapon of last resort. Section 91(14) fell, therefore, to be strictly construed. It should be read in conjunction with the first and most important provision of the 1989 Act, namely s 1(1), which made the child's welfare the court's paramount consideration when determining any question concerning the child's future. The judge had to ask himself in every case whether the best interests of the child required interference with the fundamental freedom of a parent to raise issues affecting the child's welfare before the court as and when such issues arose.

Re P (A Minor) (Residence Order: Child's Welfare) (2000) CA

A residence order had been made in favour of a child's foster parents, who were of the Christian faith. The child's parents were of the Orthodox Jewish faith and they wished the child to be brought up in that faith. An application was made to vary the residence order. It was dismissed on the ground that the child, then aged 17, and who suffered from Down's Syndrome, lacked the capacity to understand or appreciate her religious heritage, and that other matters involved in her upbringing by the foster parents outweighed any particular religious considerations. A restriction was imposed under s 91(14) Ch A 1989, which prevented the child's natural parents from making any further residence applications without the leave of the court. The natural parents appealed.

Held: the appeal would be *dismissed*. Religious heritage may be relevant, but it was not paramount in determining the welfare of the child. It was necessary to read the court's power to impose restrictions on making residence applications alongside the welfare principle outlined in s 1(1) Ch A 1989. The court's power could be exercised in a pre-emptive manner where the interests of the child demanded that this be done. The degree of restriction should be proportionate to the harm it was intended to avoid, and the court was obliged to consider carefully the extent of the restriction and specify, where appropriate, the type of application to be restrained and the duration of the order. It had been suggested that s 91(14) might infringe the Human Rights Act 1998 and Art 6(1) of the Convention for the Protection of Human Rights by depriving a litigant of the right to a fair trial, but that submission was not correct, in that the applicant was not denied access to the court.

12.7 The contact order

Note

The contact order (which replaced the access order) requires the person with whom a child lives, or is to live, to allow the child to visit or stay with a person named in the order, or for that person and the child otherwise to have contact with each other: s 8(1) Ch A 1989.

Re D (Contact: Mother's Hostility) (1993) CA

The mother (M) and father (F) of a child were unmarried. M had left F when she was six months pregnant. There had been several incidents of violence by F involving M during the short relationship and his hostility continued after the birth of the child. One year after the child's birth, F made application for contact. The application was opposed by M who was sure that F's attitude would result in disturbing the child. F's application was dismissed and he appealed.

Held: F's appeal would be *dismissed*. M's continuing hostility, resulting from F's behaviour, would result in a severe risk of emotional harm to the child. That in itself was a factor which constituted appropriate reasons for denying the contact order. It was also essential to consider whether F had had any contact with the child since its birth: that was not so in the instant case.

Re F (Minors) (Contact) (1993) CA

H and W had been married for 14 years; there were two sons aged 9 and 12. In 1991, H made known his transsexuality and took a female name by deed poll. The marriage collapsed. H later applied for a contact order. The two children, who were distressed by the events, stated that they did not want to see H again. A psychiatrist stated that long term harm to the children was likely if they did not see H again. H's application was dismissed and he appealed.

Held: H's appeal would be *dismissed*. The real question was whether the children's sincere wishes were to be outweighed by other factors favouring contact, keeping in mind the paramountcy of the children's welfare. Considerable weight had been given, correctly, to the children's deeply-held views.

Re F (Minors) (Contact: Mother's Anxiety) (1993) CA

H and W had two children. The relationship ended in 1989. Later, H was convicted of assaulting W. By 1992 it seemed that H had mended his ways and he applied for contact. His application was dismissed: the considerable stress and strains which contact would cause to W would injure her health. H appealed.

Held: H's appeal would be *allowed*. Evidence, which had not been tested, suggesting that contact would cause stress and acute strains likely to injure W's health, would not suffice to justify the issuing of an order of much severity which would have the effect of denying contact to H.

Re W (A Minor) (Contact) (1994) CA

H and W married in 1988 and separated in 1989. Contact with the child created problems for H. Following W's second marriage, she attempted to end contact. She appeared to be instructing her child to accept that her second husband was the natural father. H applied for a contact order, but this was refused. W indicated that she would disobey a contact order if it were made. H appealed.

Held: H's appeal would be *allowed*. Contact was the child's right and, except in unusual circumstances, the judge had the duty to make an order even when faced by a mother's stubborn attitudes. By refusing to make an order, the judge had, in effect, abandoned his responsibilities under the 1989 Act.

Re D (A Minor) (Contact: Interim Order) (1995)

The magistrates had decided that a father should have interim contact with his son, aged six, pending a final hearing of his application for contact. The mother had appealed against the decision.

Held: the mother's appeal would be *allowed*. Wall J said that magistrates must consider not simply whether contact was in the child's best interests, but whether it was in his interests to make the interim order. Interim orders were unlikely to be made with a full understanding of all the facts and they were to be approached, therefore, with a degree of caution. Where the principle of contact was itself in issue, the test remained the welfare test under s 1; the principle was itself a factor to be considered in the welfare equation. The circumstances in which interim orders were likely to be made in cases where the principle of contact was in issue were broadly twofold. First, where the interim contact was perceived to be and was ordered as part of the overall adjudication process. The second category was where the court had sufficient information to be satisfied that an interim order was in the child's interests even though the possibility existed that at the final hearing the court might come to a different conclusion. In every case where contact was disputed the court should remember that it was involved in dealing with a child who was in the middle of a parental conflict and whose loyalties were likely to be torn.

Magistrates should be cautious about making interim orders where the contact principle was in dispute and should do so only if, on the material before them, they were satisfied that it was in the best interests of the child for an order for contact to be made pending full inquiry.

Re M (Care: Contact: Grandmother's Application for Leave) (1995) CA

In 1987 care orders were issued concerning two boys. In 1988 a psychiatrist's report suggested an end to contact between the boys and their mother and grandmother (G). The judge ordered, however, that contact be continued until a permanent placement could be made, but continuing problems resulted in a suspension of contact in 1991. The boys were placed with a prospective adopter in April 1992. Three years later, G made application for leave to apply for contact, but as the judge believed that her application for contact would be rejected, he refused leave to apply. G appealed.

Held: G's appeal would be *allowed*. Local authorities had to justify why there ought not to be contact between grandparents and children. The court ought not to be bound by strict criteria and should give special consideration to the type of contact sought, wishes of the parents and the local authority, and any disruption likely to be caused. The test must be whether G had an apparently sound case and whether there was a key issue to be tried.

Re L (Minors) (Care Proceedings: Appeal) (1995) CA

Care proceedings had been initiated and brought in relation to two children who, it was alleged, had been abused by members of their family. Specifically, allegations were made against the father by his eldest daughter. The judge made care orders and a 'no contact' order. The standard of proof required in relation to sexual abuse, was, according to the judge, the balance of probabilities, and evidence given had satisfied this requirement. The parents appealed against the orders, contending that the judge had applied an incorrect standard of proof and had abandoned his responsibility under the 1989 Act. The local authority appealed against the 'no contact' order.

Held: appeals against the care orders would be *dismissed*; appeal against the 'no contact' order would be *allowed*. The standard of proof required was of a balance of probabilities in proportion to the seriousness of the allegations. The court had not abandoned its responsibilities since the final decision was to be that of the local authority. A termination of contact order ought to be made where there was no possibility of rehabilitation. In this case the order was not in line with the known intentions of the local authority.

Re O (A Minor) (Contact: Imposition of Conditions) (1995) CA

M and F were unmarried and had cohabited for three years. They separated before the birth of their child, who was aged three at the date of proceedings. F had been convicted in relation to the breach of a non-molestation order concerning M. M was totally opposed to any contact between F and the child. In 1994 the judge made an order for indirect contact which required M to send photographs of the child to F every three months together with reports on progress at school, and to pass on letters and presents sent by F. M appealed on the ground that there was no jurisdiction to attach conditions of this nature to the order.

Held: M's appeal would be *dismissed*. It was for the court to make a decision as to whether indirect contact was in the best interests of the child; there were sufficient powers under ss 8(1), 11(7) of the 1989 Act to make such contact orders possible. M's clear unwillingness to co-operate ought not to be allowed to defeat the court's powers. It was perfectly justifiable that the parent with care of the child ought to be obliged to report to the absent parent on the child's progress so as to invest the indirect contact with some positive meaning in these particular circumstances.

Re S (A Minor) (1996) CA

An order had been made that a father (F) should have no contact with his daughter, aged six. F's appeal was based on his argument that the judge had exercised his discretion incorrectly and his decision was clearly wrong. The authorities' interference, he claimed, constituted victimisation and the delay in hearing his appeal was to his disadvantage.

Held: F's appeal would be *dismissed*. His challenge concerning earlier orders was outside the ambit of the court's frame of consideration. As he was a litigant in person the court had examined the detailed background to the case and concluded that his treatment had not been out of order in any way. There was no victimisation in relation to the order of 'no contact' and, further, he had not been prejudiced in any way by the delay in hearing the appeal.

Re P (Minors) (Contact) (1996) CA

An order had been made that F should have only indirect contact with his children because of the antagonism of the mother, M. F contended that the judge had exercised his discretion incorrectly by giving too much weight to M's feelings and to the possibility that resulting anxiety would affect her health and cause psychological harm to the children. F appealed.

Held: F's appeal would be *allowed*. The judge had not made any mistake in relation to the principle of the case, but the Court of Appeal was obliged to look at the exercise of his discretion; it would not hesitate to interfere if it could be shown that the appropriate balancing exercise had been carried out incorrectly. In almost all circumstances it was in the child's interests to have contact with a non-residential parent. The welfare of the child was the prime consideration, but weight must be given to the parents' wishes in this area. The judge had considered the relevant factors: that was not in doubt. But he had acted erroneously in giving too much weight to the possibility of risk to M's health.

Re W (Minors) (1996) CA

An application had been made by W for the discharge of a contact order made in H's favour concerning their children, aged eight and nine. The application had been dismissed. Evidence had been given by a child psychologist, suggesting that any benefit accruing to the children from maintaining contact with H was not as significant as the psychological harm resulting from that contact. W contended that although the judge was empowered to reject expert evidence, in this particular case the evidence had been given by a psychologist who had extensive involvement with the family. Further, the judge's decision was out of line with recommendations made by the court welfare officer. W appealed.

Held: W's appeal would be *allowed in part*. The judge was perfectly entitled to reach his decision on the facts, but the order was not appropriate in the circumstances. Contact would be made less frequent.

T v W (Contact: Reasons for Refusing Leave) (1996)

X cohabited with M, the mother of a young boy, C. (X was not C's father.) Cohabitation ended but X maintained contact with C. M wished to bring this to an end. X applied for leave to apply for contact under s 10(9) Ch A 1989. This was refused by the magistrates but no reasons were given. In the meantime, M became engaged to marry Z. X appealed.

Held: X's appeal would be *allowed*. The magistrates' failure to give reasons for their decision weakened it. The terms of r 21(5)(6) Family Proceedings Courts (Children Act 1989) Rules 1991 are mandatory. Reasons must be given. Further, M's engagement to Z was a new factor which could affect the application for leave. The matter would be remitted for rehearing.

Re S (A Minor) (Adopted Child: Contact) (1999)

Y, aged nine, had been adopted by M in 1994. S, her half-brother, aged seven, who suffered from fibrosis, had been fostered by R from 1991 and, a year later, was adopted by her. In 1995 Y's behaviour indicated distress because of the separation from S. R would not allow contact because she considered that this would not be in the interests of S. Y then applied for leave to bring proceedings which would result in the granting of a contact order.

Held: Y's application for leave was *dismissed*. There seemed to be a substantial risk that the application would disrupt S's life to a degree that, within the meaning of s 10(9), he would be 'harmed' by it. If leave were to be granted, the welfare of S, and not Y, would be the court's paramount consideration. There was enough evidence to indicate that the court might hold that contact would not be in the best interest of S; because S was adopted, it would be for Y to show that a refusal to allow contact was unreasonable or was against S's interests to an extent that the court would be justified if it were to override the power to make parental decisions available to R under the adoption order. Y seemed to have no arguable case in relation to this matter.

Re F (Children) (Care: Termination of Contact) (2000)

Three children had suffered harm as a result of considerable neglect, and care orders were then made in relation to them. Under a care plan, the local authority suggested their placement for purposes of adoption. Leave was sought by the local authority to end contact by the mother (M) with them, under s 34(4) Ch A 1989, given her opposition to the care plan and the possibility of her acting so as to destabilise it. Permission was granted to the local authority and M appealed, arguing, inter alia, that the decision to end contact was an infringement of her rights under Arts 6.1 and 8, European Convention on Human Rights 1950. M argued that the local authority's decision to end contact subsequent to the making of the order would constitute an administrative order against which she would have no remedy.

Held: M's appeal was *dismissed*. The justices had acted correctly in taking into account the long term welfare of the three children and granting leave to end the contact. Although the 1989 Act established the principle that a child was best brought up by his parents at home, application of this principle in the present case would not be in the children's long term interests. Further, the justices, in applying the 1989 Act, had given appropriate consideration to the Convention, and there had been no infringement of any of its articles. The use of the Convention as a method of seeking to support an appeal ought to be discouraged.

12.8   The prohibited steps order

Note

A prohibited steps order is an order that no step which could be taken by a parent in meeting his parental responsibility for a child, and which is of a kind specified in the order, shall be taken by any person without the consent of the court: s 8(1).

Croydon Borough Council v A (1992)

Children had been removed, under an emergency protection order, from the care of their parents. The local authority asked for an interim care order which would have allowed the children to be placed with their mother. That order was refused and, following the hearing, the court went on to make two prohibited steps orders which prevented the children's father from having any contact with them, and prohibited the mother from having any contact, verbal, written, personal, with the father. The local authority appealed, contending that they had received no prior information suggesting that orders of this nature might be made, and, therefore, they had been unable to present appropriate submissions.

Held: the appeal of the local authority would be *allowed*. Magistrates in these circumstances are expected to take the opportunity to inform parties of their intention to consider making a prohibited steps order, and time must be given to enable parties to make submissions on the suitability of such an order. In this case, the orders would be quashed.

Nottinghamshire County Council v P (1993) CA

The eldest of three sisters had complained of sexual abuse by her father (F) and had made allegations that he had abused another of the sisters. Emergency protection orders were obtained by the local authority and a prohibited steps order was sought which would have ordered F to leave home and to have no contact with his daughters except under supervision of the local authority. The authority did not, however, apply for care or supervision orders. The judge would not make a prohibited steps order because it was not in accordance with s 9. He used his residual power under s 10(1)(b) and made a residence order requiring F to leave home, with the condition that contact with the daughters would be supervised. All the parties appealed.

Held: the local authority's appeal would be *dismissed*, but the appeals by F and the children would be *allowed*. A local authority was prohibited from obtaining residence or contact orders (see s 9(2)), and (under s 9(5)) could not obtain a prohibited steps order intended to have the same effect. It was the task of the local authority to apply under Part IV of the 1989 Act. The local authority's application for a prohibited steps order would not be granted. The residence order was merely artificial and, in the circumstances, without relevance.

Re H (Minors) (Prohibited Steps Order) (1995) CA

C, the youngest of a family of six children was found to have been abused by P, who was, at the time, the mother's partner. A care order was made concerning C. Supervision orders in relation to the other children were made subject to a condition that there was to be no contact between P and any of the children. A prohibited steps order was made against the children's mother to prevent any contact between P and the children. The judge decided that he lacked jurisdiction to make a prohibited steps order against P because P was not a party to these particular family proceedings. The guardian ad litem appealed.

Held: the appeal of the guardian ad litem would be *allowed*. Because a prohibited steps order against the mother would have the same results as a contact order which required her not to allow contact between the children and P, it would contravene s 9(5)(a). Further, conditions could not be attached to a supervision order. A prohibited steps order against P, requiring him not to have contact with the children, would not contravene s 9(5). Finally, a prohibited steps order could be made against a person who was not party to the proceedings; in such a case, leave *could* be given for application for variation or discharge of the order.

Re D (Prohibited Steps Order) (1996) CA

H, W and their three children were living in France. Following divorce proceedings characterised by much bitterness, W and the children returned to live in the UK. H remained in France. W sought a prohibited steps order, intended to prevent H from staying overnight in the matrimonial home when he visited the children at weekends. An order was granted. H appealed.

Held: H's appeal would be *allowed*. There is no jurisdiction allowing the making of an ouster order under Ch A 1989. Under s 11(7), an order under s 8 may make such incidental, supplemental or consequential provisions as the court thinks fit, but this is merely ancillary to the making of such an order; it does not permit the bringing in 'through a side door', of matters dealt with by MCA 1973 or any adjustment of rights of occupation enjoyed, in this case, by F.

Re J (A Minor) (Prohibited Steps Order: Circumcision) (1999)

F, a Muslim, wished to arrange for the circumcision of J, his son, aged 5. M, J's mother, applied for a prohibited steps order.

Held: M's application was *granted*. Where there was a dispute between parents exercising parental responsibility in relation to circumcision, the court should decide the matter, taking into account the principle of the child's welfare under Ch A 1989. Each case would be decided on the basis of its own facts. J lived with M, who was not a Muslim, and J would not be brought up as a practising Muslim. Further, there were no medical grounds for the operation.

Q How would you define 'welfare' in relation to the grant of an order under s 8?

13 Orders Under s 8 Children Act 1989 (continued)

13.1 The specific issue order

Note

A specific issue order is an order giving directions for the purpose of determining a specific question which has arisen, or which may arise, in connection with any aspect of parental responsibility for a child: s 8(1).

Pearson v Franklin (1994) CA

F and M, unmarried parents of two children, had a joint tenancy of a house which was owned by a housing association. The relationship between them collapsed, and M and the children left the house. She later made application for a specific issue order under s 8 of the 1989 Act, requesting that she be permitted to stay with the children in the home during F's absence. Her application was refused and she appealed.

Held: M's application would be *dismissed*. Questions involving the residence of children could be determined on application under s 8(1), always provided that the order would not constitute an interference in the occupation rights of any person. But the order being sought by M was substantially, in relation to F, an ouster order. That type of order ought not be made under the mask of a specific issue order. Given the particular circumstances of the case, the court would not exercise its inherent jurisdiction so as to grant M exclusive possession of the house. However, M could apply under s 15 Ch A 1989 for an order which would require F to effect a transfer to her of his interest in the joint tenancy of the house for the benefit of their two children.

Re F (Minors) (1994) CA

F and M cohabited as joint tenants in a small house owned by a housing association. Their relationship began to founder; M left F and took the children away to live in her parents' home. She later applied for a specific issue order allowing her to live in the housing association's house, but without F. Her application was rejected. The judge held that he had no powers to grant this order. M appealed.

Held: M's appeal would be *dismissed*. If it were possible that a right of occupation might be subjected to interference, then questions of where children ought to reside were not appropriate for determination by the court on an application for a specific issue order because, essentially, if granted, that order would be an ouster order.

Re J (A Minor) (Specific Issue Order) (1995)

J, aged 17, requested leave, under s 10(8) Ch A 1989 to apply for a specific issue order on the ground that he should be recognised as a child in need and that the local authority should make an order for him. His application was made *ex parte*, but appropriate notice had been served on the local authority. The local authority was not prepared to accept J's argument that he was a child in need, under the 1989 Act, nor would they support the application generally, because they thought that it had no chance of success.

Held: J's application would be *rejected*. Whether or not a child was to be considered in need was a question for the local authority to decide. It was inappropriate for the court to grant a specific issue order requiring the local authority to exercise its responsibilities under Part III Ch A 1989. Section 100(2) of the 1989 Act prohibits in specific terms any use of the inherent jurisdiction of the court to utilise a specific issue order so as to enforce the duty of a local authority to accommodate a child considered to be in need.

Re K (Specific Issue Order) (1999)

M, mother of K, had separated from his father, F, an alcoholic, a few months after K was born. She did not want K to have any contact whatsoever with F, or even to know him. M told K, when he was aged five, that his father was dead. A year later, F wrote to M asking for contact with K, but M refused. The following year, F made application to the court for contact, on the ground of M's unremitting hostility. In 1996, when K was 11, F made application for a specific issue order that K be told of his paternity. The Official Solicitor maintained that it was in K's interests to be told the identity of his father, but this could not be done in an appropriate manner without the full co-operation of M.

Held: F's application was *rejected*. M's hostility to F meant that any advantage to be derived by K from knowing the identity of his father would be completely outweighed by the extensive disruption that would be caused in his life by being informed at this stage.

Re A (Children) (Specific Issue Order: Parental Dispute) (2001) CA

A specific issue order had been made that E and M, children of H, who was French, and W, were to be educated at a French school in London so as to meet their bicultural requirements. W appealed against the order, maintaining that a change of school for E and M was not necessary for them, and that the judge had not given sufficient weight to the principle of dependence for a parent with care. An interview with the welfare officer ought to have been arranged so as to ascertain E's wishes and, further, greater attention ought to have been paid to the opinions of E's headmistress.

Held: W's appeal would be *dismissed*. W had no long term plans to leave London, and the choice of a school for E and M had not been restrictive in any way. The children's welfare had been paramount in the judge's decision, keeping in mind the importance of maintaining contact with F and his native land. The judge's decision not to arrange an interview with the welfare officer resulted from the exercise of his discretion and was justified, given the extra pressure that would have been placed on E. The views of the headmistress had been given adequate consideration.

13.2   The residence order

Note ——————————————————————————————————————

A residence order is an order settling the arrangements to be made as to the person with whom a child is to live: s 8(1).

13.2.1   The welfare and best interests of the child

Re W (A Minor) (Residence Order) (1993) CA

H and W separated in 1989 when the child was aged three and was left by W with its grandparents. The court welfare officer said that the child was well, wanted to stay in the grandparents' home and that the existing situation should be maintained. The judge found that the risk of a change in the child's circumstances was insufficient to negate the general presumption that the child ought to be brought up by its natural parents. A residence order was made in H's favour and the grandparents appealed.

Held: the grandparents' appeal would be *allowed*. The presumption concerning the bringing up of children could be displaced by the particular needs of a child in a specific set of circumstances.

Re K (A Minor) (1995) CA

C was a girl aged three whose mother had died when she was two. The violence of the father was such that he had been prevented by the mother during the last three months of her life from seeing C. C's grandmother, uncle and his wife applied for residence orders. The father's application for a parental responsibility order was granted, and a residence order was made in favour of C's uncle. The father appealed, contending that it was most important to take into account that a child ought to be brought up in its formative years by a natural parent.

Held: the father's application would be *dismissed*. He was obviously not a suitable person to be given care of C, and it was in the best interests of C for the residence order to be granted to C's uncle, a highly responsible individual.

Re F (Minors) (1996) CA

A residence order had allowed two young children to live with their father, H. This would have involved a change of residence for them. W, who was appealing against the order, was cohabiting with a person who had a criminal record, but she argued that he was making a sincere attempt at rehabilitation and that he cared for the children. W contended that the children had been well looked after and that, in general, young children should be raised by the mother. W appealed.

Held: W's appeal would be *dismissed*. In delicately-balanced cases, young children should live with the mother, but each case must be judged on the basis of its own particular facts, and the child's welfare was the paramount consideration. The judge was correct in finding that the temporary disturbance likely to be suffered by the children in changing homes would be outbalanced by the benefits of an upbringing by a responsible father, such as H, rather than by one who may not necessarily have shed his criminal habits.

13.2.2 The children's views

Re M (A Minor) (1993)

C, the second child of H and W, was born in 1981. In 1989 H and W were divorced and both children lived with W. In 1992 C went to live, following his own wishes, with H but returned to W after a few weeks. H applied for a residence order. The welfare officer supported the idea of C living with H. The magistrates saw C in private and recommended that C should live with W. H appealed.

Held: H's appeal would be *allowed*. Although the court was obliged to consider C's feelings and wishes, it ought not to be necessary, save in exceptional circumstances, for the magistrates to see a child in private where a welfare officer was involved. Insufficient weight had been given to the welfare officer's report and the magistrates had given no explanation as to why they did not accept the precise findings and suggestions set out in that report.

Re M (Family Proceedings) (1995) CA

C, aged 12, lived with W (her mother) and another sister, but had contact with H (her father) at his parents' home. H had made application for a residence order in relation to C who had told him that she wished to stay with him. A welfare officer's report recommended that C ought to stay with W since she appeared to be unclear as to what would be involved in living with H alone and not at his parents' home. The judge considered C's views but apparently put little weight on them, and made a residence order in favour of W. H appealed.

Held: H's application would be *dismissed*. The judge had taken C's views into account but he was not obliged to do precisely as C wished since that might not necessarily be in her best interests. It could not be said that the judge had acted incorrectly in any way.

13.2.3 Application for residence order by a child

Re T (Child Case: Application by Child) (1993)
C, a child, was adopted at the age of nine and entered into foster care when she was 13. She applied for a residence order (under r 9.2A Family Proceedings Rules 1991). Her solicitor said that C was capable of giving and understanding appropriate instructions in relation to the proceedings which involved C's wish to live with an aunt and grandparents.

Held: this was a difficult case and it was doubtful, given C's age, whether she had sufficient understanding to play a part in the proceedings without the assistance of a guardian ad litem. In this case, because proceedings had been transferred to the High Court, it would be appropriate for C's guardian to be the Official Solicitor.

Re A, J and J (Minors) (Residence and Guardianship Orders) (1993)
W had four children, and was divorced from H (the father of the 12 year old child) who was living abroad. In 1992, the father of the two younger children killed W, tried to kill those two children and then killed himself. The children had survived and then lived for a short time with their grandmother. The eldest child, C, wished to share parental responsibility for her sisters with X, a friend of W. X made application for an order appointing her as guardian of the two younger children and a shared residence order in favour of C, involving the girl aged 12.

Held: X *would* be appointed as guardian of the two younger children and a residence order *would* be issued in relation to them in favour of C. A joint residence order in favour of X and C would be made in relation to the child aged 12. X could *not* be appointed guardian of the child aged 12 because that child had a surviving parent with parental responsibility.

13.2.4 Shared residence orders

Re WB (Minors: Residence) (1993)
M and F were unmarried and had lived together for 10 years. There were two children aged 8 and 11. Care of the children was shared, following the breakdown of the relationship. F's contact with the children ceased following a severe disagreement with M. An application was made by F for a residence order and an order prohibiting the removal of the children

from the jurisdiction. Later, DNA tests seemed to indicate that F was not the genetic father of the children. A residence order was made in M's favour and another order was made allowing F to have holiday staying contact and alternate weekend contact. F appealed.

Held: F's appeal would be *allowed in part*. There should be a prohibited steps order preventing removal of the children. Further, the magistrates were acting correctly in not making a shared residence order: once it had been decided that F ought to have limited contact only, it would have been wrong to have made a shared residence order for other purposes.

N v B (Children: Orders as to Residence) (1993)

M and F were cohabitants. There were two children who considered F as their father. F commenced proceedings for a shared residence order and a prohibited steps order preventing the removal of the children from England. A series of blood tests showed later that F was not the children's father. A residence order was made in favour of M, with access to F; no prohibited steps order was made. F appealed.

Held: *allowing* F's appeal *in part*: it was very important for the children that their main home be with their mother (M), so that it would be wrong to make a shared residence order merely to give F parental responsibility. An order preventing removal of the children from this country was also made.

G v G (Joint Residence Order) (1993)

H and W were married in 1978; there were two children, aged 9 and 12. W left the matrimonial home in 1989; the children stayed with H, and W looked after them when H was working shifts. The children favoured a continuation of the arrangements. W applied for a joint residence order.

Held: a residence order *would be made* in favour of H and W. A shared residence order was uncommon, but, given H's work arrangements, this was an uncommon case. A joint residence order seemed in the best interests of both children if disturbance to their lives was be avoided.

Re H (A Minor) (Shared Residence Order) (1994) CA

M and F were cohabitants. There was one child, aged 14, who had lived with M from the age of five, and had contact with F on alternate weekends and during school holidays. Interim contact orders proved ineffective and F made application for a shared residence order. This was refused and F appealed. Cazalet J stated that it was clear that, following s 11(4) Ch A 1989, the court was empowered to make a shared residence order relating to residence in favour of two people who were not living together. Nevertheless, such an order ought not to be made in normal conventional circumstances of parents who have separated. There may be cases where a shared residence order can be made which will aid because it may reduce the difference between the parties. But almost invariably, circumstances will require that a child should have his settled home with one parent rather than another. This means that there ought to be a residence order in favour of one parent, with a contact order in favour of the other.

> It seems to me that, for the reasons given by the judge, it is important that this child should have a settled home and should not pass to and fro between his parents, in particular when there are differences between them. In the present case, in my view, the court acted entirely properly in making the order that it did, by granting residence to the mother with an order for contact in favour of the father.

Held: F's appeal would be *dismissed*. The child's shuttling from M to F was not in its interests, particularly in view of the unsatisfactory relationship between M and F.

Re D (Children) (Shared Residence Orders) (2001) CA

H and W had married in 1986 and were divorced in 1995. There were three children, aged 13, 11 and 9. The children lived with W, but had maintained substantial contact with F, including staying contact for half their holidays, and during the week. H and W had returned to the court on several occasions so as to settle matters concerning education of the children and problems relating to passports. The judge at Watford County Court had made an an order for shared residence, having concluded that the difficulties between H and W arose from W's having sole residence. W appealed, arguing that there were substantial issues between the parties which had not been resolved, so that the shared residence order was premature. Shared residence orders, she contended, were appropriate only in exceptional circumstances.

Held: W's appeal would be *dismissed*. There was no requirement either under Ch A 1989 or in the case law that a shared residence order was appropriate only in exceptional circumstances. Where children spent a significant amount of time with both parents, intentionally or by accident, such an order would be appropriate if in the children's interests. In the present case the children had a settled home with H and W; the arrangement had worked well and had lasted for a considerable period of time, giving rise to a positive benefit for the children.

13.2.5 Interim residence orders

Re Y (A Minor) (Ex Parte Residence Order) (1993)

M lived with her child, C, aged eight. In November 1992, M had phoned her mother in a highly excitable manner, so that M's mother, G, then came to collect C. G made an *ex parte* application later that day requesting leave to apply for a residence order. Leave was granted and the magistrates made a residence order in G's favour which was to endure until February 1993. M appealed.

Held: M's appeal would be *allowed*. The magistrates were in error in making an *ex parte* three month residence order without arranging for an earlier hearing *inter partes*. Because both G and M were present, the court would make a decision as to where C ought to live until the hearing arranged for February 1993 took place.

Re G (Minors) (Ex Parte Interim Residence Order) (1993) CA

W had been given custody of her four children; H was granted access. The children told H, during a visit, that W and her visitors were taking drugs. H obtained an *ex parte* residence order which was continued by the judge. W appealed.

Held: W's appeal would be *dismissed*. An *ex parte* residence order related to very unusual circumstances only; the children ought not to have been removed from W before she had been given a chance to present her case to the court. But the children's short term protection did require that they live with H during an appropriate investigation into all their allegations concerning drugs.

Re S (A Minor) (1995) CA

Following a police protection order, C, aged eight, was removed from the care of his mother, W, and an interim residence order was made in favour of the father, H. Following the divorce of H and W, a joint custody order, giving care and control to W, was made. W failed to respond to social services' enquiries concerning C, and eventually W was arrested and hospitalised under s 4 Mental Health Act 1983. W was released and appealed against the interim residence order.

Held: W's appeal would be *dismissed*. It was not the common habit of the Court of Appeal to interfere with an interim residence order. C's safety and well-being necessitated his living with H until a full hearing could be arranged. A psychiatrist would be appointed to look into C's needs and to assess the possible negative effect on him of being removed from W.

Re G (A Minor) (Leave to Appeal: Jurisdiction) (1999) CA

F and M, both Scottish, separated after their child was born. M went with the child to England, but he was placed in foster care under an interim care order, as the result of M's inability to look after him. The local authority wished to consider F and his new wife as carers for the child, and application was made under Sched 2, para 19 Ch A 1989 for leave to place the child outside the jurisdiction with F under a care order. The judge considered that the most effective way of finding out whether F was a possible carer was by way of an interim residence order. M asked for leave to appeal, contending that the judge's short cut through the procedure required under Sched 2, para 19 was unwarranted.

Held: M was *refused* leave to appeal. The court was entitled to dispense with unnecessary difficulties of procedure so as to achieve what was in the child's best interests. It would be much better for the child to remain with F rather than with short term foster parents. There was no possibility of M's appeal succeeding since all the evidence from Scotland suggested clearly that the child was flourishing under F's care.

13.2.6 The court's discretion

Re M (A Minor) (Immigration: Residence Order) (1995)

F came to the UK, with his child, C, aged 10, from Zaire to seek asylum. He did not fulfil all the terms of a temporary admission order and was placed in detention. C was abandoned by F and was then placed with a foster mother in March 1992. In September 1992 the local authority was informed that F and C were to be deported. C's foster mother made application in October 1992 for a residence order.

Held: the foster mother's application would be *allowed*. The court had to be satisfied that the application was not intended to evade the requirements of the immigration rules. If, then, the court was satisfied that the application did not breach the interests of public policy, the court would intervene only where the relevant factual situation was of an exceptional nature. Given the facts, a residence order would be granted, in the discretion of the court, until C had reached the age of 18.

Re B (A Minor) (Residence Order) (1995) CA

H and W had four children. Following the separation of the parents, one of the children, C, resided with H at an address which was near to where W was living. W applied for a residence order concerning all the children, H made a cross-application. The judge decided that C should continue to live with H, and the three other children should live with W. W appealed.

Held: W's appeal would be *dismissed*. There could be no intervention by the Court of Appeal in the decision of the judge unless it was clear that he had exercised his discretion incorrectly or that his eventual decision was erroneous. In this case the judge had considered the importance of enabling the children to be together and had balanced this by taking into account the general upset likely to be experienced by them in moving between H and W.

Re PB (Children Act: Open Court) (1996) CA

H appealed against the decision of a county court judge that his application for a residence order should be heard in private. He argued that, under the principle of open justice, and under Arts 6 and 10 of the European Convention on Human Rights, the judge's discretion ought to have been exercised so as to allow evidence to be heard in open court.

Held: H's appeal would be *dismissed*. Proceedings relating to the welfare of children should, in general, be heard in private: see r 4.16(7) Family Proceedings Rules 1991. This was in no way contrary to the right to a public hearing and to the freedom of expression under the European Convention, which is subject to provisos. A judge had discretion to hear a case in public when there was a clear need for this, but this discretion was to be exercised only in exceptional circumstances.

13.3 The welfare checklist

Note

Ch A 1989, s 1(3), sets out a checklist of matters to which the court is to have particular regard. The checklist should be taken into account where the making, variation or discharge of an order is opposed, and where the court is considering making, varying or discharging an order under Part IV of the Act: s 1(4).

13.3.1 The child's ascertainable wishes, feelings, needs (physical, emotional and educational) (s 1(3)(a), (b))

Adams v Adams (1984) CA

The judge had granted custody of the two children of H and W to H, deciding that they should be brought up together because of their closeness in relationship and age and because the anxieties they had experienced on the divorce of H and W might be lessened if they were allowed to remain together. W appealed, arguing that it was generally desirable that a girl be raised and instructed by her mother.

Held: W's appeal would be *dismissed*. The children should not be allowed to feel that they were called upon to decide whether they should live with H or W. Where appropriate, the court will override the wishes of children. *Per* Dunn LJ:

> The pressures on children were quite sufficient when a marriage has broken down and one of the parents has left home, without putting on them the additional burden of being made to feel that they have to decide their own future.

C v C (Custody) (1988) CA

H and W had two children, C1 and C2. Following the parents' separation C1 remained with H, and C2 stayed with W. Interim custody orders were issued in favour of H and W in relation to C1 and C2. The judge made an order which divided the care and custody of the two children between the parents, allowing them access. W appealed.

Held: W's appeal against the split order would be *allowed*. After a divorce, siblings ought to be raised together, where that is possible, so that they can give each other a measure of support. The judge appeared to have erred, however, by omitting the appropriate consideration of C1's long term interests in being raised together with C2 in the same surroundings. Purchas LJ stated that where a judge decides to go against a decision in which young people have a satisfactory and available home together, with one parent acting as a custodial parent, then any departure from that course merits a specific reference as to the reasons why he decided not to accept such a course.

Re A (A Minor) (Custody) (1991) CA

H and W had separated. W took the daughter, aged 12, with her; H was left with a boy and a girl aged six. A psychologist's report made a recommendation that the girl aged six and the boy should remain with H, and that the other girl should remain with W. Custody of the two girls was awarded to W and custody of the boy was awarded to H. H appealed against the custody order in relation to the girl aged six.

Held: H's appeal against the custody order concerning the girl aged six would be *allowed*. It was merely a point to be considered rather than a presumption, that the mother of young girls ought to be looked upon as having responsibility for their care. It was not in the best interests of the girl that she should be taken from the custody of H.

Re P (A Minor) (Education: Child's Views) (1992) CA

H and W separated and their boys, C1, aged 14 and C2, aged 10, lived with W for some five years. C1 then decided to reside with H. H later informed W that he could no longer meet C1's private school fees, and suggested a day school as a possible substitute. The mother applied for an order stating that C1 should go to a boarding school, as she and H had agreed previously. H appealed, and C1's wishes and views were received as evidence.

Held: H's appeal would be *allowed*. It was the duty of the court to take into account the views of older children, particularly if they were mature and sensible. *Per* Butler-Sloss LJ:

> The courts, over the last few years, have become increasingly aware of the importance of listening to the views of older children and taking into account what children say, not necessarily agreeing with what they want nor, indeed, doing what they want, but paying proper respect to older children who are of an age and the maturity to make their minds up as to what they think is best for them, keeping in mind that older children very often have an appreciation of their own situation which is worthy of consideration by, and the respect of, the adults, and particularly including the courts.

13.3.2 Likely effect on the child of changes in his circumstances (s 1(3)(c))

S v W (1981) CA

H and W had married in 1970; the marriage was dissolved in 1978 on the grounds of two years' separation by consent. There were two children, a boy aged eight and a girl aged five. Disruptive behaviour on the part of the children had been evident and H claimed that it was the result of W's attitudes. Psychiatrists had interviewed the children and tended to agree with H. Some of the children's teachers, however, observed that, away from their home, the children behaved normally; they suggested that custody should be given to W. In 1980, the judge decided to grant custody to H; and altered W's access arrangements. W appealed.

Held: W's appeal would be *allowed*. Clearly, the children wanted to live with W who could provide a good home. The children were normal and were reacting as might be expected to difficulties in their situation. They needed a new beginning in a new environment. *Per* Ormrod LJ:

> The more satisfactory the status quo, the stronger the argument for not interfering. The less satisfactory the status quo, the less is required before deciding to change.

Stephenson v Stephenson (1985) CA

In 1979 H and W married. In 1981 the marriage broke down when W left the matrimonial home. H continued to care for the child, aged three at the time of the hearing, and was helped by his cohabitant. In the belief that the child was being ill-treated, W decided not to return her, following access. W's allegation was proved untrue after investigations by paediatricians and a welfare officer, who recommended that she be returned to H. The judge decided, however, that it would be best for her if she were to stay with W. H appealed.

Held: H's appeal would be *allowed*. The judge had not given any of his reasons for disagreeing with the welfare officer. It seemed clear, moreover, that there were risks to the child for the future in W's home – W was living with a person with a criminal record – which would not exist if the child were to return to H.

13.3.3 The child's relevant characteristics, eg age, sex, background (s 1(3)(d))

Re W (A Minor) (1983) CA

C was born in 1980. The parents, H and W, separated in 1981 when W left the matrimonial home. H had prevented W from taking C with her. Custody of C had been granted to H, with daily access to W. A supervision order was also made. The judge, considering the situation in the long term, transferred custody to W. H appealed.

Held: H's appeal would be *dismissed*. The specific features of individual cases were often unique, so that any so called principle which suggested that younger children ought to live with their mothers had to be modified often in the light of those features. But when a fine weighing exercise had been undertaken in order to decide whether a child had to be removed from a parent's keeping, it was important to view the results in the light of the importance of not interfering with the child's upbringing. In this case it seemed that it would not be right to prevent W from being involved in C's upbringing. The order transferring custody of C to W would not be interfered with.

Re B and G (Minors) (Custody) (1985) CA

A decree nisi had been granted to H and W, who were Scientologists and the parents of a boy aged 10 and a girl aged 8. H was awarded custody of the children. In 1981 W and the stepfather withdrew from their membership of the Church of Scientology. In a later hearing, W contended that if H brought up the children they would be damaged by exposure to the doctrines of Scientology. H argued that a state of affairs which had lasted for five years ought not to be disturbed. The judge held that the doctrines were dangerous and that it was not in the children's best interests to be exposed to them. This, he said, tipped the balance in favour of granting W care and control. H appealed.

Held: H's appeal would be *dismissed*. It was in the interests of the children that the judge should seek to make relevant findings concerning Scientology, otherwise he would be unable to assess possible risks to the children if they continued their contact with H. There was ample evidence, further, that the judge was entitled to form a view that H could not be relied upon to fulfil his promises concerning the upbringing of the children. There were, therefore, no grounds for interfering with the judge's decision.

13.3.4 Harm which the child has suffered or is at risk of suffering (s 1(3)(e))

Note ───

In this context, harm is taken to mean ill-treatment or the impairment of health or development. In determining whether the harm suffered is significant, the child's health is to be compared with that which could reasonably be expected of a similar child. See s 31 of the 1989 Act.

H v H (Child Abuse: Access) (1989) CA

After the divorce of H and W, W was given custody of the three children, with reasonable access granted to H. Later, W formed suspicions that H had been sexually abusing the daughter, and she prevented further access.

H denied all the allegations and made application for an access order. The judge held that H had abused the daughter in a serious manner, but he granted H access to the three children for one day a month, under the continuing supervision of the local authority. W appealed.

Held: W's appeal would be *dismissed*. A finding of sexual abuse by a parent is a highly significant factor to be taken into account in considering the general future of a child, but it should not always lead to a denial of access to a parent. Each case must be considered on its own particular facts. A delicate balancing exercise had been undertaken and all relevant matters had been considered by the judge. There seemed to be no reason to interfere with the exercise by the judge of his discretion.

Re M (Minors) (Contact) (1995)

H and W were married in 1982; there were two children. Following separation in 1989, both children remained with H and, as a result of problems arising from contact, the court welfare officer recommended that all contact between the children and W should cease. W agreed to the recommendation and contact ended in 1992. In 1993 W applied for contact. Another welfare officer reported that contact would have a significantly negative effect on both children. A contact order was refused. W appealed.

Held: W's appeal would be *dismissed*. It was necessary for the court to be aware of the need for a child to enjoy the advantages of a permanent relationship with its parents but also to keep in mind the possibility of harm resulting from the implementation of a contact order. The judge was quite entitled to decide that the possibility of the children experiencing emotional disturbance tipped the scales against contact.

13.3.5 Capability of each of the child's parents and other relevant persons in meeting the needs of the child (s 1(3)(f))

Scott v Scott (1986) CA

Following H's petitioning for divorce, a consent order was made by which interim custody of the child was given to W, with reasonable access to H. Access was a failure and H applied for custody. The judge heard H and W and their cohabitants. He found that W had made a sustained attempt to turn the child against H, that W's cohabitant had a serious criminal record and had committed acts of indecency against the child. The judge was impressed with H and his cohabitant. Although there was a risk in taking the child from its mother, that seemed a lesser risk than allowing her to remain with W and her present cohabitant. Custody was granted to H. W appealed.

Held: W's appeal would be *dismissed*. The judge's decision had been made on the basis of his impression of the parties involved with the child.

That decision which also took into account possible risk to the children should stand.

Re K (Minors) (Access) (1988) CA

H and W were educationally subnormal and were unable to provide care for their children without assistance given by social services. The local authority wished to have the children committed to care so as to place them with foster parents, with the object of adoption. H and W sought access with a view to rehabilitation. The judge decided that this was not realistic, but he did not wish to break the ties between H, W and the children. He gave leave for a placement with foster parents and ordered access until further order, subject to a six-monthly review. The local authority appealed.

Held: the appeal of the local authority would be *allowed*. The children would not be rehabilitated with H and W. Their best long term interests involved placement with foster parents and subsequent adoption. The local authority would be granted leave for placement with a view to adoption.

Re H (Minor) (Custody Appeal) (1991) CA

During a custody hearing in relation to a child aged 14, H accused W of adultery and a variety of offences, including theft and perjury. The judge had found that W had committed adultery, but he refused to make any finding on the allegations of crime. H appealed, arguing that the judge was wrong in not making a finding against W, which would have shown clearly that she ought not to have custody of the child because of her general unfitness of character.

Held: H's appeal would be *dismissed*. Objectionable conduct by W did not necessarily mean that she could not provide the appropriate level of care for the child. There was no evidence to suggest that the child was affected adversely by W's behaviour. It was not necessary to make any findings against W. She had looked after the child well during the past three years. Further, it was not realistic to suggest that H could care for the child in these circumstances.

Q Do you consider that the meaning given in s 31(9) Ch A 1989 to the term 'harm' is realistic?

14 Care and Supervision Orders

14.1 Essence and aspects of the care order

Note ──
Fundamental to Part IV of Ch A 1989 is s 31(1): 'On the application of any local authority or authorised person, the court may make an order (a) placing the child with respect to whom the application was made in the care of a designated local authority, or (b) putting him under the supervision of a designated local authority or of a probation officer.'
──

Re TB (Minors) (Care Proceedings: Criminal Trial) (1995) CA
A hearing of care proceedings was delayed by the judge, pending the result of the trial of the parents who had been charged with criminal neglect of the children. The local authority and guardian ad litem appealed.

Held: the appeal would be *allowed*. It ought not to be supposed that care proceedings would be adjourned whenever a parent was the defendant in criminal proceedings. Each case would be considered on its specific set of facts and the welfare of the child would be considered as more important than any disadvantage suffered by a defendant in such proceedings. It was essential that the children be settled as soon as possible. The care proceedings would be reinstated swiftly.

Re S and P (Discharge of Care Order) (1995)
Care orders had been made on W's two children. The orders had been made by consent, and W applied for their discharge and, alternatively, applied for contact. The local authority submitted that W's application had no real chance of success so that there was no case to answer.

Held: W's application would be *dismissed*. The real question to be answered was whether the magistrates, who had accepted the local authority's argument, had behaved unfairly in the exercise of their discretion by refusing to allow the case to be heard in full. Grounds did exist, however, to support the findings of the magistrates that W's application had no chance of success.

Re A (Care Order: Discharge of Application by Child) (1995)
Care proceedings had been transferred by the judge to the High Court in order to determine whether a child who was the subject of a care order required leave to make an application for the discharge of that order.

Held: the case would be *remitted* to the county court. Under s 39(1)(b) Ch A 1989, a care order can be discharged on application of the child himself and there was no requirement that the subsection was subject to any initial procedure necessitating the granting of leave.

Re D (A Minor) (Basis of Uncontested Care Order) (1995)

Application had been made by a local authority for a care order concerning a child whose sister had died in circumstances which were not yet clear. The local authority had expressed concern as to the possibility of a connected future issue arising concerning an unborn child. This matter promised to be complicated by any finding of fact with reference to the undecided case.

Held: the court had no specifically defined duty in this area in relation to an unborn child. A declaratory judgment on this question would *not*, therefore, be appropriate. A care order which would end any contact between the child and his parents would be made without any further delay.

Manchester City Council v B (1996)

A child, C, was born in May 1994. In August 1994 medical investigation indicated injuries to C's head. H and W denied that the injuries were non-accidental and C was discharged into his grandparents' care. Medical evidence as to the cause of the injuries was of an ambiguous nature and the local authority made application for a care or supervision order.

Held: a care order would be *granted*. The burden of proof was on the local authority to show whether the injuries were non-accidental; the standard of proof would be 'a balance of probabilities commensurate with the serious nature of the allegations'. Although C's injuries were life-threatening, H and W were a significant feature in his life. A supervision order would also be made, in the circumstances.

P v Bradford Borough Council (1996)

Care orders were made in relation to M's children. She applied, two years later, for their discharge and, alternatively, for contact. The local authority contended that M was in the habit of associating with offenders and that her role as parent was less than satisfactory. M gave evidence, at the conclusion of which the local authority argued that there was no prospect of the orders being discharged. The case was stopped by the magistrates and M's applications were then dismissed. M appealed.

Held: M's appeal would be *dismissed*. M was a poor witness and the magistrates had acted correctly in stopping the case. Applications for the discharge of care orders were to be decided generally, but not always, on adequate evidence. The court had to take into account the sufficiency of evidence and the prospects of success for M's application.

Re EC (Disclosure of Material) (1996)

Care proceedings had been brought by a local authority concerning a child whose sibling had died of injuries of a non-accidental nature. It had not been possible for the police to determine which of the relatives (parents, uncle, grandmother) had been responsible for the death; the Crown Prosecution Service had recommended that no further action be taken. The police did not consider their investigation to have been ended. A care order was made. The local authority were allowed by the judge to inform the police of the father's admission that he had caused the injury leading to the child's death. The police made application to obtain a transcript of proceedings and copies of the parents' statements and medical evidence.

Held: the application would be *allowed*, but *in part only*. The court has a discretion as to whether to disclose to the police matter covered by s 98(2) of the 1989 Act so as to allow the police to consider the range of their enquiries into an alleged criminal offence. But an important factor in the exercise of that discretion is the public interest in furthering frankness in criminal proceedings by the preservation of confidentiality. Public interest was a predominating factor in the instant case and some transcripts would not be passed to the police. So far as the request for medical evidence was concerned, the public interest in maintaining confidentiality would give way to the public interest in the prevention and investigation of crime. The medical evidence would be passed to the police.

North Yorkshire CC v Wiltshire CC (1999)

C was born in 1990 in Wiltshire where her parents, F and M, resided. She suffered from cerebral palsy and needed special care. She was legitimate and her parents had parental responsibility. F and M separated some two years after C's birth, and C was voluntarily placed with foster parents who moved to North Yorkshire. WCC made payments to them for foster care and applied for a care order which was contested by M. The court was asked to decide which local authority ought to be designated in the order and this involved deciding for purposes of s 31(8)(b) the meaning of 'ordinarily resident'. M had moved to the Isle of Wight, F had moved to Leicestershire. NYCC was designated as the appropriate authority and appealed, contending that the area in which C had been ordinarily resident at the moment she was provided with accommodation remained the area in which she was ordinarily resident, irrespective of later changes.

Held: the appeal was *dismissed*. For the purposes of the Act, 'ordinarily resident' could not refer to the place in which neither C nor her parents were living and to which they did not intend to return. Section 105 precluded the movement of a child to the area of another authority from affecting her residence with that original authority, or her remaining there from affecting that residence. The court had acted correctly in finding that C had ceased to be resident in Wiltshire; it was entitled, in the exercise of its discretion under s 31(8)(b), to designate NYCC as the appropriate authority for purposes of the order.

Plymouth City Council v C (2000)

J, a child, was born in Plymouth. The parents, F and M, had a profound and chronic drug problem, and the local authority immediately obtained an emergency protection order which was converted swiftly into an interim care order. F and M moved to live with the maternal grandmother and then moved to a residential assessment centre in Plymouth. Some four months before a court hearing, J and M were separated and J was then placed with her paternal grandmother in Liverpool. It was held, at first instance, that J's 'ordinary place of residence' was Plymouth, where M lived. Plymouth CC was considered to be the designated local authority. F appealed.

Held: F's appeal was *dismissed*. A newly born child cared for by her mother was incapable of establishing an ordinary residence apart from that of the mother; accordingly, the mother's residence was the child's ordinary residence of dependency. To determine which local authority had primary statutory responsibility, ss 31(1) and 105(6) Ch A 1989 should be construed so that the child's ordinary area of residence was the area of residence immediately prior to the period to be disregarded under s 105(6), for purposes of the Act.

14.2 Threshold criteria

Note

A court may only make a care order or supervision order if it is satisfied (a) that the child concerned is suffering, or is likely to suffer, significant harm; and (b) that the harm or likelihood of harm is attributable to (i) the care given to the child, or likely to be given to him if the order were not made, not being what it would be reasonable to expect a parent to give to him; or (ii) the child's being beyond parental control: s 31(2) Ch A 1989.

Re J (Minors) (Care: Care Plan) (1994)

The local authority was asking for final care orders in relation to M's four children. The judge was satisfied that the threshold criteria had been met and that, in the interests of the welfare of the children, they should be removed from M's care and final orders made. A care plan made by the local authority had been modified a few days before the hearing. It proposed placements with foster parents, although no complete matching of the children and foster parents had been undertaken. The guardian ad litem opposed final care orders, suggesting the alternative of interim care orders.

Held: final care orders *would be made*. The local authority plan must be in line with guidance structures issued by the Department of Health. The threshold criteria had clearly been satisfied and, on the facts, final care orders as issued seemed to be the appropriate course of action to be taken in relation to the four children.

Re B (Minors) (Care Proceedings) (1994)

M had three young children, C1, C2 and C3. C2, a girl born in February 1988, died in July 1988. C1 and C3, both boys, had different fathers. C1 was admitted to hospital suffering from a condition connected with a concentration of sodium. A post mortem on C2 found that she had been injected with a salt solution. C3 had also been injected with a harmful substance. M was found to be suffering from Munchausen's syndrome by proxy (a pathological condition involving the inducing of illness in another so as to elicit attention and sympathy). Care orders were sought by the local authority in relation to C1 and C3 with a view to placement with their fathers. M sought contact. The local authority and guardian ad litem objected.

Held: it was *not necessary* to make any order for contact. The threshold criteria had been satisfied and the welfare of C1 and C3 necessitated the making of care orders. M's contact with the younger boy would not be to his advantage, and contact with him would be ended. The local authority were to ensure reasonable contact of M with C1.

F v Leeds City Council (1994) CA

A care order had been made in relation to M when she was 15. She was then detained in secure accommodation, following involvement in drug abuse and prostitution. She gave birth to C while under the age of 18 and the local authority were granted a final care order in relation to C. M appealed.

Held: M's appeal would be *dismissed*. The judge had held correctly that C's welfare was the paramount consideration. C was considered to be at risk of significant harm from M's general neglect. Time did not allow any attempt at rehabilitation and assessment; the making of a care order was right in the circumstances.

Re T (A Minor) (Care Order: Conditions) (1994) CA

A care order was applied for by the local authority in relation to a very young child, C, whose seven sisters were in care. An interim care order was made, to be followed by an assessment. The threshold criteria were satisfied and C's parents contended that a supervision order was appropriate in the circumstances. A supervision order was made with conditions which were not stated in the order. The local authority appealed.

Held: the appeal would be *dismissed*. Any conditions attached to a supervision order ought to be specified in that order. Conditions could not be attached to a care order once the criteria set out in s 31(2) had been satisfied.

Re M (A Minor) (Care Order: Threshold Conditions) (1994) HL

The mother of a very young child, C, was murdered by the father, F. C was then fostered and a residence order was made in relation to C and three siblings in favour of the mother's cousin, X. F was convicted and recommended for deportation. X applied for a residence order. F agreed with the making of a care order which was granted. X's appeal was allowed by the Court of Appeal and the care order, was discharged and replaced by a residence order in favour of X. F appealed to the House of Lords.

Held: F's appeal would be *allowed*. The Court of Appeal did possess the jurisdiction to enable it to make a care order. The care order should be restored so as to allow C's general progress to be monitored by the local authority. The relevant date under s 31(2) Ch A 1989 on which the court had to be satisfied of threshold conditions was the date on which the local authority had commenced protective arrangements concerning C.

Re C (A Minor) (Care Order Appeal) (1995)

A care order was made which effectively reduced contact between H and W (the parents) and their child, C. H and W appealed, contending that no order should be made which would allow C to live with the foster parents who had previously looked after her. It was agreed that the threshold criteria had been met; no findings on this matter had been made.

Held: the parents' appeal would be *dismissed*. It was not in accord with practice that no findings seemed to have been made in relation to threshold criteria. No other criticism of the magistrates could be sustained in this case.

Re P (Emergency Protection Order) (1996)

C, aged two months, was admitted to hospital after receiving injuries which appeared to be non-accidental. The judge concluded that M, one of the parents, was responsible. An emergency protection order was obtained by the local authority, but an extension was refused by the magistrates. M appeared to be suffering from Munchausen's Syndrome by proxy. The parents withdrew their vigorous objections to the grant of a care order.

Held: a care order *would be made*. The court had to be satisfied that the threshold criteria had been met on a balance of probabilities. Where the magistrates had refused to extend an emergency protection order there appeared to be no effective procedure under the 1989 Act whereby the local authority could challenge their decision.

Lancashire County Council v A (A Minor) (2000) HL

A, a baby girl, had been cared for by a child-minder while her parents were out at their place of work. After a period of two months, it was found that A had serious non-accidental head injuries. Applying for a care order, the local authority relied on s 31(2)(b)(i) Ch A 1989, which allowed the court to make an order of this nature where the harm or likelihood of harm was attributable 'to the care given to the child'. The authority relied solely on injuries sustained during the two month period by A. The application was dismissed, the judge holding that, for purposes of s 31, it was necessary to satisfy the court by evidence that the significant harm sustained by A was to be attributed to the care, or absence of care, given to the child by the parent against whom the order would be made. The Court of Appeal reversed the decision. The parents of A then appealed to the House of Lords, contending that 'the care given to the child', in s 31(2)(b)(i), referred to care given by the parents or other primary carers. The local authority (and A's guardian) argued that no words of limitation of this nature could be read into the provision; the phrase meant care given by any person who played some part in the care arrangements for A.

Held: the appeal would be *dismissed*. If the parents' arguments were to be accepted, this would produce the result that where a child had sustained repeatedly non-accidental injuries, the court would be unable to intervene by making a care order if unable to identify which of the child's carers had inflicted the injuries. Parliament could not have intended this result, for such an interpretation would mean that the child's future health would have to be hazarded on the chance that the non-parental carer, rather than a parent, had inflicted the injury. A preferable interpretation would be that 'care given to a child' referred primarily to the care given by parents or other primary carers; that was the norm. Different norms might apply in the case of shared caring, and, in such a case, 'care given to the child' might embrace the care given by any carers.

Where, therefore, a child whose care is shared among its parents and some other carer, suffers some harm, for purposes of s 31(2)(b)(i), it was possible for the court to make a care order, even though there existed no more than a mere possibility that the parents, rather than the other carer, were responsible for the child's injuries.

Re D (Child: Threshold Material) (2000) CA

It was held that a judge could, in appropriate circumstances, permit a local authority to re-open an issue of the threshold criteria for the making of a care order although the particular issue had been determined by agreement at the first part of a split hearing and there was no new evidence to consider.

14.2.1 'Significant harm'

Re O (A Minor) (Care Order: Education: Procedure) (1992)

O was a persistent truant. In 1991 her parents were prosecuted and fined for not sending her to school. An interim care order was made later but did not have the desired effect. The local authority then applied for a care order under s 31. O and her parents appealed, contending that no impairment of intellectual or social development had been established by the local authority and that any harm suffered by O was not significant and little more than might be expected in the case of a similar child.

Held: the appeal would be *dismissed*. Per Ewbank J:

> In my view it was entirely open to the justices to come to the view, as they did, that O's intellectual and social development was suffering and was likely to suffer, and that the harm which she was suffering from or was likely to suffer from, was significant ... What one has to ask oneself is whether O suffered significant harm by not going to school. The answer, in my judgment, as in that of the justices, is obvious. The second threshold condition is that the harm, or likelihood of harm, is attributable to the care given to the child not being what it would be reasonable to expect a parent to give him, or that the child is beyond parental control. In my judgment, where a child is suffering harm in not going to school and is living at home, it will follow that either the child is beyond the parents' control or that they are not giving the child the care that it would be reasonable to expect a parent to give ... In this appeal O and her parents have wholly failed in their endeavour to show that the justices came to the wrong decision.

Humberside County Council v B (1993)

H and W, whose child, C, was born in October 1991, suffered from a form of schizophrenia, for which they received medical treatment. Following discovery of facts showing that C had been left alone in the house in January 1992, the local authority carried out an assessment and found evidence of bruising to C which appeared to be inconsistent with non-accidental injury. An interim care order was made by the magistrates.

Held: the same principles applied to interim as to full orders, except that in the case of an interim order the court had to be satisfied only that there were *reasonable grounds* to suggest that the child was likely to suffer significant harm. There were grounds for believing this in the case of C, but the magistrates had not abided by the welfare criteria; nor had they taken into account whether or not to make an order in any event.

Re M (A Minor) (Care Proceedings: Appeal) (1995) CA

C, aged six, was admitted to hospital with multiple bruising. She suffered a renal failure. The local authority argued that the child's injuries had been caused by punching. The mother and her cohabitant denied this, stating that C had sustained injuries as the result of a fall. The judge found that the threshold criteria had been satisfied, that the mother had not sought medical help for C and that there were growing and justifiable anxieties as to C's welfare. He did not make a care order, but issued a residence order to the mother, on the condition that she should continue to live with her cohabitant's parents. The local authority appealed.

Held: the local authority's appeal would be *dismissed*. The judge had directed himself correctly in holding that the local authority had to prove their case on a balance of probabilities; but he was entitled, in considering the threshold criteria, to hold that the local authority had *not* made out their case adequately in relation to the more serious allegations made against the mother.

14.2.2 'Is suffering ... or is likely to suffer ...'

Re H (Minors) (Child Abuse: Threshold Conditions) (1996) HL

W had four children, all girls. C1 and C2 were fathered by H, whom she had married in 1979; C3 and C4 were fathered by X, with whom she had lived after separating from H in 1984. In 1993, C1, aged 15, complained to the police, alleging that she had been sexually abused by X since the age of eight. X was charged with rape and C1 was then placed with foster parents. In 1994 the local authority made application for care orders in relation to C2, C3 and C4. X was acquitted of rape, but the local authority proceeded with their application which was based on the alleged abuse of C1 by X. The local authority asked the judge to find that X had sexually abused C1, or, at least, that there was a substantial risk that he had done so. The application was dismissed and the Court of Appeal dismissed the local authority's appeal. The local authority appealed to the House of Lords.

Held: the appeal of the local authority would be *dismissed*. In order to establish that a child was likely to suffer significant harm in the future (within the meaning of s 31 of the 1989 Act) so as to enable the court to make a care or supervision order, there had to be a real possibility of risk, *based on actual facts rather than mere suspicion*.

Lord Nicholls said that he could not accept the argument that 'likely' within the meaning of s 31 meant 'probable'. 'Likely' was used in the sense of a real possibility, one which could not be sensibly ignored, having regard to the nature and gravity of the feared harm in the particular case. The standard of proof required here was the ordinary civil standard of balance of probabilities. To decide that C2, C3 and C4 were at risk because there was a possibility that C1 was abused would be to base a decision not on fact, but on the suspicion that C1 *might* have been abused. That would be to lower the threshold prescribed by Parliament. Parents were not to be at risk of having a child taken from them and removed into the care of the local authority on the basis of suspicions only.

Lord Browne-Wilkinson (dissenting) said that if legal proof of actual abuse was a prerequisite to a finding that a child was at risk of abuse, the court would be powerless to intervene to protect children in relation to whom there were the gravest suspicions of actual abuse but the necessary evidence legally to prove such abuse was lacking.

Lord Lloyd (dissenting) said that the question was whether, on all the evidence, the court considered that there was a real possibility of the child's suffering significant harm in the future. If so, the threshold criteria were satisfied. The court did not have to be satisfied on the balance of probabilities that the child had in fact suffered significant harm in the past, whether by sexual abuse or otherwise, even where the allegation of abuse was the foundation of the local authority's case for a care order.

Re M (Care Order: Parental Responsibility) (1996)

C, a five day old child had been abandoned outside a health centre. It proved impossible to trace any person who might have been responsible for him. A thorough medical examination indicated that C was suffering from neurological and cardiac deficiencies. Concern for his condition had increased in spite of the excellent care he had received from foster parents. The local authority proposed that C be placed for adoption and made application for a care order.

Held: the application by the local authority would be *granted*. The threshold criteria set out in s 31 Ch A 1989 had been satisfied. In answer to the question whether, when the protective arrangements made by the local authority had been initiated, C was suffering or likely to suffer some significant harm, it appeared that the very fact of C's having been abandoned (which in itself amounted to ill-treatment) showed that C was suffering from significant harm. Further, at the very time of his being abandoned, it could be said that he was likely to suffer significant harm in the future because of the need to undergo medical treatment. There was a clear need for some person to be given parental responsibility for C, so that important decisions concerning his future could be made. The general powers under ss 20–24 of the 1989 Act seemed inadequate in this case and it would be in the best interests of C that the care order be made, rather than no order at all.

14.3   The 'two stage' test

Re M and R (Minors) (1996) CA

The court had been asked to make four full care orders on the basis of allegations of sexual abuse in the past, and had refused. Surrey County Council and the guardian ad litem appealed.

Held: the appeal would be *dismissed*. When considering whether to make a care order the court could have regard, under s 1(3)(e), to any harm that the child had suffered or was at risk of suffering if satisfied on the balance of probabilities that such harm, or risk of harm, in fact existed.

Butler-Sloss LJ said that where a court was faced with an application for a care order under s 31, it first had to consider whether the requirements of the section had been met. If they had been met, the court was given a discretion as to what to do, but in exercising that discretion the court had to act in accordance with s 1. These two stages had been described as the 'threshold' stage and the 'welfare' stage. If there was a dispute as to whether the child had suffered or was at risk of suffering harm, the judge, when deciding whether to make an order under s 8 or s 31, had to resolve this matter. The court had to reach a conclusion based on facts, not mere doubts or suspicions. It was for the court to decide whether the evidence established harm or the risk of harm. The final decision was for the judge, as were all questions of relevance and weight. When the judge is of the opinion that a witness's expertise is required to assist him to answer the fundamental questions, then the judge can safely rely on such evidence while never losing sight of the fact that the final decision is for him.

14.4 The non-adversarial nature of care proceedings under Ch A 1989

Re L (A Minor) (Police Investigations: Privilege) (1996) HL

C, the child of H and W, who were drug addicts, became ill after ingesting methadone. W's excuse was that this was accidental. The local council obtained interim care orders in relation to C and her brother. On the application of H and W, the district judge made an order stating that H and W had leave to disclose to a medical expert the court papers, for the purposes of a report concerning the frequency of taking methadone. W's solicitors instructed a chemical pathologist, whose report cast considerable doubt on W's excuse concerning C's taking the substance. The police asked to be provided with a copy of the report. W appealed against disclosure, contending that the judge had no jurisdiction to order disclosure because the report was protected by legal professional privilege, and that the judge had exercised his discretion incorrectly.

Held: W's appeal would be *dismissed*. Since proceedings under Part IV Ch A 1989 were *investigative and non-adversarial* and placed the child's welfare as the primary consideration, an expert's report obtained by a party to care proceedings was not protected by legal privilege.

Lord Jauncey said that if litigation privilege were to apply to the report, in this case it would have the effect of subordinating the child's welfare to the interests of the mother in preserving its confidentiality and that would seem to frustrate the primary purpose of the Act. On the question of self-incrimination, W had voluntarily initiated the process concerning the report and did not appeal against the order when it was made. She had to be taken, therefore, to have waived any claim against self-incrimination consequent upon the order of the judge. On the matter of the judge's exercise of her discretion, she had taken the view, which was entirely justified, that C's best interests would be served by disclosure, and it could not possibly be said that she had acted in error in reaching such a decision.

14.5   The supervision order

Note

A supervision order is made by the court on the application of any local authority or authorised person, placing the child under the supervision of a designated local authority or a probation officer: s 31(1)(b). The criteria in ss 1 and 31 must be satisfied.

14.5.1   Duration of the supervision order

M v Warwickshire County Council (1994)

Care proceedings had commenced in relation to C1, aged 11, and his brother, C2, aged 13. Interim supervision orders had been made. C1's social worker had recommended that there should be a six month supervision order. C1's mother agreed. The magistrates held that a 12 month supervision order was needed. All the parties appealed.

Held: the appeal would be *allowed* and a six month order substituted. Schedule 3, Part II, para 6(1) Ch A 1989 provided that a supervision order would cease to have effect at the end of a period of 12 months beginning with the date of the order. This could mean either that the order must endure for 12 months, or that it could be made for a maximum of 12 months. The uncertainty could be ended by the court using the interpretation likely to be of real advantage in the situation. This meant that the maximum period should be 12 months in the circumstances of this case.

Re A (A Minor) (Supervision Order: Extension) (1995) CA

C, aged 11, lived with her mother and was placed under a 12 month supervision order. During the currency of the order an extension was applied for by social workers. A care order in place of the supervision order was recommended by the guardian ad litem. The local authority and C's mother opposed the application. The court held that it had no authority to make a care order on an application for an extension of a supervision order. The mother appealed.

Held: the mother's appeal would be *allowed*. An application for the extension of a supervision order was not to be equated with an application for a supervision order within s 31(5)(b). The court was not entitled, on application being made to extend an order, to decide to substitute an interim care order.

14.5.2 Supervision of contact by means of a supervision order

Re DH (A Minor) (Child Abuse) (1994)

H and W had a son, C, aged almost two. During the first year of C's life, W, who was suspected of suffering from Munchausen's Syndrome by proxy, was sentenced to three years' probation for cruelty involving C. The court ordered that W should have contact for one hour every two weeks with C, to be supervised by H. The local authority sought the ending of all contact between W and C.

Held: there was a likelihood of significant harm to C, and the threshold conditions for a supervision order were met. In more serious cases where the matter of child protection was involved, a supervision order could be made. While, generally, it was not desirable for contact to be supervised over a long period, it would be *appropriate* in the instant case.

14.5.3 Supervision orders and role of guardian ad litem

Re K (Supervision Orders) (1999)

Following the death of M's youngest child in suspicious circumstances, three children were removed from her. The local authority accepted, during care proceedings, that it was not possible to infer that M was clearly responsible for the child's death. M was prepared to accept, however, that the threshold criteria were satisfied by, for example, her unsuitable relationships. She accepted also that a one year supervision order ought to be made. The guardian ad litem, appealing, contended that no order should be made if no findings concerning the death were to be made and, in the alternative, because the local authority were meeting the children's needs under Part III Ch A 1989, no order need be made.

Held: the appeal would be *dismissed*. A guardian ad litem should approach with care the question of whether it was appropriate to disturb an agreement between a local authority and parents, or advance alternative and arguable proposals. The evidence showed that the threshold criteria were met, and it was possible that the children would come to harm were an order not to be made. There was sufficient evidence to suggest that, were a supervision order not to be made, M would not co-operate with the local authority and this would be to the disadvantage of the children. In this case a supervision order was preferable to no order.

14.6   Investigation of the child's circumstances

Note

Where in family proceedings in which a question concerning the child's welfare arises and it seems to the court that a care or supervision order might be appropriate, an investigation of the child's circumstances can be directed: s 37(1).

Re H (A Minor) (Section 37 Direction) (1993)

A lesbian couple requested a residence order in relation to a child who had lived with them in their home since being born there.

Held: the situation would be regularised as far as was possible by *the grant* of interim supervision and interim residence orders. The local authority was directed, under s 37(1) to make an investigation of the child's circumstances. The phrase 'child's circumstances' should be construed in a wide sense so as to include any situation which might affect the possibility of the child's being likely to suffer any significant harm in the future.

14.7   Interim orders

A v M and Walsall Borough Council (1993)

Because of W's poor record concerning her parental ability and H's violence towards their child, the local authority made application for a care order. In the event, a series of interim care orders was made. Prior to the final hearing the local authority made application for an order ending contact between W and the child. According to the magistrates, there was no reasonable prospect of W caring adequately for the child, and contact was ended. W appealed.

Held: W's appeal would be *allowed*. The magistrates had made their decision at an interim hearing. Except for cases of grave risk to a child, contact ought to be continued pending a final hearing.

Re S (Children: Interim Care Order) (1993)

W had three children, aged two, three and four. Because of her violent relationship with H, father of the younger two children, all three children had been placed on the child protection register. Later, W took the children to H and asked him to look after them; she attempted suicide later that day. The local authority sought interim care orders; the children were to remain with H and contact with W would be carefully supervised. An eight week interim care order was made. H appealed.

Held: H's appeal would be *dismissed*. At the interim stage, the magistrates need satisfy themselves only that there were *reasonable grounds* for believing that the children were suffering or were likely to suffer significant harm. Further, at that stage, the magistrates should be careful not to prejudice a future final hearing and should make sure that their reasons for making the order were sufficient and appropriate.

Re G (Minors) (Interim Care Order) (1993) CA

H and W were inadequate parents, unable to care for their two sons, and the local authority obtained an interim order, following which the children were placed with foster parents. W applied for the discharge of the interim order, and the local authority applied for the striking out of W's application as an abuse of the process. The local authority sought a further interim order. The judge would not make such an order and granted a prohibited steps order which, effectively, prevented the local authority from altering the existing placement of the boys.

Held: the appeal of the local authority would be *allowed*. An interim care order was a useful and impartial method of preserving the status quo; it did not confer any temporary advantage on parties. The problem of deciding which type of order was to be made would be resolved on the basis of the principles in s 1 Ch A 1989, allowing the court to make an appropriate choice as to the alternatives which would be available at the final hearing. *Per* Waite LJ:

> Parliament intended the regime of an interim care order to operate a tightly run procedure closely monitored by the court and affording to all parties an opportunity of frequent review as events unfolded during the currency of the order. That purpose would be frustrated if a practice were to be allowed to grow up under which renewals of interim care orders were sought routinely by local authorities without any attempt to keep the court up to date with progress, or granted by the court perfunctorily without any of the enquiries necessary to eliminate the risk of essential disclosure being lost through administrative lethargy.

Re C (A Minor) (Interim Care) (1994)

C, a very young child, was the fourth of M's children. At her birth in February 1993, the local authority was granted an interim supervision order. In May 1993, C sustained injuries when dropped on the street pavement by M's mother. The local authority succeeded in its application for an *ex parte* order which changed the interim supervision order into an interim care order. The care order was confirmed at an *inter partes* hearing; it was to be reviewed one month later. M appealed against the *inter partes* interim care order.

Held: C's welfare at the time of the hearing required that she *should return* to M. M gave an undertaking that her mother would not be allowed to have contact with C. An interim supervision order was substituted; it would contain a condition making it necessary for M to attend a day centre twice every week.

14.7.1 Assessment of child in relation to interim order

South Glamorgan County Council v B (1993)

C, aged 15, was beyond parental control. Medical consultants stated that because of her behaviour it was essential that she be taken from her home. C refused to attend the appropriate adolescent unit and directions were given by the judge, under s 38(6), that she be assessed at the unit. The local authority asked that the court exercise its inherent jurisdiction so as send C forcibly to the unit. C's father argued that s 38(6) gave C the right to refuse to submit to an assessment, so that it ought not to be authorised.

Held: it was clear that the High Court *could override* a child's wishes and give its consent to medical assessment. C's welfare was the paramount consideration. It seemed clear that C had to attend the unit in her own interests. The local authority was given leave to remove C forcibly to the unit for assessment.

Re C (A Minor) (Interim Care Order: Residential Assessment) (1997) HL

C, aged four months, was admitted to hospital suffering from fits. Severe non-accidental head injuries were diagnosed. No satisfactory explanation had been given by the parents who were aged 16 and 17, were immature and lacked appropriate family backing. At the contested care proceedings, the judge decided that C's interests necessitated the making of a residential assessment of C and the parents under s 38(6). The Court of Appeal allowed an appeal by the local authority: attention was drawn to *Re M (Minors) (Interim Care Order: Directions)* (1996), in which the Court had held that there was no power to order the assessment of any other person in relation to the child. (Section 38 Ch A 1989 provides: 'Where the court makes an interim care order, or interim supervision order, it may give such directions (if any) as it considers appropriate with regard to the medical or psychiatric examination or other assessment of the child ... (6) ... A direction under subsection (6) may be to the effect that there is to be (a) no such examination or assessment ...') C's parents appealed to the House of Lords.

Held the parents' appeal would be *allowed*. Lord Browne-Wilkinson said that, in *Re M*, the Court of Appeal had construed s 38(6) and (7) narrowly, and had held that 'other assessment of the child' had to be construed as *ejusdem generis* with 'medical or psychiatric examination'. This construction ought *not* to be accepted. It was necessary to construe the statute *purposively* so as to give effect to Parliament's underlying intentions. There seemed to be no reasons here for the application of the *ejusdem generis* principle; indeed, it was not possible to find the genus to which it could apply. A young child could not be assessed properly by divorcing him from his environment. The interaction between C and the parents was an essential element in making an assessment of him. It was necessary to construe sub-ss (6) and (7) in a *broad manner*. They conferred on the court a jurisdiction to order (or prohibit) any assessment involving a child's participation and involved providing the court with material necessary to reach a proper decision at the final hearing of the application for a full care order. The judge had adopted a satisfactory course.

14.7.2 Duration of interim orders

Note

The duration of interim care and supervision orders is based upon s 38(4), (5) Ch A 1989. Maximum duration is eight weeks; the length and number of subsequent orders seem uncertain.

Gateshead Borough Council v N (1993)

Interim care orders had been made in relation to two children. It was intended that the orders should elapse seven weeks and four days following the date of the original interim orders. The magistrates would not agree to the making of a further interim order for a period exceeding three days. They supported their decision by stating that it derived from s 38(4) Ch A 1989, under which an interim care order could be made for a maximum period of eight weeks from the date on which the original order had been issued. The local authority appealed.

Held: the appeal of the local authority would be *allowed*. It was clear that a second or subsequent care order would expire four weeks after it was made or eight weeks from the date on which the original order was made, if that was later.

Q Do the threshold criteria set out in s 31(2) Ch A 1989 appear to you to be adequate in the context of the purpose of care and supervision orders?

15 The Guardian Ad Litem; and Wardship

15.1 The basis of the appointment of the guardian ad litem

Note ───────────────────────────────

For the purposes of any specified proceedings, the court shall appoint a guardian ad litem for the child concerned unless satisfied that it is not necessary to do so in order to safeguard his interests: s 41(1) Ch A 1989. The guardian ad litem is under a duty to safeguard the child's interests in the manner prescribed by rules of court: s 41(2)(b). Under the Family Proceedings Rules 1991, r 4.11, the guardian is required, *inter alia*, to appoint a solicitor, give appropriate advice to the child and to instruct the solicitor on matters relevant to the child's interests.

15.1.1 Aspects of the work of the guardian ad litem

R v Pontlottyn Juvenile Court ex p Reeves (1991)

M made application for access to her two sons from whom she had been parted for 13 years. M's solicitors, knowing that the local authority would oppose the application, proposed a pre-trial review, the joining of the sons as parties and the appointment of a guardian ad litem. The solicitors were under the impression that the appointment of a guardian would not be opposed. The magistrates rejected M's application and did not state their reasons. M applied for judicial review.

Held: the proceedings had been *unfair*. Further, the only person able to represent the sons' interests and views, given the local authority's opposition to M's application, was a guardian ad litem. The case for the appointment of a guardian was clear and urgent. An order of certiorari would be made, ordering that the sons be joined as parties and represented by a guardian ad litem.

R v Cornwall County Council (1992)

A letter was sent to all guardians ad litem informing them that no more than 65 hours were to be spent on each child's case. Authorisation would be needed for any excess time. Where a guardian spent more time without authorisation, no extra payments would be made. The Panel of Guardian Ad Litem Reporting Officers requested judicial review.

Held: an order of certiorari *would be made* so as to quash the decision. The director of social services had abused his powers and had sought to interfere with the independence of the guardians in a manner which would have restricted their ability to carry out their duties. *Per* Brown P:

> The role of guardian ad litem is of primary importance in the implementation of the Children Act 1989 ... The position of the guardian has become a matter of greater importance than hitherto. It is vital that the independence of the guardian in carrying out his or her duties should be clearly recognised and understood.

Re S (A Minor) (Independent Representation) (1993) CA

A child had been involved in inconsistent contact and resident order applications made by his parents. He made application to the court to be permitted to represent himself himself without the Official Solicitor acting in the capacity of his guardian ad litem. The child's application was dismissed; the judge decided that the parents should be heard.

Held: the child's appeal would be *dismissed*. The parents had neither an express nor an implied right to be heard, but a judge had the discretion to hear any party where he considered this to be necessary in the interests of justice. The question to be answered was: had the child sufficient understanding to make a wise choice in relation to issues arising concerning its own interests? Where judgment necessitated maturity and understanding, the court would not always accept that the child had a maturity which allowed the guardian ad litem to be dispensed with. *Per* Sir Thomas Bingham:

> The 1989 Act enables and requires a judicious balance to be struck between two considerations. First is the principle, to be honoured and respected, that children are human beings in their own right with individual minds and wills, views and emotions, which should command serious attention. A child's wishes are not to be discounted or dismissed simply because he is a child. He should be free to express them and decision makers should listen. Second, is the fact that a child is, after all, a child. The reason why the law is particularly solicitous in protecting the interests of children is because they are liable to be vulnerable and impressionable, lacking the maturity to weigh the longer term against the shorter, lacking the experience to measure the probable against the possible ... The judge has to do his best, on the evidence before him, to assess the understanding of the individual child in the context of the proceedings in which he seeks to participate.

Re T (A Minor) (Wardship: Representation) (1993) CA

T, aged 13, had been adopted and now wanted to live with her aunt. The solicitor whom she consulted was confident that he could accept T's instructions, and was granted leave to apply for a s 8 residence order. T's adoptive parents then applied for leave to issue proceedings for wardship against T. The judge directed that the Official Solicitor be appointed T's guardian ad litem. T appealed.

Held: T's appeal would be *allowed*. The court had power to appoint a guardian ad litem where circumstances were such as to necessitate protection of the child, but there were no special circumstances in this case which justified exercise of the power.

Re M (Prohibited Steps Order: Application for Leave) (1993)

C, aged 14, had repeatedly run away from home. The local authority obtained an emergency protection order and a guardian ad litem was appointed. The guardian asked for leave to apply for a prohibited steps order. The application was granted; there appeared to be no record of the magistrates' findings and the local authority appealed.

Held: the appeal would be *allowed*. The appointment of a guardian ad litem concerned specific proceedings, and these did not include applications for prohibited steps orders. Further, the magistrates ought to have recorded their findings under the Family Proceedings Court (Children Act 1989) Rules 1991, r 21.

Re F (A Minor) (Care Order: Withdrawal of Application) (1993)

An oral application to withdraw an application for a care order was made by a local authority in the absence from the proceedings of the child's guardian ad litem. The guardian later made it clear that he would have opposed the local authority's application to withdraw. The guardian appealed.

Held: the guardian's appeal would be *allowed*. The withdrawal of care proceedings requires as much and as careful consideration as any other application which might be made under the provisions of the Ch A 1989. The obligation to take into account the child's welfare necessitates, by its nature, a duty to consider expert evidence from the guardian ad litem, prior to the making of a decision to withdraw proceedings. Under the 1991 Rules, r 15, the guardian ad litem must be present in court where an oral request to withdraw proceedings is made.

Re H (A Minor) (Role of Official Solicitor) (1993)

The parents of H, aged 15, made him a ward of court. He was later joined as a party with the Official Solicitor who was acting as the guardian ad litem. A significant problem had arisen concerning the relationship of H with a person who was being tried for sexual offences in relation to another boy. The expert instructed by the Official Solicitor alleged that the relationship between the man on trial and H was of a harmful nature. H made an application to remove the Official Solicitor from the proceedings, claiming that his views were not being made known. He wished to defend himself.

Held: H's application would be *granted*. Whether H had sufficient understanding to take part in proceedings without the assistance of a guardian ad litem had to be examined in the context of all the circumstances in the particular case. Past and future circumstances in relation to H had also to be examined. The court was not obliged in this particular case to consider what might be in the best interests of H. In the circumstances which applied, the Official Solicitor would act as *amicus curiae* and be given the relevant papers and the authority to make whatever applications he thought might be necessary.

Re P (Minors) (Interim Order) (1993) CA

Interim care orders had been made in relation to two girls, aged four and six. The judge at the final hearing accepted that the threshold criteria in s 31 had been met and that it seemed to be in the best interests of the girls to travel with the mother and her new cohabitant to Northern Ireland where they intended to make their permanent home. The guardian ad litem had expressed his wish to continue being involved in the case so as to monitor the situation in relation to the children. The judge gave his approval to the plan to move the children to Northern Ireland, but he refused to make a full care order. An interim care order was made. The local authority appealed.

Held: the local authority's appeal would be *allowed* and a full care order would be made, It was the duty of the court to act as swiftly as was possible in the interests of justice and the welfare of the children. It was a misuse of the court's power to adjourn proceedings to do so (by indicating that a series of interim orders would be made) for the purpose of keeping the guardian ad litem in office. It was not right to seek to effect a policy of granting future interim orders; each order had to be considered in the light of whatever circumstances existed at the time of application.

Re M (Minors) (Care Proceedings: Child's Wishes) (1994)

Care proceedings had been commenced concerning C1, a boy, aged 12, and C2, a girl, aged four. No directions had been sought from the court concerning the separate representation of the guardian ad litem. C1 had expressed the wish to return to his home so that he could stay with C2, but his guardian considered that separation of the children was necessary. Care orders were made after it became clear that C2 had been sexually abused by a member of her family.

Held: the court had a *duty to appoint* a guardian ad litem for C1 unless satisfied that such an appointment was not necessary in order to safeguard C1's interests. Where there appeared to be no conflict between the child and his guardian, a solicitor for the child would be appointed by the guardian under the 1991 Rules, r 4.11(2). Where a child was instructing his solicitor directly and was capable of conducting proceedings on his own behalf, the guardian should inform the court of this fact.

Re J (Adoption: Appointment of Guardian Ad Litem) (1999) CA

M, C's mother, made application for leave to appeal against the decision of a county court judge to appoint G as guardian ad litem, in proceedings to free C for adoption. C was aged eight. M was unsure as to G's suitability for discharging the duties of a guardian ad litem so as to safeguard C's best interests, because G had already participated in a meeting relating to adoption and had appeared to show signs of bias. The county court judge did not consider G to have shown bias, and considered him an appropriate person to act as guardian ad litem. M accepted that the judge could exercise his discretion in relation to such an appointment. M contended, nevertheless, that the practice guidance manual did stress the need for a guardian to demonstrate independence without any previous involvement in the case. M appealed.

Held: M's application would be *dismissed*. The judge had not been in error in the exercise of his discretion. G was unbiased, and his previous knowledge of the case and his familiarity with C were all advantageous in the circumstances.

Re M (Terminating Appointment of Guardian Ad Litem) (1999)

G, guardian ad litem in two cases heard in the Family Proceedings Court, had been the subject of complaints. The appropriate complaints procedure was activated by the Guardian ad litem Panel. Discussions were held with the care judge and it was decided that a new guardian should be appointed and the cases transferred to the county court. G then applied to be reinstated, contending that the correct procedure had not been followed, that the court ought not to terminate her appointment, and that, had the appointment been terminated correctly, she should, nevertheless, be reinstated.

Held: G's application would be *granted*. The correct procedure had not been followed. The appointment of a guardian ad litem could be terminated only if the appropriate procedure were to be followed accurately. The cases had been transferred to the county court at the time the decision was taken and, therefore, G's appointment could be terminated lawfully by the Family Proceedings Court only in accordance with the Family Proceedings Courts (Ch A 1989) Rules 1991, r 14. The complaints procedure had commenced and it was not appropriate for the court to investigate at this stage the complaints against G.

Re A (A Child) (Contact: Separate Representation) (2000) CA

The National Youth Advocacy Service (NYAS) appealed against a decision refusing to appoint it as the guardian ad litem of G, aged four. G was involved in contact proceedings between her parents. NYAS argued that a guardian ad litem ought to be appointed because there had been no proper investigation of allegations of abuse of G by her father, and there was a conflict between the interests of G and those of her parents.

Held: the appeal would be *allowed* in part. The appointment of a guardian ad litem would be in G's best interests, particularly where there was a conflict of interests between the child and parents. But because of prior contact of NYAS with G's parents, and the possibility of this being interpreted as bias, the Official Solicitor, rather than NYAS, would be asked to act as guardian.

15.1.2 The guardian ad litem and disclosure of records and reports

Note

The court may take account of any statement contained in a report made by a guardian ad litem: s 41(11)(a) Ch A 1989. The guardian ad litem has the right to examine records held by a local authority, or an authorised person, compiled in connection with an application concerning a child: s 42(1), as amended by Sched 16, para 18 Courts and Legal Services Act 1990.

Re T (A Minor) (Guardian Ad Litem: Case Record) (1994) CA

C, the child of H and W, was born in 1989. Two years later, W committed suicide. H was unable to care adequately for C. The local authority made application for a care order and interim care orders, which were granted. In pursuance of its plans for the adoption of C, a record concerning one set of prospective adopters was shown to C's guardian ad litem. A second set of adopters was interviewed, and approved. Records concerning the approved adopters were not shown to the guardian ad litem. The judge made a care order, holding that the guardian did not have any right to see the records. The guardian ad litem appealed.

Held: the appeal would be *allowed*. Section 42 Ch A 1989 was clear. It entitled the guardian ad litem to examine and take copies of records held by the local authority which related to a child involved in proceedings such as those which were under way. It was not possible for the guardian ad litem to perform his duties under the 1991 Rules, r 4.11, unless he had access to case records. The right of access to the records prevailed over claims of privilege and confidentiality. The judge had not acted correctly in making a care order in the absence of a report from the guardian ad litem in relation to possible effects on C's interests of C's placement with selected adopters.

Re D (Minors) (Adoption Reports: Confidentiality) (1995) HL

H and W had two children. Following divorce, H remarried and, with his second wife, made an application to adopt the children. W, who opposed the adoption, asked to see a report of the guardian ad litem, under the Adoption Rules 1984, r 53(2), and, in particular, two sections concerning the feelings of the children towards the parents. W's application was refused, and her application to the Court of Appeal was dismissed on the ground that there was a presumption that information contained in the report was confidential, and that the burden rested on the party requesting disclosure to justify the removal of confidentiality. W appealed to the House of Lords.

Held: W's appeal would be *allowed* and the question of disclosure would be remitted to the trial judge. A party is entitled to disclosure of all those materials which require to be considered by the court when taking decisions which may be adverse to the party. Adoption proceedings are of particular significance. The court should consider whether disclosure of material prepared by the guardian ad litem might involve the chance of significant harm to the children. Where the court is satisfied that the interests of the children are such as to warrant non-disclosure, such consideration ought to be weighed against the interest of the parent in being given an opportunity to examine and respond to the material in the report of the guardian ad litem.

Re C (Minors) (Guardian Ad Litem: Disclosure of Report) (1996)

Following the making of care orders in relation to two children, application was made under the 1991 Rules, r 23, for the disclosure of a report prepared by the guardian ad litem to the family centre which was to be responsible for the children's therapeutic treatment. The guardian ad litem did not raise objections to this course of action but requested that disclosure be of a limited nature. The local authority appealed, arguing that, since it was a party to the proceedings, it was entitled to disclose the full contents of the report to its officers.

Held: the appeal would be *dismissed*. Confidentiality of the report of the guardian ad litem was an overriding principle which had to be carefully maintained. The court ought to be told for whom disclosure of the report was requested. The family centre included a number of persons who would be able to peruse the report; some statement as to the identity of those persons was essential.

Oxfordshire County Council v P (1995) CA

M, who had been involved in care proceedings under the 1989 Act, made an admission to the guardian ad litem that she was responsible for the injuries to the child, upon which the proceedings were based. The guardian ad litem reported M's statement to a social worker who informed the police. The guardian ad litem was interviewed by the police. He made a witness statement relating to the admission. Later the Crown Prosecution Service said that it intended to rely on that statement for the purpose of criminal proceedings pending against M. M then made application under the 1991 Rules, r 4.10(9) for the termination of the appointment of the guardian ad litem on the ground that co-operating with him had become impossible in the circumstances which now obtained.

Held: M's application would be *granted*. The confidentiality enjoyed by a guardian ad litem related to information obtained for purposes of the report. The guardian ad litem had been in error in making a witness statement to the police without seeking and obtaining the prior leave of the court.

Re T (Children) (Care Proceedings: Guardian Ad Litem) (2000) CA

Care proceedings had commenced in relation to two children. The children's father, F, was joined as a party and was cross examined by S, a solicitor acting for the guardian ad litem. F became aware that S had acted for him in an unrelated case some years earlier. F then made application for an order that S be not heard. The application was dismissed, and F appealed.

Held: F's appeal would be *dismissed*. S would be removed only if there was a possibility of injustice emerging. S did not remember having represented F in any earlier case, and checks made on records at the office of S's firm indicated no likely conflict of interest or a risk of injustice in this case, in which she was acting for the guardian ad litem.

Re R (A Child) (Care Proceedings: Disclosure) (2000) CA

G, R's guardian ad litem, asked for access to a report made by the Area Child Protection Committee, concerning the events surrounding the death of R's brother and the method of approach to the problems of R's family by the interagency. The local authority would not allow access to the report on the ground that G had no right to examine it. Under s 42(1)(b) the judge ordered the local authority to grant G access to the report. The local authority appealed on the ground that the report ought not to be disclosed as a matter of policy, since it might affect an assessment of the agency's work.

Held: the appeal of the local authority was *dismissed*. It was a record held by a local authority so that G did have a right to read it, under s 42(1)(b). Exercise of G's right must not be taken to mean, however, that sensitive information ought to be disclosed.

15.2 Wardship

Note

Wardship, fundamentally a creature of the common law, involves 'a system whereby any person may, by issuing proceedings for the purpose, make the High Court guardian of any child within its jurisdiction, with the result that no important steps in the child's life can be taken without the court's leave, and the court may make and enforce any order or direction consistent with the principle that the first and paramount consideration is the welfare of the child': *Law Commission* (1987).

15.2.1 Aspects of wardship

Re D (A Minor) (Wardship: Sterilisation) (1976)

C, aged 11 at the time of the hearings, was born with Sotos syndrome, involving epilepsy and severe behavioural problems. The mother and a gynaecologist arranged that C should be sterilised. The educational psychologist involved with C made her a ward of court and applied for an order continuing the wardship so as to delay or prevent the operation on her.

Held: The order would be *granted*. Because C was unable to give an informed consent, the court was able to exercise its protective powers, and because the operation was not medically necessary, and it was quite likely that C would be able to understand its implications when she was older, it would be postponed. *Per* Heilbron J:

> I have first of all to decide whether this is an appropriate case in which to exercise the court's wardship jurisdiction. Wardship is a very special and ancient jurisdiction. Its origin was the Sovereign's feudal obligations as *parens patriae* to protect the person and property of his subjects and particularly those unable to look after themselves, including infants. This obligation, delegated to the Chancellor, passed to the Chancery Court, and in 1970 to this Court. The jurisdiction is very wide, but there are limitations. It is not in every case that it is appropriate to make a child a ward, and counsel for the mother has argued ... that as this case raises a matter of principle of wide public importance ... continuation of wardship would be inappropriate ... The type of operation proposed is one which involves the deprivation of a basic human right, and, therefore, it would, if performed on a woman for non-therapeutic reasons, and without her consent, be a violation of such a right [to reproduce] ... This operation could, if necessary, be delayed or prevented if C were to remain a ward of court ... I think that this is the very type of case where this court should 'throw some care around this child', and I propose to continue her wardship which, in my judgment, is appropriate in this case ... It is quite clear that once a child is a ward of court, no important step in the life of that child can be taken without the consent of the court, and I cannot conceive of a more important step than that which was proposed in this case.

Re D (A Minor) (Justices' Decision: Review) (1977)

In 1972, C, aged three, was committed into the care of the local authority. The magistrates, some four years later, acting on an application by C's parents, discharged the order; directions concerning C's place of residence and supervision were made. The local authority commenced proceedings to make C a ward of court. The question arose as to whether the court should exercise its wardship jurisdiction, notwithstanding that the magistrates had declined to make a care order.

Held: the court *could* exercise its wardship jurisdiction; it was empowered to take into account, as a matter of paramount importance, C's welfare.

Re E (A Minor) (Wardship: Court's Duty) (1984) HL

In 1977, C's mother, W, left him, and in 1982, when C was six, wardship proceedings were commenced by the county council. The council sought an order that C be committed to its care and control, prior to his being adopted. H, C's father, opposed the adoption proposal and asked that care and control of C be committed to him. The judge found in favour of H. The council appealed successfully to the Court of Appeal. H appealed to the House of Lords.

Held: H's appeal would be *allowed*. At no point in the proceedings had consideration been given to a recommendation that a period of access might be granted to H under the welfare officer's supervision, so as to ascertain whether H and C were able to develop an appropriate relationship. The order in favour of the council would be set aside and the matter would be remitted to the judge with directions to implement the recommended course of action.

Lord Scarman reminded the court exercising its wardship jurisdiction that it was exercising a wardship, not an adversarial, jurisdiction. The duty of the court was not limited to the parties' dispute, rather has it the duty to act according to its judgment 'to serve the true interest and welfare of the ward'.

Re JS (A Minor: Boy Soldier) (1990)

J, who was born in 1972, joined the armed forces in 1988. Following the onset of severe medical and psychological problems, he left barracks and returned home without permission of his superior officers. His mother made him a ward of court and applied for care and control.

Held: J was clearly subject to military law and it would, therefore, be *inappropriate* to continue the wardship jurisdiction of the court as it related to him.

Re J (A Minor) (Wardship: Medical Treatment) (1990) CA

J, a ward of court, had been born prematurely and had suffered severe brain damage. The medical staff who were caring for him were questioning whether they ought to reventilate him should his breathing cease. The judge, in the exercise of the court's *parens patriae* jurisdiction, ordered that J should be treated with antibiotics in the circumstances envisaged but that he should not be reventilated if he developed any chest infection, unless his doctors deemed it appropriate. The Official Solicitor appealed.

Held: the appeal would be *dismissed*. *Per* Lord Donaldson:

The court when exercising the *parens patriae* jurisdiction takes over the rights and duties of the parents, although this is not to say that the parents will be excluded from the decision-making process. Nevertheless, in the end, the responsibility for the decision whether to give or withhold consent is that of the court alone. It follows from this that a child who is a ward of court should be treated medically in exactly the same way as one who is not, the only difference being that the doctors will be looking to the court rather than to the parents for any necessary consents. No one can dictate the treatment to be given to J, neither court, parents nor doctors. These are the checks and balances ... Choice of treatment is in some measure a joint decision of the doctors and the court or parents ...

Per Taylor LJ:

I consider that the correct approach is for the court to judge the quality of life J will have to endure if given the treatment and decide whether in all the circumstances such a life would be so afflicted as to be intolerable to that child. I say 'to that child' because the test must not be whether the life would be tolerable to the decider. The test must be whether the child in question, if capable of exercising sound judgment, would consider the life tolerable. The circumstances to be considered would, in appropriate cases, include the degree of existing disability and any additional suffering or aggravation of the disability which the treatment itself would superimpose ... To add distress and the risk of further deterioration to an already appaling catalogue of disabilities is clearly capable in my judgment of producing a quality of life which justified the doctors' stance and the judge's decision ... This appeal should be dismissed.

Re A (A Minor) (Wardship: Criminal Proceedings) (1990)

A, a ward, had admitted committing a number of offences. A decision was taken to administer a caution rather than prosecute him. The Official Solicitor in his capacity as guardian ad litem asked for directions as to who ought to consent to such a caution.

Held: the decision to caution A was a matter of significance for him and, therefore, the decision to consent to a caution ought *not* to be taken without the consent of the wardship court since it had the ultimate parental responsibility in relation to A. Consent to the caution ought to have been sought when the police interviewed the ward or as soon as possible after that event.

Re J (A Minor) (Wardship: Medical Treatment) (1992) CA

J was aged 16 months. He was microcephalic, blind and severely epileptic. Medical opinion was unanimous in advising that he could well deteriorate and that his expectation of life, although uncertain, must be short. The local authority were granted leave under s 100 Ch A 1989 to invoke the inherent wardship jurisdiction of the High Court so as to determine whether artificial ventilation and/or life-saving measures should be given to J if he suffered a life-threatening event. The judge had ruled that, pending a further hearing, the *status quo* should be observed. The local authority appealed.

Held: the authority's appeal would be *allowed*. *Per* Lord Donaldson:

The fundamental issue in this appeal is whether the court in the exercise of its inherent power to protect the interests of minors should ever require a medical practitioner or health authority to adopt a course of treatment which in the *bona fide* clinical judgment of the practitioner concerned is indicated as not being in the best interests of the patient. I have to say that I cannot conceive of any circumstances in which this would be other than an abuse of power as directly or indirectly requiring the practitioner to act contrary to the fundamental duty which he owes to his patient. This, subject to obtaining any necessary consent, is to treat the patient in accordance with his own best clinical judgment, notwithstanding that other practitioners who are not called upon to treat the patient may have formed a quite different judgment or that the court, acting on expert evidence, may not agree with him ... I have no doubt that all the doctors concerned [in this case] would agree that situations can change, and that if and when a decision whether or not to use mechanical ventilation has to be taken, it must be taken in the light of the situation as it then exists. This is what clinical judgment is all about ... So long as those with parental responsibilities consent to J being treated by the health authority's medical staff, he must be treated in accordance with their clinical judgment.

Re R (A Minor) (Wardship: Restrictions on Publication) (1994) CA

H took away R from W, to whom care and custody had been granted in wardship proceedings. Later H was arrested and committed for trial on a charge of having abducted R. During the wardship proceedings an order had been made which acted so as to restrain publication of any material involving R. H made application for a removal of the order so as to make possible the publication of reports concerning his trial. The judge decided that publicity in these circumstances would have a negative effect on the welfare of the ward, and, further, that any order made by the trial judge would be unlikely to afford the measure of protection resulting from an order emerging from wardship proceedings. An order was issued forbidding publication of material relating to R. H appealed.

Held: H's appeal would be *allowed*. Reports of criminal trials should be restrained only in the interests of the administration of justice. The trial judge was entitled to decide whether it was necessary in the circumstances to restrict in any way reports of H's trial.

Re W (Wardship: Discharge: Publicity) (1995) CA

An application by H for the discharge of the wardship of his four sons and against an order which prevented him and the sons from providing the media with information concerning the proceedings, was dismissed. The sons had criticised the Official Solicitor in an article in a newspaper. The care and control of the sons was with H; they did not wish to have any contact with their mother, W, who had been granted an injunction prohibiting H from using his house as a refuge for men at a time when the sons were living there. The sons applied for the termination of the appointment of the Official Solicitor; this was dismissed.

Held: the appeal concerning wardship would be *dismissed*. The protection of the sons resulting from a continuation of the wardship was of a better quality than that which would result from the use of Ch A 1989. The Official Solicitor would continue to be involved in the situation. The appeal concerning publicity was allowed in part and the restraint order would be altered so as to prevent identification of the sons. Public interest, however, did not necessitate publicising of the family's identity.

Re K (A Child) (2000)

K left his grandmother's care and joined a religious cult. He was made a ward of court on his grandmother's application, the Official Solicitor being appointed as the guardian ad litem. Media representatives gave publicity to the case, and K recorded an interview with the BBC. K's grandmother, fearing that he would cease contact with her, obtained an injunction preventing the BBC broadcasting the interview. The BBC applied for a discharge of the injunction, while K's grandmother contended that such an interview was 'an important step' in K's life which ought not to have taken place without leave of the court. Since the BBC knew that K was a ward of court, the interview constituted a contempt of court.

Held: the argument that the BBC required leave of the court before broadcasting the interview with K was *rejected*. The 'important step' in K's life was his leaving home and joining the cult, not giving an interview to the BBC, so that there was no case for injunctive relief. Munby J stated that no major step in the life of a ward should be taken without the court's prior consent, and to undertake or facilitate such a step without the court's consent was a contempt. So long as the media took care to avoid any breach of the restraints imposed by s 12 Administration of Justice Act 1960 and s 97(2) Ch A 1989, no contempt was committed by a media interview of a ward of court. Publication of information concerning a ward, even if he was known to be a ward, was not, of itself, and without more ado, a contempt of court.

Re T (A Minor) (Wardship: Medical Treatment) (1996) CA

T was born in April 1995 suffering from biliary atresia, a life-threatening liver defect. He could not live beyond the age of two and a half without a liver transplant. Medical opinion suggested unanimously that the chances of a successful transplant were good and that it would be in T's best interests to undergo the operation. The parents, both health care professionals, who were living abroad, did not wish the operation to be performed on T. The judge had said that he understood the mother's refusal to give consent, but he was of the opinion that her refusal to accept the doctors' unanimous advice was not the conduct of a reasonable parent. The judge directed that the mother present T at a hospital for assessment for transplant surgery. The mother appealed.

Held: the mother's appeal would be *allowed*. Butler-Sloss LJ said that a long line of cases from 1981 indicated that when an application under the inherent jurisdiction was made to the court, the welfare of the child was the paramount consideration. The parents' consent or refusal of consent was an important consideration to weigh in the balancing exercise to be carried out. But the court could overrule the decision of a reasonable parent. In this case the judge had erred. He had accepted the medical opinion and assessed the reasonableness of the mother's decision against it. He did not weigh in the balance reasons against the treatment which might be held by a reasonable parent on much broader grounds than the clinical assessment of the likely success of the proposed treatment. The mother had concentrated on T's present peaceful life without the pain and upset of intrusive surgery. It was doubtful whether the judge was correct in deeming the mother to be unreasonable in her assessment of the broader perspective of whether the transplant ought to be performed.

The child's welfare was the paramount consideration and it was necessary to recognise the very strong presumption in favour of a course of action which would prolong life and the inevitable consequences for T of consent not being given. To prolong life was not the sole objective of the court and to require it at the expense of other considerations might not be in the best interests of the child. The effect of the evidence of one of the doctors concerning the mother's decision and the prospect of forcing the mother to accept the prospect of invasive surgery had resulted in the conclusion that it was not in T's best interests to give consent and require him to be brought back to England for purposes of a transplant. T's best interests required that his future treatment be left in the hands of his parents.

15.2.2 Minors within the jurisdiction can be made wards

Re F (In Utero) (1988) CA

A mentally disturbed woman who was disposed to drug abuse became pregnant. The local authority made an application *ex parte* for leave to ward her unborn child. The local authority appealed after the application had been dismissed.

Held: the appeal of the local authority would be *dismissed*. A foetus had no right of action and could not be a party to the proposed action. *Per* May LJ:

> I have considerable sympathy with the local authority in their position on the facts of the instant case, but I am driven to the conclusion that the judge was right and that the court has no jurisdiction to ward an unborn child. If the courts are to have this jurisdiction in a sensitive situation such as the present, I think that this is a matter for Parliament and not for the courts themselves. I do not think that even if the courts were minded to extend the jurisdiction in this type of case, they could in law or in practice limit this, as counsel suggested, to children having a gestation period of not less than 28 weeks.

Re BM (A Minor) (Wardship: Jurisdiction) (1993)

F, the British father, and M, the German mother, of a child, C, were unmarried. Following the end of their relationship, F applied for parental responsibility and contact. M went to Germany with C, and F commenced proceedings relating to wardship. The court made a seek and search order which was served on M. She failed to return to England and F issued a summons under the Hague Convention, Art 3, asking for a declaration that the action of keeping C in Germany was wrongful.

Held: because F did not have parental responsibility, M was C's sole custodian until wardship proceedings were begun. The English court possessed jurisdiction in wardship in these circumstances if C was either in England or M and C were habitually resident in England at the date of the wardship order. It was clear that M had not changed her habitual residence in England by the date of the wardship order. Because the custody of the child was vested in the court from the date of the wardship order, M was guilty of wrongful retention of C after service of the order.

15.2.3 In general, any person, including the child himself, can apply to make a child a ward of court

Re AD (A Minor) (1993)

Following the breakdown of her parents' marriage, a child, aged 14, left home to live with a friend's parents. The child then made application under s 8 Ch A 1989 and the matter was sent to the High Court. The child's mother commenced wardship proceedings and the Official Solicitor was appointed as the child's guardian ad litem.

Held: the child would *remain* a ward of court and the Official Solicitor would remain as her guardian ad litem.

15.3 Inherent jurisdiction of the High Court

Note

No court shall exercise the High Court's inherent jurisdiction with respect to children, so as to require a child to be placed in the care, or put under the supervision, of a local authority, or so as to make a child who is the subject of a care order a ward of court: s 100(2)(a)(c) Ch A 1989.

Re O (A Minor) (Medical Treatment) (1993)

A child, born prematurely, suffered from respiratory distress syndrome. The doctor attending her considered that a blood transfusion might be necessary. The parents, because of religious beliefs, refused to give their consent. An emergency protection order was made by the court. It was a matter of urgency to establish whether the court should act so as to override the declared objections of the parents, and what legal steps were needed to allow the court to make its decision.

Held: it was the duty of the court to issue appropriate directions to ensure that the child *would* receive blood transfusions in accordance with medical advice. The order which would authorise the medical treatment would be made under the inherent jurisdiction of the court rather than under Ch A 1989.

Devon County Council v S (1995)

X was married to M, the mother of nine children. X had a record of sexual offences but M did not consider him as a threat to her children. The local authority viewed X as a risk because of his paedophilic tendencies, and took the decision to make application in wardship proceedings for leave to invoke the court's inherent jurisdiction. The district judge rejected the application, holding that there was no jurisdiction to do this, and, in any event, the local authority could commence care proceedings in relation to M's children. The local authority appealed.

Held: the local authority's appeal would be *allowed*: s 100 Ch A 1989 had no application in this case because the local authority were not seeking protective powers, merely asking the court to consider the exercise of powers of that kind. *Per* Thorpe J:

> Any member of the family or any other with a sufficient standing might apply to the court to exercise its inherent power to protect these children. Where no one else invokes that protection, it seems to me quite wrong that the local authority should be excluded from doing so by a restrictive construction of s 100.

A care order might be less than helpful because it would interfere with M's parental role. There was good reason to believe that if the court's powers were not exercised, the children might suffer harm. Leave to request the exercise of the court's inherent jurisdiction would, therefore, be granted.

Q How might the office of guardian ad litem be extended in its scope in the interests of children?

16 Adoption

16.1 Essence of adoption

Note ————————————————————————————————————

Adoption involves the termination of a child's legal rights and duties in relation to his natural parents and the substitution of similar rights and duties in relation to his adoptive parents. The law concerning adoption is consolidated in the Adoption Act 1976, together with amendments of the Ch A 1989.

16.1.1 Who may apply for an adoption order and who may be adopted

Note ————————————————————————————————————

Schedule 10, para 4 Ch A 1989 allows adoption in some cases where one of the adopting spouses is at least 18. In the case of a joint application, it must be made by a married couple: s 14(1) AA 1976. A single person aged 21 or over may adopt if the requirements concerning domicile are satisfied: s 15(1) AA 1976. Children under 18 who are not and have not been married can be adopted: ss 12(5), 72(1) AA 1976.

R v Secretary of State for Health ex p Luff (1991)

H and W, aged 53 and 57 respectively, had visited Romania and wished to adopt two very young children seen by them in orphanages there. The Home Secretary examined the question of the children's adoption, taking into account H's poor health and a recent coronary bypass operation. The Department of Health considered the requirements of s 6 AA 1976, which demand, *inter alia*, that first consideration be given to the need to safeguard and promote the welfare of the child throughout his childhood. The Department of Health advised that H was not a suitable person to make application for adoption of the children. The Home Office refused admission to the children and H asked for judicial review. H argued that the Department of Health had given too much weight to his life expectancy and that the decision was irrational, given the urgency of the children's position in Romania.

Held: H's application would be *dismissed*. H's life expectancy was one factor among others which were taken into account. The decision of the Secretary for Health was rational in that the stability which would be essential for children with a disturbed background would be disrupted by the possibility of H's death during their teenage years.

Re KT (A Minor) (Adoption) (1993)

M, the mother of the child, C, was unable to provide appropriate care for him. C had been brought to England by his grandparents. C's aunt, A, lived with C's grandparents and made application to adopt him. Following her leaving the grandparents' house, A continued to visit C during the week; at weekends C stayed with A. A made the principal decisions relating to C's upbringing. Section 13(1) AA 1976 prohibits the making of an adoption order unless the child concerned has had his home with the applicant at all times during the preceding 13 weeks.

Held: M's agreement to C's adoption would be *dispensed with*. An adoption order *would be made*. For purposes of s 13 it would be assumed that C had resided with A and that he had done so for a considerable period of time. C's situation was analogous to that which would have obtained had he attended a boarding school for most of the week.

Re B (A Minor) (Adoption Order: Nationality) (1999) HL

B, aged 14, came to the UK from Jamaica in 1995 with her mother. She had been given leave to enter for six months and when her mother returned to Jamaica she remained with her grandparents. An extension of leave was refused and the grandparents decided to adopt her in order for her to obtain British citizenship, with a right of abode, to allow her to finish her schooling. In spite of the opposition of the Secretary of State, an adoption order was made, but was discharged by the Court of Appeal which held that the judge was in error in concentrating on the benefits of achieving British citizenship as part of the welfare consideration in s 6 AA 1976. The grandparents appealed.

Held: the appeal would be *allowed*. In considering the requirement of s 6 that first consideration be given to the need to safeguard and promote the welfare of the child throughout his childhood, the court ought not to ignore the benefits likely to accrue to B following an adoption order. The concern of the Secretary of State relating to principles of immigration policy did not justify in itself the refusal to make an order, and the judge who made the order had given these benefits first consideration.

Re C (A Minor) (Adoption: Illegality) (1999)

X wished to adopt C, a Guatemalan child, and commissioned a study report prepared by an independent social worker. X was separated, had no children and had been rejected as a suitable adopter on two occasions because of her health and because it was felt that she was unsure as to the essence of adoption in the UK. Guatemalan lawyers had helped her to make application to adopt C.

Held: it *was appropriate* to grant an adoption order in X's favour. The commissioning of a study report was the making of an arrangement for facilitating C's adoption within s 72(3) AA 1976. Payments to the report's author and Guatemalan lawyers constituted breaches of law under ss 11, 57 AA 1976; X had committed criminal offences. Although this was to be taken into account by the court it did not constitute an absolute bar to the granting of an adoption order. The lawyers involved supported X's application as being in C's best interests, a matter which would be taken into account when the court exercised its discretion.

B v P (Adoption by Unmarried Father) (2000)

B made application to adopt his child, C. B and P, parents of C, separated after a short period of cohabitation, and B was unaware of P's pregnancy. Following C's birth in October 1998, C was put up for adoption. B learned of this and was assessed as a suitable carer for C, who was placed with him in December 1998. He then applied for an adoption order, but this was opposed by the Official Solicitor who contended that the welfare requirements of C would be satisfied by granting a residence order to B, thus restricting P's exercising parental responsibility.

Held: B's application was *allowed*. P had continued to reject C and had declared that she was uninterested in C's upbringing and would agree to B's adopting C. The adoption order would be made under s 15(3) AA 1976.

Re AMR (Adoption: Procedure) (2000)

A was brought up in Poland by X, her great grandmother. X was appointed A's guardian by an order which removed parental authority from N1 and N2, A's natural parents. A came to England with X and was placed in the care of her great aunt, Y. Y later applied to adopt A. The court was asked to decide whether consent was needed from N1 and N2, or X. It became necessary to decide whether the Polish order giving guardianship to X, and depriving N1 and N2 of parental authority, ought to be recognised under English law.

Held: the consent of N1 and N2 was *not required*, but that of X *was*. The Polish concept of parental authority was broadly similar to that in English law, so that it was appropriate and in accordance with the doctrine of comity for the Polish order to be recognised. N1 and N2 were no longer 'parents', for purposes of AA 1976; hence, their consent was not required.

Re N (A Minor) (Adoption: Foreign Guardianship) (2000)

N, a Romanian boy, aged 12 at the time of the hearing, had been abandoned by his mother at birth and was placed in an orphanage in Bucharest. A, the applicant, an unmarried English woman, had worked in the orphanage, and decided in 1994 that she wished to adopt N. The Bucharest court made a declaration of abandonment, transferring parental rights to the orphanage, and N's mother signed a declaration giving consent under Romanian law to A. A and N moved later to England.

Held: the Bucharest orphanage was capable of constituting a guardian within the meaning of s 16 AA 1976, and was, therefore, capable of approving of, and consenting to, N's adoption by A. The court was satisfied that it would be in N's best interests *to make the adoption order*.

Re H (A Child) (Adoption Disclosure) (2001)

Local authorities made an application for guidance concerning notification of proceedings to the natural fathers of the children, H and G. The unmarried mothers of the children had commenced adoption proceedings, but both refused to disclose the identities of the fathers of the children (who had been placed by the mothers for adoption at birth).

Held: directions were *granted*. Neither father had a parental responsibility order, and neither had a right to consent or withhold consent to the adoptions, nor had they a right to notice under the Adoption Rules 1984. Notice was not normally given to the natural father; but the court took into account Sched 1, Part 1, Arts 6, 8 Human Rights Act 1998. H was a part of a family unit with his father, so that an absence of notice would breach rights under Arts 6, 8. H's mother would therefore be asked to disclose the father's identity to the local authority voluntarily. No similar tie existed in the case of G, and it was not necessary that G's father be given notice.

16.1.2 Aspects of adoption: the welfare principle; conditions

Re Adoption Application (Non-Patrial: Breach of Procedures) (1993)

W was able to obtain possession of a small child during a visit to El Salvador. The child was brought to England so that W and her husband, H, could make arrangements to adopt him. Proceedings were commenced under the AA 1976. The question emerged as to whether H and W had acted in breach of the AA and, if they had, whether the breach might be set aside.

Held: the court did *not* possess the power to waive any breaches of the Act. W's action in handing the child to H so that he could be adopted, constituted a placing of the child for adoption contrary to the provisions of the Act. However, a breach of this nature was not necessarily a bar to the making of an adoption order. On balance, in the particular circumstances of the case, the child's welfare ought to take precedence over the parents' having acted in breach of the Act.

Re U (A Minor) (1993) CA

C's grandparents wished to adopt her and the local authority made application for a freeing order. The local authority's adoption panel had rejected the grandparents' application to be approved as adoptive parents. The local authority's application for a freeing order was dismissed; a residence order was made under Ch A 1989, s 10(1). The local authority appealed, arguing that the judge had no power to use a two-stage approach. If, according to the adoption agency, adoption was in the child's best interests, the judge ought to have made an adoption order after noting that the matters set out in AA 1976, s 18(1)(a)(b), were satisfied.

Held: the local authority's appeal would be *dismissed*. The primary concern of the adoption agency and the court was the child's welfare. Only where the court decided that the child's welfare would be furthered by adoption would the next stage, which involved considering whether parental consent could be dispensed with, be examined. There were no different tests for applications for freeing and for adoption.

Re S (A Minor) (Adoption Order: Conditions) (1995) CA

H and W, who were active Jehovah's Witnesses, wished to adopt S. The judge raised the matter of the possibility of H and W withholding their consent to blood transfusions for S, should he become ill. A condition was imposed on the adoption order, requiring H and W to give an undertaking not to withhold consent without making application to the court. H and W appealed.

Held: the appeal of H and W would be *allowed*. Conditions attached to adoption orders ought not to be imposed against the adoptive parents' wishes, particularly where they could result in breaking their relationship with the adopted child.

Re G (Adoption: Illegal Placement) (1995) CA

The child, G, had been placed for adoption in circumstances which breached AA 1976, s 11. Following an application to adopt, made to the county court, the judge decided against transferring the case to the High Court. The guardian ad litem appealed.

Held: the guardian's appeal would be *allowed*. It was not possible for any court to authorise retrospectively a placement which breached the provisions of s 11. But there was no bar to the High Court authorising a placement which otherwise would be in breach of s 11. Transfer of the case to the High Court was essential.

Re B (A Minor) (Adoption Application) (1995)

C was a child born in the Gambia to Gambian parents. She was brought to Britain to spend an extended holiday with potential adopters, and a guardian ad litem was appointed. Agreements signed by the parents suggested that they might not have understood the significance and implications of the term 'adoption', which differed markedly from the Gambian concept of adoption. The question of the future of C was transferred to the High Court.

Held: C's welfare was the first consideration; but the court had to look at matters other than those directly related to welfare, such as the legal status of adoption in the Gambia and immigration status. It appeared that the parents had not intended that C be adopted, in the sense of that term as used in English law. C's welfare required that *she return to the Gambia* in spite of the emotional links made with the prospective adopters with whom she had spent almost 18 months.

16.2 Consent to adoption order

Note ──────────────────────────────────

The court will not make an adoption order unless the child is free for adoption, under 18, or, in the case of each parent or guardian, the court is satisfied that he freely, and with full understanding of the matters involved, agrees unconditionally to the making of an adoption order or his agreement has been dispensed with on a ground set out in s 16(2).

16.2.1 Parent or guardian cannot be found or is incapable of giving agreement (s 16(2)(a))

Re R (Adoption) (1967)
The natural parents of a child were living in a country which was governed by an oppressive totalitarian regime. Efforts to locate them had been extensive but had failed.

Held: the agreement of the parents would be *dispensed with*. There was no practical method of contacting the parents because of insuperable difficulties of communication. Further, it was obvious that they could not give consent to a proposal of which they were in total ignorance.

Re F (An Infant) (1970) CA
Some steps had been taken so as discover the natural mother prior to the making of an order for adoption. The search had been unsuccessful.

Held: it had to be shown that, in the search for the mother, *all reasonable and proper steps* had been taken. In this case, however, all such steps had not been taken. Thus, in the search for the natural mother, the applicants had not been in touch with the father, with whom the mother remained in sporadic contact.

16.2.2 Agreement has been withheld unreasonably (s 16(2)(b))

Re C (An Infant) (1964) CA
C, an illegitimate child, was put into care and later placed with a view to adoption. The mother, after giving consent, withdrew it, wishing to find a foster mother for C. Medical evidence suggested that that C could suffer adversely if separated from the prospective adopters who had very good relations with her.

Held: adoption would be *granted*. The mother's consent was being withheld unreasonably, particularly in view of C's uncertain future with her. *Per* Pearson LJ:

> We are not concerned in cases of this kind, where the question is simply whether the mother's consent is being unreasonably withheld, with, in itself, the question as to which course would be in the child's best interests. It is not enough to show – indeed it is not strictly a relevant consideration by itself – that, in the child's interests, it would be better that the child should remain with foster parents or that the child should be taken by the mother. What is relevant is the mother's attitude to questions concerning the child's welfare. Counsel for the applicants has pointed out that there are two aspects to this case. The judge in the first instance has decided primarily that the mother unreasonably withheld her consent, having regard to the medical evidence, which she had an opportunity of seeing and considering, and, indeed, did see and consider. The second aspect raises the question whether the mother's attitude of withholding consent was reasonable in relation to the arrangements, or lack of them, which had been made for the child's future in the event of the child's being returned to her.

Re B (1967)

H, who was Spanish, and W, who was English, were married in 1959. C1 was born in 1960 and, in 1961, W left H and returned to England where C2 was born. W arranged for C2 to be placed with prospective adopters when she was one week old. C2 had remained with the prospective adopters for several years. H had provided no financial assistance. The prospective adopters applied for an adoption order and asked to dispense with H's consent.

Held: H's consent *would* be dispensed with and an adoption order would be made. *Per* Goff J:

> H has not paid or offered to pay anything towards C2's maintenance. He has not made any enquiry as to her whereabouts or how she is being looked after and brought up. He has not sought access or sought to bring C1 and C2 together ... It is all symptomatic of complete neglect ... I suggested in argument that it was fair to say that H had washed his hands of C2 and I still think that is the only inference.

Re W (An Infant) (1971) HL

M gave birth to C, an illegitimate son who was taken into care and had been since that time with foster parents with whom he had settled well. M gave consent to C's adoption but later withdrew and asked to take care of C. Evidence indicated that M lived in an unstable style. If C were returned to her there were real doubts as to whether she would be able to cope with the tasks involved. The county court judge decided that M was withholding her consent unreasonably and made the order. M's appeal to the Court of Appeal was upheld. The applicants appealed to the House of Lords.

Held: the applicants' appeal would be *allowed*. *Per* Lord Hailsham:

The test is reasonableness and nothing else. It is not culpability. It is not indifference. It is not failure to discharge parental duties. It is reasonableness, and reasonableness in the context of the totality of circumstances. But though welfare *per se* is not the test, the fact that a reasonable parent does pay regard to his child's welfare must enter into the question of reasonableness as a relevant factor. It is relevant in all cases if and to the extent that a reasonable parent would take it into account. It is decisive in those cases where a reasonable parent must so regard it ... The question in any given case is whether a parental veto comes within the band of possible reasonable decisions and not whether it is right or mistaken. Not every reasonable exercise of judgment is right, and not every mistaken exercise of judgment is unreasonable. There is a band of decisions within which no court should seek to replace the individual's judgment with his own.

Re V (A Minor) (Adoption: Consent) (1986) CA

H and W had one child, C, whom W took to live with the applicants when she left H. She later left C with the applicants and went to live with her second husband. When she left the second husband she asked for the return of C, but this was refused by the applicants who then made application for the adoption of C. W refused to give consent, stating that she hoped to be reunited eventually with C. An adoption order was made dispensing with W's consent, but making provision for regular access by W. W appealed.

Held: W's appeal would be *allowed*. On the facts of the case, the judge was in error in dispensing with W's consent, Further, the access order would act so as to strengthen C's bond with W, and this would contradict the purpose of the adoption order.

Re B (A Minor) (Adoption: Parental Agreement) (1990) CA

Care orders were made in relation to C1 and C2 following general neglect by the mother, M. C1 and C2 were placed with foster parents and access was granted to M. C1 settled down, but C2 was disruptive and unsettled.The foster parents sought to adopt C1. M refused to give consent although the judge found that adoption would be in the best interests of C1. He was unable to say that M's refusal was outside the band of parental decisions. The foster parents appealed.

Held: the foster parents' appeal would be *allowed*. *Per* Butler Sloss LJ:

In refusing the adoption the judge referred to the possible effect of a Pyrrhic victory and the possibility that it might bring about the cessation of the very contact that M was wishing to have. He does not, however, appear to have considered that aspect of the problem within the situation of the mother and her refusal to consent. At the age of this child, his view of being in touch with his mother with or without an adoption would carry a great deal of weight with these appellants and with any court who might in future consider whether access should be granted. M's position for herself and her child in respect of contact with the other child is more likely to be secure with adoption than in a situation where the adoption was refused ... In my judgment the judge misdirected himself in putting [M's grievance] into the balance. There can, in my view, only be rare instances when a sense of grievance can justifiably have an important effect and I find it difficult to envisage when that could occur.

Re D (A Minor) (Adoption: Freeing Order) (1991) CA

The freeing for adoption of C, a child in their care, was the basis of an application made by the local authority; the application was opposed by the mother. According to the judge, two questions had to be answered: was adoption in C's best interests, and was the mother's consent being unreasonably withheld? It mattered not whether the questions were considered together or separately. The application was dismissed and the local authority appealed.

Held: the appeal of the local authority would be *allowed*. In the case of an opposed application it was necessary to consider first the question of the child's welfare. That should be considered *separately* from the question of whether the mother was unreasonably withholding her consent. The judge had been in error. The mother's consent would be dispensed with and C would be freed for adoption.

Re EH and MH (Step-Parent Adoption) (1993)

M and W were married in 1975. Their two daughters were aged 12 and 15 at the time of the proceedings. In 1980 H and W separated soon after the second child was born. In 1982 W remarried. H had very little contact with the children after 1986. W and her second husband wished to adopt the children but H withheld his consent.

Held: the adoption order would be *granted*. There appeared to be no precedent concerning the dispensing with parental agreement in circumstances in which a step-parent adoption was under consideration. It was necessary for the court, therefore, to have recourse to the principles used to dispense with consent in other cases. Clearly, the children felt that H was no part of their lives. Given those views it would seem that H's withholding of consent was not within the group of decisions which a reasonable parent might be expected to make in these circumstances. H's consent would be dispensed with.

Re CD (A Minor) (1996) CA

An adoption order was made in relation to M's daughter, C, aged nine, allowing C to be adopted by C's father and his wife. The court dispensed with M's consent which it considered to have been unreasonably withheld. M was allowed restricted contact with C. M appealed, contending that her withholding of consent was reasonable since she had consented to a residence order, and the general advantages of adoption over residence were minimal.

Held: M's appeal would be *dismissed*. Given the facts, the judge was entitled, within the exercise of his discretion, to conclude that the welfare of C *did* necessitate the making of an adoption order, and that a reasonable mother would have put her child's welfare before her own considerations and would have given her consent to the adoption.

Re AB (A Minor) (Adoption: Unmarried Couple) (1996)

C, a child, in the care of the local authority, lived with foster parents who wished to adopt him. Only the foster father could apply for an adoption order, since he and the foster mother were unmarried. Both foster parents applied for a joint residence order, which would allow the foster mother to obtain parental responsibility. C's mother, M, did not oppose the joint residence order. She wanted C to continue living with the foster parents, but she withheld consent from the adoption order.

Held: evidence showed clearly that C had made excellent progress in his foster parents' home and that they were able to meet his needs adequately. He had stated clearly that he wished to stay with them. In these circumstances, C's welfare necessitated that M be displaced so far as C was concerned. M's consent would be *dispensed with* as it was being withheld unreasonably.

Re O (A Minor) (Adoption: Withholding Agreement) (1999) CA

F, S's father, was not aware of the existence of S until he learned about impending adoption proceedings. At that time S was 18 months old, and had flourished and was establishing bonds with the proposed adopters, A, and their other adopted child. F, who was living in a stable relationship, wanted to look after S and opposed the adoption. S's mother supported the adoption. An adoption order was made by the judge, who found F's withholding of consent to be unreasonable. F was granted a parental responsibility order and an order for yearly contact with S. F appealed; A cross appealed the parental responsibility order.

Held: appeal and cross appeal were *dismissed*. The judge was correct in concluding that, given S's bonding with A, it was right that he should live with them, in his best interests; that an adoption order was necessary to ensure S's continuing stability; and that F was acting unreasonably, since a reasonable individual would have given priority to S's welfare and would have understood the significance of stability in S's life.

Re A (A Child) (Adoption of a Russian Child) (2000)

A, born in Russia, was placed in a children's home by her mother, M, two days after her birth, and she was then put up for adoption. E, an English couple who were involved in commerce in Russia, adopted A one year later, following an adoption order from the Russian court. M knew of the hearing but did not attend. The Russian order was not recognised in the English courts and E needed to obtain an adoption order in England. A's guardian ad litem noted that M had given her consent to A's adoption within a period of six weeks following A's birth, and this was contrary to s 16(4) AA 1976. The Russian court stated that any attempt to make contact with M might lead to E's becoming involved in proceedings concerning an allegation that E had violated M's right to confidentiality. E applied for M's consent to be dispensed with.

Held: the application was *granted* and an adoption order issued. The court was obliged to consider the practicality of steps proposed to obtain M's consent. In the circumstances it would not be reasonable to expect that consent to be sought. An adoption order was appropriate, given the bonds which had developed between E and S.

Re B-M (A Child) (Adoption: Parental Agreement) (2001) CA

The biological parents of C, aged 12, made an appeal against an order dispensing with their consent to C's adoption, and against an adoption order made in M's favour, M having fostered C for 10 years. The parents contended that they had been reasonable in withholding consent because an adoption order would have removed the fundamentals of the legal relationship existing between C and her mother, who was intending to emigrate to the USA, and would remove from the mother the opportunity of introducing C into the new jurisdiction as her natural daughter. Further, she argued, the judge was in error when considering whether the mother's consent had been unreasonably refused.

Held: the mother's appeal would be *dismissed*. The child's immediate need for a measure of security certainly outweighed a hypothetical restriction on her ability to reside in the future in the USA with her parents, and the court had been correct in concluding that considerations of C's welfare were sufficiently significant so as to override the withholding of consent by the parents.

16.2.3 Persistent failure to discharge parental duties, abandonment or neglect of child, persistent ill-treatment of child (s 16(2)(c), (d))

Watson v Nicolaisen (1955)

M had given her illegitimate daughter to foster parents. The child showed considerable confidence in the foster parents and they wished to adopt her. During the period in which the child was with the foster parents, M had made no financial contribution to the child's support. She had visited the child on one occasion only. The question was whether, for the purposes of adoption and consent, M had abandoned the child.

Held: M had *not* abandoned the child. She did genuinely desire that the child should remain with her. *Per* Lord Goddard:

> Unless and until an adoption order was made, and it never was, [M] had not only not parted with with all her rights in the child, but had certainly not divested herself of her responsibility towards the child. She may have thought that she had rid herself both of the child and all her responsibilities to that child, but in that she was mistaken ... In my opinion, therefore, the justices were right in coming to the conclusion that [M] had never abandoned her child before the case came before them.

Re P (Infants) (1962)

M parted with each of her two children a few weeks after each was born. She never had either of them to stay with her and made few enquiries as to their progress. Travelling to see them would have been an easy matter but M apparently preferred not to visit them. The natural and moral obligations of a parent were held by the court not to have been carried out by M. The financial obligations on M were disregarded by her almost completely. In these circumstances the court's discretion would be exercised so as to *dispense* with M's consent to an adoption order.

16.3 Freeing for adoption

Note ──

The 'freeing for adoption' procedure involves the court in making an order declaring that a child is free to be adopted, where the court is satisfied that the parent or guardian has understood freely and fully the making of an adoption order, save where his consent has been dispensed with: s 18(1).

Re C (Minors) (Adoption: Residence Order) (1993) CA

The court had made an order in relation to C's children which freed them for adoption. The father, F, was convicted of rape and brought an action in relation to a residence order for the children under Ch A 1989. A trial of the preliminary issue was ordered by the judge, to consider whether a parent whose children are the subject of an order which has been made freeing them for adoption may request a residence order. It was held that F would require the leave of the court, under Ch A 1989, s 10(2)(b)) if he wished to make such an application. F appealed.

Held: F's appeal would be *dismissed*. Where children have been freed for adoption in accordance with AA 1976, their natural parent loses parental responsibility, for the purposes of the 1989 Act, s 10(4). He therefore will have no power to make an application for a residence order unless granted leave by the court.

Re P (Minors) (Adoption: Freeing Order) (1994) CA

A freeing order in relation to M's twin children was applied for by the local authority. M refused to give her consent. The judge decided that the welfare of the twins would certainly be promoted by the process of adoption but that, nevertheless, they would derive advantage from continuing their contact with M. The order sought was made and M's consent was dispensed with under AA 1976, s 16(2). The local authority were directed to search for potential adopters who would be prepared to accept continuing contact of the children with M, together with its implications. M appealed.

Held: M's appeal would be *allowed*. It appeared that the judge had attempted to make contact a prerequisite of adoption. But if there were no continuing contact M would not be acting unreasonably in withholding her consent to the adoption of the twins. The judge ought not to have dispensed with M's consent.

Re C (Minors) (Contact: Jurisdiction) (1995) CA

F was the father of three children and had applied for an extension of time so as to enable him to make an appeal against the terms of an order which varied the contact aspects of a freeing for adoption order. The original order had allowed the parents contact with the three children 12 times each year, but a variation of the order had reduced this to three times each year. F appealed.

Held: F's appeal would be *allowed*. The making of a contact order meant that family proceedings within the terms of Ch A 1989 would not continue. A judge did not have, therefore, any jurisdiction to vary the order under s 10. However, in the circumstances of the case, the court would use its powers to vary the order so as to allow F contact three times each year, pending further review by the High Court.

H (A Minor) v Oldham Borough Council (1996) CA

An order was made freeing M's son, C, aged three and a half, for adoption. M's consent had been dispensed with by the judge on the ground that she was withholding it unreasonably. M was later convicted of the wilful neglect of C. The father, F, applied for contact and parental responsibility orders; his applications were dismissed. The judge had considered the possibility of adverse consequences for C arising from a rehabilitation programme for M. M contended that the judge's conclusions were unduly strict in relation to her failure to look after C. The local authority, she claimed, had moved too swiftly in their desire to obtain a placement for C.

Held: the appeal would be *dismissed*. The judge had not erred and there were no grounds for questioning his general approach to the case. M's contentment ought not to be attained at the cost of insisting upon C's return home when it was clear that he needed a new life with persons who would provide him with the level of care which was required.

Re G (Adoption: Freeing Order) (1996) CA

C had been born to a teenage mother; the local authority had obtained a care order. C was placed with prospective adopters and, in November 1993, a freeing order had been made under s 18. The prospective adopters did not proceed and C was placed in a school for children who were severely disturbed. In June 1995, X and Y, friends of C's mother, M, asked for leave under Ch A 1989, s 10(9) to apply for a contact or residence order, but this was refused. In October 1995, M's application under AA 1976, s 20, for a revocation of the freeing order was rejected. M, X and Y appealed.

Held: the appeals would be *dismissed*. The applications of X and Y were very unlikely to succeed. Further, the court's power of revocation of a freeing order is discretionary. In the light of s 6 AA 1976, the judge's refusal of M's application was a proper exercise of his discretion.

Re J (A Child) (Adoption: Revocation of Freeing Order) (2000)

Application was made by a local authority for the revocation of a freeing order concerning J, made in June 1999. It was contended that the order was no longer of any relevance because of changes in circumstances. It had been intended that J would be placed for adoption, but he was now well settled in a foster placement and the authority now wished him to remain there for the long term without any need for adoption. Only J's mother, M, could make application for a revocation of the order once the year-long period since the order was made had ended. There was little possibility of M applying, and the local authority contended that the court ought to exercise its inherent jurisdiction in revoking the order, since this would be in J's best interests.

Held: the appeal would be *allowed*. There was no reason within the AA 1976 why the court could not exercise its inherent jurisdiction in circumstances of this nature, and it was in J's interests that, because adoption was no longer appropriate, the local authority should make long term plans for him.

Re F (Minors) (Adoption: Freeing Order) (2000) CA

The county court judge had refused a freeing order relating to an adoption order concerning C, aged two, on the ground that C's natural father had withheld consent. In considering the reasonableness of the father's attitude, the judge had taken into account the matter of C's contact with her three older siblings who would remain in care.The father claimed that the isolating of C from her natural family would be to her disadvantage.

The guardian ad litem appealed against the refusal, arguing that the judge was wrong in his consideration of what a reasonable parent might do, and had not given sufficient attention to the advantages for C of adoption.

Held: the appeal would be *allowed*. The judge appeared to have given too much attention to the issue of contact with siblings. Thorpe LJ stated that the opposition of the father to adoption did not begin to satisfy the strong needs that C had for a permanent placement that would enable her to make those attachments of which she had so far been deprived.

Re R (A Child) (Adoption: Duty to Investigate) (2001)

The guardian ad litem raised an issue in freeing proceedings as to whether a local authority was obliged to contact the mother's relatives so as to investigate them as potential carers of a child. The mother was determined, from the outset, that she had no wish for her family to know anything about the birth of the child, since such knowledge could create very difficult problems. The mother, who was unmarried, had refused also to identify the child's father.

Held: there was no statute or regulation which imposed an absolute duty on a local authority or guardian to inform or investigate a family in the circumstances of this case. Such an investigation would confer no benefit on the child and might jeopardise co-operation with the family, to the detriment of the child. Further, to impart confidential information to persons from whom the mother wished it to be kept would be a gross interference with the mother's right to have her private life respected.

16.4   Setting aside of an adoption order

Re B (Adoption Order: Jurisdiction to Set Aside) (1995) CA

B's parents were Arab. He had been placed with, and adopted later by, a Jewish couple. Several years later he learned that his parents were Arabs and made application for an order which would nullify the adoption order. B's application was refused on the ground of a lack of jurisdiction. B then appealed.

Held: B's appeal would be *dismissed*. The court did not have the jurisdiction which would have enabled it to nullify the adoption order, which had been made in a correct manner, simply because of a mistake relating to B's ethnic origins. If such an application were to be allowed it would assist in the impairing of the adoption system which accepted adoption orders as existing for life. An order might be set aside only where it clearly involved a denial of natural justice.

16.5 Adoption contact register

Note

Under AA 1976, s 50, the Registrar General is obliged to set up and maintain a separate register of adoptions. Records concerning connections between names on the register may be examined only with the leave of the court: s 51.

R v Registrar General ex p Smith (1991)

S had been adopted when he was nine weeks old. As an adolescent he became mentally disturbed and evinced severe hatred for his adoptive parents. He was convicted on a charge of murder and while serving his sentence killed another prisoner, under the delusion that he was killing his adoptive mother. Following his transfer to Broadmoor he applied under s 51 for a copy of his birth certificate. His application was refused by the Registrar General on grounds of public policy. He made an application for judicial review.

Held: S's application would be *refused* because there was justified and serious concern that in the future S might use the information gained through a perusal of the register, in order to commit a serious offence.

Re X (A Minor) (Adoption Details: Disclosure) (1994) CA

After the making of an adoption order, the local authority made application for an order which was intended to prevent details concerning the adoptive parents being entered on the register, under s 51. The local authority feared that the adopted child's mother might use the register so as to obtain these details and disrupt the child's life. The application was refused and the local authority appealed.

Held: the local authority's appeal would be *allowed*. The court did not possess any power to make modified entries on the register, but the inherent jurisdiction of the High Court could be exercised so as to prevent the Registrar disclosing any information during the minority of the child without first seeking leave of the court.

D v Registrar General (1996)

M's child, C, had been adopted some 17 years earlier. M had requested information concerning C from the local authority which had taken over the records of the defunct National Children's Adoption Agency. The local authority refused to supply M with information and she made application to seek an order under AA 1976, s 50(5)(a) that the Registrar General should provide her with appropriate information. The Registrar General claimed that his office could not carry out the appropriate search. M appealed.

Held: M's application would be *dismissed*. The test to be applied was whether M had made out a case which would convince the court that the order she was seeking was reasonable. The significant point was that there had to be shown some benefit or need relating to C rather than M. This had not been shown; indeed, C had not taken the opportunity to place her name on the register and had shown no curiosity concerning her adoption.

Q 'There is a lack of consistency in the law. The Adoption Act 1976 and the Children Act 1989 are not consistent in their approach. Different approaches must be taken depending on the type of application. In some cases the needs of the children will be paramount and in others they will be taken into account.' (White Paper *Adoption – A New Approach*, Cm 5017, 2000, para 2.11.) Illustrate the significance of this statement by reference to some of the leading cases.

17 Child Abduction

17.1 Parental child abduction across frontiers

Note ───

Child abduction involves, in the context of this part of family law, removal of a child, without the appropriate permission, and taking him across national frontiers. The Hague Convention, signed in 1980, is concerned with securing the prompt return of children wrongfully removed to or retained in any of the contracting states and ensuring that rights of custody and access under the law of contracting states are effectively respected. The European Convention 1980 seeks to recognise and enforce custody decisions in contracting states. The Child Abduction and Custody Act 1985 is concerned with the ratification of the international Conventions.

───

17.1.1 Paramountcy of child's welfare

Re F (A Minor) (Abduction: Jurisdiction) (1990) CA

H, who had dual British and Israeli nationality, married W, an Israeli national, in 1979. There were two sons. H and W separated in 1989 and H brought one of the sons to England, thereby breaching W's rights under Israeli law. W applied for an order requiring H to return the child to Israel. (Israel was not, at that time, a party to the Hague Convention.)

Held: the order would be *granted*. The welfare of the child was paramount and the child ought to go to the jurisdiction in which he was habitually resident. The court was aware that the Israeli courts would apply principles which were acceptable to the English courts and that there would be no risk of discrimination or persecution in relation to the child.

17.1.2 The child's 'habitual residence'

C v S (Minor) (Abduction: Illegitimate Child) (1990) HL

M had removed her child from Western Australia, the country of origin, to England. Under the law of the country of origin, M was, at all material times, the sole custodial parent. M had no intention of returning to Australia.

Held: the removal of the child was *not wrong* under CACA 1985, and the retention of the child in England was *not wrongful* since the removal was not wrongful and the child's habitual residence was no longer in the country from which M had taken him.

Re B (Child Abduction: Declaration) (1994) CA

H and W separated in 1992. B, their child, was born in Canada in 1991 and remained with W. In December 1992, H and W made an agreement under seal, giving W interim custody of B. H consented to W and B returning to England where they would live. W took B to England in December 1992 so as to settle there, but, at the end of the month, returned to Canada in order to seek a reconciliation. This failed and, without H's knowledge or consent, W and B returned to England. H gave notice of termination of the 1992 agreement and applied for B's return under the Hague Convention.

Held: H's application would be *dismissed*. B was not habitually resident in Canada immediately prior to his being taken to England in 1993; his removal was not wrongful under the Convention. On returning to Canada for the attempted reconciliation, W had no fixed intention of returning there. Hence, neither W nor B, who was in W's sole custody, became habitually resident in Canada as a result.

Re V (Abduction: Habitual Residence) (1995)

H and W lived together from 1981 and were married in 1991. H managed a hotel in Corfu. In March 1995, H returned from London to Corfu on the understanding that W would follow with the child in one month's time. W, however, had commenced divorce proceedings in early April. She stayed in London with the child. H made application under CACA 1985 and the Hague Convention for the return to Greece of the child.

Held: H's application would be *rejected*. The parties were habitually resident in Greece for part of each year and habitually resident in England for the remaining months of each year. At the date on which W was expected to take the child to Greece, the child was habitually resident in London. Hence the child had not been wrongfully retained in a contracting country which was not the one in which he was habitually resident under the Hague Convention, Art 4.

Re A (Abduction: Habitual Residence) (1996)

H and W had three children. H was an American serviceman stationed in England; W was British. Following the termination of H's posting in England, the family spent two months in Michigan before H was posted to Iceland where the family followed him in 1993. Following the collapse of the marriage, W brought the children, wrongfully, to England. H and W commenced divorce proceedings in Michigan and England. H asked for the return of the children to Michigan on the ground of their habitual residence there. He claimed that the Hague Convention had application in the circumstances. W contended that the children had been habitually resident in what was then a non-Convention country, Iceland.

Held: H's application would be *dismissed*. H had not remained resident in Michigan throughout the period of his army service (which he claimed was the situation under Michigan law). His sole family home was in Iceland where the family had been resident. Article 4 of the Convention demands residence in a contracting state immediately before the wrongful removal. Residence in an American base did not prevent the operation of Iceland's law. H could not be deemed, therefore, to have been a resident of an American State throughout the period under consideration. The family was habitually resident in Iceland and the Convention had no application. The children were settled well in England and W was pregnant, which would involve difficulties for her if the family went to America. It was not in the family interests, therefore, to order a return to Michigan.

Re M (Abduction: Habitual Residence) (1996) CA

H and W had married in India and had been habitually resident in England. Their child was born in 1992 and they separated in January 1994. They made an agreement whereby the child would be brought up by paternal grandparents in India. In February 1994, the child was taken to India. In July 1995, W decided to withdraw her consent to the child's residing in India. She made the child a ward of court and asked to invoke the jurisdiction of the High Court. The judge held that W's change of mind effectively ended the child's habitual residence in India and gave him habitual residence in England. W thought that as a result she had the right to order the child's return to England. H appealed.

Held: H's appeal would be *allowed*. Habitual residence is to be viewed as a question of fact which should be decided by reference to all the circumstances. A person cannot acquire habitual residence in a country without actually residing there. W's decision that the child was to return to England was insufficient to make him habitually resident there without his returning to live there. At the date of W's application, the child was habitually resident in India, and the court had, as a result, no jurisdiction.

17.2 Wrongful removal and retention as separate concepts

Re H (Minor) (Abduction: Custody Rights) (1991) HL

H, the Canadian father of a child in the custody of his mother, W, had failed to return him to W, and, in breach of an order of the Canadian court, had removed the child out of the jurisdiction to England. W made application to the English court for the return of the child under CACA 1985, and the Hague Convention 1980. The application was dismissed by the judge and the Court of Appeal upheld his decision. W appealed to the House of Lords.

Held: W's appeal would be *dismissed*. The correct construction of the Hague Convention shows that the removal and retention of a child in breach of custody rights are to be seen as single and exclusive events occurring on a particular occasion. Hence, because the child had been removed from the state in which he had his habitual residence on a date before the Convention came into force, the court lacked the jurisdiction under the 1985 Act, s 2(2) to order his return.

17.2.1 Effective cause of child abduction

R v A (Child Abduction) (1999) CA

C, aged 15, had left her home and travelled to London with the appellant, A, in his car, living together for nine days. Evidence was given of previous travel of this nature with A. On the morning of C's disappearance, A had told C's mother that he had come to tell C that she could not go away with him. A contended that he had taken C to London to stop her doing harm to herself. He denied that he had deceived the mother by pretending that he was trying to stop C leaving. In summing up, the judge had told the jury that they had to be sure that A had taken C, that is, caused C to accompany him, but they did not need to be satisfied that A was the sole or even the main cause, provided that A's actions amounted to something more than merely inconsequential. A was convicted and he appealed.

Held: A's appeal was *dismissed*. The question was whether A had taken C out of the lawful control of her mother. There was sufficient evidence allowing a jury to conclude that C's decision to accompany A was not the sole cause of her doing that.

17.3 Risk of harm to the child

Re F (Child Abduction: Risk if Returned) (1995) CA

H and W were married in Colorado in 1987; H was an American citizen, W was British. C, their child, was born in December 1990. C had observed violence perpetrated by H against W, and had been assaulted by H. W obtained in 1994 from the Colorado court a judgment which was, effectively, an ouster order. In July 1994 she returned with C to England. The court granted in December 1994 an application by H for C's return to Colorado. W appealed, arguing that C's removal was not in breach of H's rights of custody, since it was lawful under Colorado legislation. Further, C's return would result in a serious risk of his sustaining physical or mental harm.

Held: W's appeal would be *allowed*. Under Colorado law both H and W had equal, although separate, custody rights concerning C. Whether or not C's removal amounted to a breach of H's rights of custody was a matter of Convention law as interpreted and applied by the English courts. Because Colorado law made void F's rights, as a result of C's removal, that removal was in breach of H's rights of custody and was wrongful. In the singular circumstances of this case, where there was evidence of a highly adverse effect on C when he learned of his possible return to Colorado, the court would not order his return under Art 13(b).

Re K (Abduction: Psychological Harm) (1995) CA

W, an English parent, had wrongfully removed her child, K, from America, thus breaching the terms of an order. She appealed against an order for the return of K to her American father, H, in pursuance of the Hague Convention. She argued that K's position would be intolerable, within the meaning of Art 13. Further, she had insufficient notice of H's application for custody.

Held: K was to be *returned*. There was no evidence to establish that K would be placed in an intolerable position or that the order would result in physical or psychological harm being caused to her. Adequate notice had been given to W but she had not responded within the appropriate period of time as required under law.

Re G (A Minor) (1996) CA

H and W were British subjects who had moved in 1992 to Florida, following their marriage. There were two children. Following a holiday in Britain, W refused to move back to Florida and H and the children went back there without her. H divorced W in America and was granted a residential parent, with W enjoying visiting rights. H later remarried and an order was made allowing the children to visit W in Britain for two months in 1995. At the end of the visit, the eldest child returned but the other child remained in Britain. In response to the order, W agreed to return to America with the child. Evidence was given that the child became upset on hearing of this, and W contended that returning the child to America would result in psychological harm.

Held: W's appeal would be *dismissed*. Under the terms of the Convention it was intended that children would be returned to the country in which they were habitually resident; it was for the courts of that country to make a decision concerning where the children ought to live. There was no evidence of the possibility of a severe risk of psychological harm resulting to the child.

Re C (Minors) (Abduction: Grave Risk of Psychological Harm) (1999) CA

Following the dissolution of the marriage of F and M, they were given joint custody of their two children. A court in California ordered that the residence of the children was not to be changed without the consent of F and M, or the court. F was found later, by a Californian court, of having caused serious physical harm to the children. M was given permission to visit England. She took the children there and failed to return to California. F commenced proceedings under the Hague Convention for the children's return. M relied on Art 13(b), contending that there was a grave risk of the children being exposed to physical or psychological harm if they returned, and, in any case, they did not wish to return. The judge decided that it was not appropriate to order a return because of the risk of psychological harm and the consequent strain on M. F then appealed.

Held: F's appeal was *allowed*. Strict tests necessitating clear evidence of the likelihood of substantial harm had to be applied, and this evidence had not emerged. The argument concerning the unwillingness of the children to return required consideration in the context of the fact that they were influenced by M and their stepfather. It was the duty of the court to implement the Convention, and it was for the court in California to weigh up the certainties and uncertainties in the case and decide the future of the children.

17.4 Consent and acquiescence

Re A (Minors) (Abduction: Custody Rights) (1992) CA

H and W lived in Australia where they were divorced. W took the children to England. H wrote to W stating that he was aware that W's action was unlawful but that he did not intend to contest the matter because he did not wish to upset the children. H later submitted an application to the Australian courts for the return of the children under the Hague Convention and the CACA 1985. W contended that the court ought to exercise its discretion so as not to return the children to Australia because of H's acquiescence. This argument was rejected by the judge who ordered that the children be returned. W then appealed.

Held: W's appeal would be *allowed*. Acquiescence could be active or passive, signified by precise and unambiguous statements or silence and inaction. Acquiescence could be effective only where the parent was aware of the child's removal *and* knew that the action was unlawful *and* was aware of his rights against the other parent. This seemed to be the essence of the situation in this case. An acquiescence could not be retracted after having become known to the other party.

Re M (Minors) (1996) CA

F and M were cohabitants and had lived in Australia. In August 1995 M took their two children to England on holiday. F had indicated his consent to this arrangement. M had agreed to return to Australia in October but phoned F, stating that she intended to remain in England until the beginning of 1996. F gave his consent to the arrangement and wrote to M suggesting that she extend her vacation as long as was necessary so that she could consider her future carefully. He wrote again, requesting M to keep to the terms of the original arrangement. In September 1995 F was granted, in an *ex parte* hearing, a sole custody and guardianship order together with an order for M to return to Australia no later than October 1995. In the exercise of his discretion, the judge held that the children were to be returned despite F's earlier apparent acquiescence. M appealed.

Held: M's appeal would be *dismissed*. The judge had exercised his discretion correctly. The judge was entitled to make his decision, keeping in mind that a hearing *inter partes* had been fixed in Australia for December 1995.

Re C (Abduction: Consent) (1996)

H, an American, and W, who was British, lived in Alaska, taking frequent holidays in England with their two young children. Because of difficulties concerning the marriage, H and W had separated briefly when H brought the children to England, in January 1995. They had remained in England since that date. H sought the return of his children, contending that he had given his agreement only to a short holiday in England. W argued that H had consented to, or acquiesced in, the removal and retention of the children and that they could be at risk of suffering physical or psychological harm if they were returned to America with a view to living there.

Held: H's application would be *dismissed*. There was one problem only, that of consent, since there was nothing in H's behaviour which suggested acquiescence. The risk of serious harm could be dealt with by demanding appropriate undertakings from H. The court would, therefore, exercise its discretion under the Hague Convention, Art 13(a), by refusing to issue an order for the immediate return of the children to H.

Re D (Abduction: Acquiescence: Father's Removal from USA to England) (1999)

F, British, and M, American, were married in 1988 and lived in the USA. D, their child, was born in the USA in 1990. In 1994, F and M separated, and F and D went to live in England. D was sent twice to the USA, and back to England, following the intention of F and M that he would live where he was being sent. In June 1997 D was sent to England with a two months' return ticket. He continued to live with F and F's partner. In April 1998, F was imprisoned for importation of a classified drug. M discovered this and applied for D's return under the Hague Convention. She argued that D was in England solely for a holiday and F had wrongfully refused to return him to the USA.

Held: M's application was *dismissed*. She had acquiesced in F's wrongful retention. She had written on several occasions to D in terms which suggested that he was remaining in England and had forwarded his clothes to him. D had remained in England for 35 out of the last 47 months. His life had become unsettled, and the substantive case concerning his future ought to be determined as swiftly as possible.

Re I (Abduction: Acquiescence) (1999)

F had written to M's solicitors in Australia, stating that he had agreed, with much reluctance, to give consideration to arrangements whereby the children of F and M might remain in England, with contact arrangements in Australia to be financed by M's family. M argued that this constituted acquiescence. F commenced proceedings under the Hague Convention.

Held: the children were ordered to *return to Australia*. Negotiation was not equivalent to acquiescence. The letter by F to the solicitors was no more than a request for help and advice. F did want the children to return to Australia, and no agreement concerning their future had been made.

Re R (Abduction: Consent) (1999)

M, Scottish, had married F, American. They had two children and lived in the USA. In 1996 the marriage was collapsing, according to M because of F's continuing violence, and according to F because of M's alcoholism. In March 1997 M went to the UK with the children. F made application for their return under the Hague Convention, but M argued that F had given his consent to their removal and that their return involved the risk of grave physical or psychological harm.

Held: F's application was *dismissed*. Although written consent was not necessary, consent could be implied from conduct, always provided that it was unambiguous. A number of factors had to be taken into account, and due weight had to be given to F's having given up the American matrimonial home, and the fact that M had always acted as the children's principal carer. It seemed appropriate for them to remain in the UK.

Re B (Abduction: Acquiescence) (1999)

C, aged five, was taken from her American home by her English mother, M. The American father, F, sought legal advice in the USA, but was not told of the right to ask for summary return under the Hague Convention. He asked M for a reconciliation, and, in his letter, stated that, should there be no reconciliation, he would give his agreement to M and C settling in the UK. He then visited England and took more legal advice, but, again, was not informed of the Hague Convention. He was granted a contact order, but contact was not successful, and he made an application for C's return to the USA. M argued that F had acquiesced in C's removal, and that C's return would involve her in grave harm under Art 13(b).

Held: the application was *refused*. There was a lack of evidence to support M's argument under Art 13(b). In fact, F had acquiesced. He had failed to bring proceedings in the USA and had applied in the UK for contact only. C was settled in the UK and had begun her schooling there. It was not appropriate in all the circumstances for the court to return her to the USA in the exercise of its discretion.

Re H (Abduction: Child of 16) (2000)

C1 and C2, aged 14 and 11, had been removed wrongfully from Australia by their mother, M. The father, F, genuinely believed that they were on an extended holiday. He did not know their address, and M later moved to another address without notifying him. F applied for the return of C1 and C2. By the time of the hearing C1 had reached the age of 16, and a question arose as to whether Art 4 Hague Convention precluded the making of an order for his return. C2 had, according to M, settled down well in England and F appeared to have acquiesced in their removal from Australia.

Held: C2's return to Australia was *ordered*. C1's case was to be relisted for determination as to her views, under the court's inherent jurisdiction. M should not be allowed to benefit from her deception, and her attempts to conceal the address of C1 and C2 could not be viewed as acquiescence by F.

17.5 Aspects of the European Convention

Re A (Foreign Access Order: Enforcement) (1996)

H and W were French nationals. H lived in France, W lived in England with the two children. In 1993 H obtained an order from a French court which gave joint parental authority and provided that the children should continue to live with W and that H should have a right similar to contact for one month each year. In 1994 W was granted by the English courts an order that the children were not to be removed from England and that in all other respects the French order was to continue. H made application through an originating summons under the CACA 1985, s 15, that the French order be registered in England. The judge heard evidence that the children had made statements to the welfare officer that they did not wish to go to France. He held that the exception in the European Convention, Art 10(1)(b), had been clearly made out by W. An order was made and H appealed.

Held: H's appeal would be *allowed*. An order would be made which would recognise the French order and would register it in England. The judge did not have jurisdiction to make the order in the terms used. H's application for recognition and registration, unless it were possible to make out the exception in Art 10, should have been granted. It was correct to ascertain the wishes of the children, but these ought not to determine in any way matters of recognition and enforcement of orders. Further, the judge's giving contact in England rather than France constituted, in effect, a review of the *substance* of the French order, and this was specifically forbidden by the European Convention, Art 9(3).

Re S (Abduction: European Convention) (1996)

F and M, were unmarried. There was one child. F, whose habitual residence was in England, instituted proceedings under Ch A 1989 and these were served on M. F discovered later that M had taken the child with her to Denmark. F obtained an *ex parte* order which gave him residence and an order that the child be returned forthwith to England. He made application for a declaration under the European Convention, Art 12, that the removal of the child by M was unlawful.

Held: the declaration requested by F would be *granted*. The removal of the child by M was, in the circumstances, unlawful. It was not necessary that M be served with the *ex parte* application since both F and the child were habitually resident in England.

Re H (A Minor) (Abduction: Rights of Custody) (2000)

F, unmarried father of H, began proceedings for guardianship and access in an Irish court. He then asked for an order for the return of H, following her removal to England by the mother, M, without consent having been given by F. F argued that the wrongful removal of H constituted a breach of the rights of custody vested in the Irish court. The Court of Appeal allowed an appeal by F against the refusal of an order to return H to Ireland. M appealed.

Held: the House of Lords *dismissed* M's appeal. The Irish court did possess custody rights relating to H because of F's pending application for guardianship, under a purposive interpretation of Arts 3 and 8 Hague Convention 1980. The jurisdiction of the Irish court had been invoked by F; that court had rights of custody concerning H, and F was entitled to make application to the country to which H had been wrongfully taken, so as to order the return of H. (*Per* Lord Mackay: 'It would be more appropriate in most cases for the application to be made by the person concerned rather than the court itself having to undertake that responsibility.')

17.6 The child's wishes and interests

S v S (Child Abduction) (Child's Views) (1992) CA

H, W, and their child, C, lived in France. C had psychological difficulties which were thought to stem from her not being taught in English, her mother tongue. The marriage began to break down and W removed C to England although H and W had made an agreement that the place of habitual residence would be France and that H would have access. In her evidence, W said that she feared the possibility that H might be violent. The psychological problems of C were mentioned, but as a matter of secondary importance only. H made application for the return of C to France. W agreed that her taking C to England was unlawful and argued that there was a real risk of harm being caused to C if she were to return to France and that C objected to returning. W contended that C was sufficiently mature for her expression of views to be taken into account. The court welfare officer was asked by the judge to ascertain C's views and wishes. The judge refused to make the order for which H had asked. H appealed.

Held: H's appeal would be *dismissed*. The object of the Hague Convention was to ensure a swift return of children who had been wrongfully removed. C's objections to returning to France did have significance and it was not necessary to interfere with the judge's decision to discover C's views and the method he had chosen in order to do so.

Re E (Children) (Abduction: Non-Convention Country) (2000) CA

F and M were practising Muslims, with a habitual residence in the Sudan. Following their divorce, M brought their children to the UK, this being contrary to the order of a Sudanese court which had ordered that the children were to stay with their paternal grandmother in the Sudan, in accordance with Islamic Sharia law. M made application for a residence order but that was dismissed. F was granted wardship and an order that the children be returned forthwith to the Sudan. M appealed, contending that the children would be deprived of a natural upbringing and that they would be living under a regime which was inimical to their welfare.

Held: M's appeal would be *dismissed*. It was necessary to consider the welfare of the children within the context of whatever rules and customs obtained in the country from which they had been abducted. Sudan was not one of the Hague Convention member states, but it would not be in the interests of comity if a state whose system derived from Judaeo-Christian foundations were to condemn a system derived from an Islamic foundation when that system was conceived by its originators and operators to promote and protect the interests of its children according to its traditions and values. An abducting parent cannot be allowed to succeed in an application by attacking the principles of non-member countries, save where matters of persecution or ethnic, sex or other types of discrimination were involved.

Re T (Minors) (Abduction: Custody Rights) (2000) CA

The parents of G, aged 11, and T, aged six, were British nationals who had resided in Spain since 1993. In 1997 the mother began divorce and custody proceedings in Spain. In January 2000 the father defied the Spanish court by removing G and T from Spain to England, in breach of the mother's rights of custody. A defence under Art 13(b) Hague Convention was rejected, given G's lack of sufficient age and maturity for her wishes to be considered. She then wrote to her mother, making it obvious that she did not wish to return to Spain, and making reference to the mother's alcohol problems. The father then appealed against the decision to return the children to Spain.

Held: the father's appeal would be *allowed*. G's clear, genuine and reasoned objections to returning to Spain showed a maturity well beyond her years, and the conflict set up by the hostility of the parents to each other, combined to make out a defence under Art 13. In the case of T, there was a risk that an order to return him to Spain without G would place him in a difficult situation which might prove intolerable. In these quite exceptional circumstances the Art 13 defence was established. *Per* Ward LJ: 'The exercise of the court's discretion had to be taken in the round. Upholding the Convention was too high a price for G and T to pay.'

17.7 Delay in instituting proceedings and breach of court order

M v M (Contempt: Committal) (1992) CA

H and W were divorced, following which W was awarded custody of their child. H gave an assurance that he would not abduct the child and was then permitted access. During an access visit, H abducted the child, removing him to Australia. The child's return was effected by the court. When H returned to England he was arrested for contempt and was sentenced to 12 months' imprisonment. H appealed.

Held: H's appeal against sentence was *dismissed*. The Court of Appeal held that a sentence of that nature was not excessive in the circumstances. The removal of a child from the jurisdiction in defiance of a court order and in breach of an undertaking was a very grave contempt of court.

Re G (Abduction: Striking Out Application) (1995)

H, an English national, made an application under the Hague Convention in relation to the children of his marriage to W, an American citizen. W had gone to America with the children and an order had been issued forbidding their removal from Florida. W later returned to England with the children and the American court issued an order requiring W's return to America. W then instituted proceedings under Ch A 1989 for residence and contact orders. H commenced proceedings under Ch A 1989 and the Hague Convention. No other steps were taken by H under the Convention until a year later. W applied for the striking out of H's applications.

Held: W's application would be *allowed*. The essence of the Hague Convention concerned the swift return of abducted children to the country from which they had been wrong fully removed. H did not begin proceedings under the Convention with sufficient speed when the children were taken to England. It was not clear whether there was any point to pursuing those proceedings, particularly in view of the fact that proceedings under Ch A 1989 were soon to commence. The important, necessary procedural requirements relating to the Hague Convention had been virtually ignored; a continuation of proceedings would, therefore, in these circumstances, constitute an abuse of process.

17.8   Joinder of children as parties

Re M (A Minor) (Abduction: Child's Objections) (1994) CA

H and W had a child, C, aged 13. After H and W had separated in 1986, C stayed in Ireland with W and H returned to England. C then left home and, in hospital, stated that he had been injured by W's partner. A place of safety order was made and eventually W sought, in 1993, to have C detained in a secure unit. C absconded on eight occasions and H then brought him to England where he was put into a home. W applied for his return to Ireland under the Hague Convention. C applied to be joined as a party to proceedings, and his application was successful. He was granted leave to appeal against the order for his return. W appealed against C's joining proceedings as a party.

Held: C's appeal would be *allowed*. Only in exceptional cases should a child be made party to proceedings under the Convention, and this was such a case. H had not appealed against the order for C's return and C's own representation would be the only way for the court to seek to understand the nature of his objections to return. There was considerable evidence to support C's objections to a return and he appeared to have sufficient maturity for his views to be taken into consideration by the court under Art 13. The court was empowered to exercise its discretion so as to refuse to order that C be returned to Ireland.

Re M (A Minor) (Child Abduction) (1994) CA

In 1976 H and W were married in Australia, where their sons, C1 and C2 were born. Following the separation of H and W, W moved to England.

Two years later an Australian court awarded custody of the boys to H. In 1993 the boys were removed by W to England, and H applied for their return under the Hague Convention. A consent order for their return was made. C1 and C2 objected strongly to returning to H. C1 attempted suicide; C2 made a disturbance on the aircraft on which they were to return, leading to their being taken off. They were sent back to W and their application to be joined as parties was rejected. C1 and C2 appealed against the rejection. W appealed against the consent order.

Held: the appeal of C1 and C2 would be *dismissed*. W's appeal would be *allowed*. On the facts presented to the court there was no necessity for C1 and C2 to be joined as parties to the proceedings, and separate representation seemed unnecessary. The objections of the boys had not been presented to the judge who issued the consent order. That order would be set aside in view of the alteration in the circumstances of the parties.

17.9 Foreign orders

Re R (Minors) (Abduction) (1994)

X and Y were French nationals who had cohabited in France where they had two children aged four and six at the time of the proceedings. In 1991, following their separation, Y took responsibility for the care of the children and petitioned the court for parental authority. A few days before the final hearing, X and the children came to England. A French court held that X had taken the children without Y's consent. X's application was rejected and the children's return to France was ordered. Y made application in the English courts under the Hague Convention for the return of the children.

Held: Y's application would be *granted*. Under French law she had parental authority, and X's removal of the children was wrongful within the Convention. Even if X had established a defence under Art 13, the court would have exercised its discretion to return the children; their welfare necessitated their speedy return to France and, not unmindful of the importance of the principle of comity to the community of nations, the court considered itself obliged to lend its support to the decision arrived at by the French courts.

Re M (Child Abduction) (European Convention) (1994)

H and W, who lived in Ireland, came to England with their two children. In July 1992 H made application to the Irish court for custody and an order which would effect the children's return to Ireland. In August 1992 W presented an application to the court in England and was granted *ex parte* interim residence orders. In October 1992 the Irish court granted sole custody to H, stating that W had unlawfully taken the children out of Ireland. H then applied under the European Convention, Art 7, for enforcement of the Irish court order.

Held: H's application would be *dismissed*. The European Convention, art 7, makes clear that decisions made in one contracting state must generally be recognised and enforced in other contracting states, but the court may exercise discretion in refusing to recognise or enforce an order under art 10(1). The Irish court order for sole custody was not compatible with the English court's residence order which was unlimited in time even though it was classified as being of an interim nature. It had to be remembered that the two children had already spent some 18 months in England and concern for their welfare necessitated that the court should refuse the request for recognition and enforcement of the order.

Re D (Abduction: Discretionary Return) (2000)

M, mother of two children, made application for the return of the children to France, where they had been born and raised. Following the separation of M and F, a French court issued a residence order in M's favour; the father, F, was to have the children during their holidays. At the end of a holiday period, F kept the children in England, arguing that M had given her consent to the children residing with him in England.

Held: M's application would be *allowed*. M had given her consent to the children living with F, but the court had the right to exercise its discretion concerning an order that they be returned to France. Concern had emerged concerning the children's life with M, her partner, and his children. Further, if the court refused an order for the children to return to France, this would be in conflict with the French court's residence order, and would create difficulties if the children wished to visit France in future years. The court should exercise its discretion and allow the children to return to France in order that outstanding issues might be resolved there.

Q 'Paramountcy of the child's welfare must always dominate the courts' attitude to resolving the problems arising from an abduction.' Do you agree?

Appendix

Aspects of the Family Law Act 1996

FLA 1996 received the Royal Assent on 4 July 1996. Section 65 (power to make rules and regulations) came into force on that date. Part III has been almost entirely repealed. Part IV came into force on 1 October 1997. It is unlikely, however, that Part III (Divorce and Separation) will now be brought into force. At the time of publication of this edition, the following provisions of the 1996 Act are *not* yet in force: ss 2–21, 23–25, 60, 64, 66(1), (2) (part), Scheds 1–3, 8, paras 1–15, 16(1)–(4), 16(5)(b), 16(6)(a), 17–43, Sched 9, paras 1, 2, 5, 6, 10 (part).

1 Repeals
The following are included in the schedule of repeals (1996 Act, Sched 10):

MCA 1973	ss 1–7, 9, 10, 17, 18, 20, 22, 49, Sched 1, para 8;
DVMPA 1976	whole Act;
DPMCA 1978	ss 16–18, 28(2), 63(2), Sched 2, paras 38, 53;
Matrimonial Homes Act 1983	whole Act;
MFPA 1984	whole Act;
Ch A 1989	s 8(4)(c)(f), Sched 11, para 6(b), Sched 13, paras 33(1), 65(1).

2 Part I of the Act – General Principles of Parts II and III
The institution of marriage is to be supported. Parties to a marriage which may have broken down should be encouraged to take practical steps (eg, by seeking counselling) to save it. A marriage which has broken down should be ended with minimum distress to parties and their children. The risk of violence to parties and children should be removed or diminished: s 1. (This section *is* in force.)

3 Part II of the Act – Divorce and Separation
Two types of court order will be available: a divorce order and a separation order: s 2.

Marital proceedings commence with a *statement of marital breakdown*. But, under s 8(2), a party making a statement must (except in certain prescribed circumstances) have attended an *information meeting* not less than three months before the statement is made. That meeting is intended to provide parties with relevant information concerning divorce and to give them the opportunity of meeting a counsellor.

The statement must set out the maker's belief that the marriage has broken down, that the maker is aware of the purpose of the period for reflection and consideration, and that he/she wishes to make arrangements for the future: ss 5(1)(b), 6. The statement will be served on the other party. A statement made before the first anniversary of the marriage is ineffective for purposes of application for an order of divorce (but not separation): s 7(6).

There follows a period of 14 days (to allow for service of the statement on the other party), after which a nine month *period of reflection and consideration* begins. The objectives of this period are to allow parties to reflect on the possibility of reconciliation and to consider arrangements for the future: s 7(1). The period can be extended, eg, by joint notice under s 7(8) (possibility of reconciliation). The possibilities of mediation should be considered by the parties.

Either party may make *application for a divorce order*. The applicant must show that the marriage has broken down irretrievably, that arrangements about the information meeting and about the future have been satisfied and that the application has not been withdrawn: s 3. 'Irretrievable breakdown' will be shown by a declaration by the party that, following reflection on the breakdown, and having considered arrangements for the future, the applicant now believes that it is not possible to save the marriage.

The court must satisfy itself that there is no order under s 10 preventing divorce. Such an order may be made only if the court is satisfied that the dissolution of the marriage would result in substantial financial hardship to the other party or a child of the family, *and* that it would be wrong in all the circumstances for the marriage to be dissolved.

For the court to be satisfied that arrangements for the future have been made, there must be produced, eg, a court order dealing with financial arrangements, a negotiated agreement of financial matters, an agreement by both parties that financial arrangements have been made.

The order is then made. (There will no longer be decrees nisi and absolute.)

(This part of the Act now seems unlikely to be brought into force.)

4 Part III of the Act – Legal Aid for Mediation

The Legal Aid Act 1988 is amended so as to enable the Legal Services Commission to cover the costs of mediation for families eligible for legal aid: ss 26–29.

(This part of the Act is largely *not* in force.)

5 Part IV of the Act – Family Homes and Domestic Violence

A new concept of 'matrimonial home rights' replaces the term 'rights of occupation' formerly used in the Matrimonial Homes Act 1983. Protection is given to persons in a variety of categories (see ss 33–41) by the use of occupation orders. Section 36 covers cohabitants or former cohabitants with no existing right to occupy.

Non-molestation orders are covered in ss 42–49. The range of applicants eligible for protection is extended to include 'associated persons' (see s 62), eg, spouses, former spouses, cohabitants and former cohabitants, parents of a child. An order may prohibit specific types of molestation or molestation generally. and may be made for a specific period or until further notice: s 42(6)(7). Applications may be made with leave of the court by children under 16: s 43. Orders may be made *ex parte*: s 45. Under s 47, the court must attach a power of arrest to an order where respondent has used or threatened violence against the applicant or a child, unless this is not necessary for their protection. Schedule 6 makes it possible for the court to make an ouster order for the protection of children when an emergency protection order or interim care order is made. This allows the removal of a suspected abuser from the home, rather than removal of the child.

(This part of the Act is in force.)

6 Part V of the Act – Supplemental

Under s 64 the Lord Chancellor may make regulations providing for the separate representation of children in proceedings in England and Wales which relate to any matter in respect of which a question has arisen, or may arise, under Parts II and IV, MCA 1973, DPMCA 1978. Such regulations may provide for representation only in specified circumstances.

(This part of the Act is not yet entirely in force.)

7 Separation

On application by one or both parties to a marriage, the court will make a separation order if the requirements under s 8 concerning information meetings and under s 9 concerning arrangements for the future, are met and the marriage has broken down irretrievably. An application for a separation order must not be made by reference to a statement if a period of more than one year has passed since the ending of the period for reflection and consideration: s 5(3). The order comes into force as soon as it is made and will remain in force during the continuation of the marriage or until cancelled by the court on application of the parties: s 2. A separation order can be converted into a divorce order under the procedure set out in s 4.

(This part of the Act seems now unlikely to be brought into force.)

Index